It's a lot to expect authors themselves to live up to the magic of their words, and it's very special when they do. Philip Yancey has a way about him that can only be described as Graceful. Not vanishing at all ... very present.

BONO, lead singer of U2
and co-founder of ONE and (RED)

Every Philip Yancey book is worth reading. In the decades (!) that I have followed Philip, I have never been disappointed in his work. Just the opposite; each book has sharpened my thinking and touched my heart. He is a gift to our generation.

MAX LUCADO, pastor and author

For decades now, Philip Yancey, our finest journalist, has provided an accurate evangelical voice at the interface between Christian witness and secular assumptions. *Vanishing Grace* — given the contentious times in which we live — is critically needed. Yancey at his best. In his words, "A heartfelt plea to my tribe, mostly evangelicals, to recover the mission and the spirit that Jesus left us." On page after page he goes "from strength to strength ... full of grace and truth."

EUGENE H. PETERSON, Professor Emeritus of Spiritual
Theology Regent College, Vancouver, BC

There's not much I'd rather read about than grace. And there's no one I'd rather have tell me about it than Philip Yancey. Years ago, reading his book on the streets of Calcutta, I was introduced to the Jesus I never knew. Now he's written a manifesto to awaken the church that he loves but is very concerned about. He knows that Christians are meant to give off the aroma of Christ, but we've often smelled like something else. Allow his words to embolden you to recommit yourself to love the way Jesus did ... after all it is by our love that he said the world would know that we belong to him.

SHANE CLAIBORNE, author, activist, lover of Jesus,
www.redletterchristians.org

Philip Yancey's books are like dinner parties where you meet people you never would have known otherwise. In Philip's latest, *Vanishing Grace*, you'll meet Henri Nouwen, Francis Collins, Thomas Bruce, Joanna Flanders-Thomas, Dr. King, Craig Detweiler, Barbara Brown Taylor, Jürgen Moltmann, George MacDonald, Kathleen Norris, and so many more. Bringing everyone together is Phillip, an ever-gracious host. You'll leave the party exhilarated and inspired, charged up with hope and a call to action.

BRIAN D. McLAREN,
author of *We Make the Road by Walking*

In Yancey's book *Vanishing Grace*, I was immediately drawn into a complex issue brought to light in an uncomplicated narrative. Yancey uses his masterful writing to lead readers into a place of understanding how volatile the good news "feels" to many outside of our faith. Yet he moves the reader into a place where we can all gently deliver the Good News to the world.

CARLOS WHITTAKER, author of *Moment Maker*

VANISHING
GRACE

Also by Philip Yancey

The Bible Jesus Read

Church: Why Bother?

Disappointment with God

Finding God in Unexpected Places

Grace Notes: Daily Reading with a Fellow Pilgrim

I Was Just Wondering

The Jesus I Never Knew

Meet the Bible (with Brenda Quinn)

Prayer: Does It Make Any Difference?

The Question That Never Goes Away

Reaching for the Invisible God

A Skeptic's Guide to Faith

Soul Survivor

The Student Bible (with Tim Stafford)

What's So Amazing About Grace?

Where Is God When It Hurts?

By Philip Yancey and Dr. Paul Brand

Fearfully and Wonderfully Made

The Gift of Pain

In His Image

In the Likeness of God

PHILIP YANCEY

VANISHING
GRACE

WHAT EVER HAPPENED TO
THE GOOD NEWS?

ZONDERVAN

Vanishing Grace

Copyright © 2014 by Philip Yancey

This title is also available as a Zondervan ebook. Visit www.zondervan.com/ebooks.

Requests for information should be addressed to:

Zondervan, 3900 Sparks Drive, SE, Grand Rapids, MI 49546

Library of Congress Cataloging-in-Publication Data

Yancey, Philip.
    Vanishing grace : whatever happened to the good news? / Philip Yancey. —
1st [edition].
        pages cm
    ISBN 978-0-310-33932-8 (hardcover)
    1. Christianity — United States — Public opinion. 2. Christianity and
culture — United States. 3. United States — Church history. 4. Witness bearing
(Christianity) I. Title.
    BR517.Y37 2014
    277.3'083 — dc23   2014010695

Published in association with Creative Trust, Inc., www.creativetrust.com

Front cover image: Chris Hackett / Getty Images®
Back cover and interior image: Potapov Alexander / Shutterstock®
Cover design Belinda Bass
Interior design: Katherine Lloyd, The DESK

Printed in the United States of America

First Printing September 2014

CONTENTS

129990

See to it that no one misses the grace of God...
HEBREWS 12:15

PREFACE

I set out to write a book on the endangered state of grace and ended up writing four short books, all related and bound inside the same cover.

I began with a concern that the church is failing in its mission to dispense grace to a world thirsty for it. More and more, surveys show, outsiders view Christians as bearers of bad news, not good news. (Part One)

Next I looked for models of how we could do it better, settling on three: pilgrims, activists, and artists. From their examples we can all learn what communicates best to a culture running away from faith. (Part Two)

Then I sensed a need to step back and ask a basic question that Christians may take for granted: Is the gospel truly good news? And if so, how does it stand up in light of alternatives offered by science, New Age, and other beliefs? (Part Three)

Finally, I returned briefly to one of the main stumbling blocks of faith, the confusing role of Christians in a diverse world. For many people, Christians' involvement in politics has drowned out our message of good news for all. How can we avoid being dismissed as one more lobby group? (Part Four)

All four sections have roots in a book I wrote almost twenty years ago. Originally, I had titled it *What's So Amazing About Grace and Why Don't Christians Show More of It?* until the publisher persuaded me to drop those last eight words. The question, though, has only grown more urgent in recent years. Like a sudden thaw in the middle of winter, grace happens at unexpected moments. It stops us short, catches the breath, disarms. If we manipulate it, try to control it, somehow earn it, that would not be grace. Yet not everyone has tasted of that amazing grace, and not everyone believes in it.

In a time of division and discord, grace seems in vanishing supply. Why? And what can we do about it?

PART ONE

A WORLD ATHIRST

In the novel The Second Coming *one of Walker Percy's characters says about Christians, "I cannot be sure they don't have the truth. But if they have the truth, why is it the case that they are repellent precisely to the degree that they embrace and advertise the truth? ... A mystery: If the good news is true, why is not one pleased to hear it?"*

CHAPTER 1

A GREAT DIVIDE

In general the churches ... bore for me the same
relation to God that billboards did to Coca-Cola:
they promoted thirst without quenching it.

JOHN UPDIKE, *A MONTH OF SUNDAYS*

A
s a Christian, I have deep concern about how we represent
our faith to others. We are called to proclaim good news
of forgiveness and hope, yet I keep coming across evidence
that many people do not hear our message as good news.

I decided to write this book after I saw the results of surveys
by the George Barna group.* A few telling statistics jumped off
the page. In 1996, 85 percent of Americans who had no religious
commitment still viewed Christianity favorably. Thirteen years
later, in 2009, only 16 percent of young "outsiders" had a favorable impression of Christianity, and just 3 percent had a good
impression of evangelicals. I wanted to explore what caused that
dramatic plunge in such a relatively short time. Why do Christians stir up hostile feelings — and what, if anything, should we
do about it?

For more than a decade I've had a window into how the
modern secular world views Christians, through a book group I

---

* Sources, including Bible references, are given at the end of the book.

belong to. These informed, well-traveled readers include an environmental lawyer, a philosopher who got fired from a state university because of his Marxist views, a child-development expert, a pharmacology researcher, a state auditor, a bankruptcy attorney, a librarian, and a neurologist. Our diverse careers and backgrounds make for lively discussion.

After ranging over ideas sparked by whatever book we've just read, the conversation usually drifts back to politics—a sort of substitute religion, apparently. All but one of my book buddies lean strongly to the political left, the sole exception a libertarian who opposes nearly all government. The group views me as a source of information about a parallel universe that exists beyond their social orbit. "You know evangelicals, right?" I nod yes. Then comes a question like, "Can you explain why they are so opposed to gay and lesbian marriages?" I do my best, but the arguments I repeat from leading evangelicals make no sense to this group.

After the 2004 reelection of George W. Bush, the Marxist professor launched into a tirade against right-wing evangelicals. "They're motivated by hate—sheer hate!" he said. I suggested fear as a possible motive instead, fear of society trending in what conservatives see as a troubling direction. "No, it's hate!" he insisted, uncharacteristically raising his voice and turning red in the face.

"Do you know any right-wing evangelicals personally?" I asked.

"Not really," he admitted a bit sheepishly, though he said he had known many in his youth. Like most of those in my book group, he had grown up in the church, in his case among Seventh-day Adventists.

Many similar conversations have taught me that religion represents a huge threat to those who see themselves as a minority of agnostics in a land of belief. Nonbelievers tend to regard evangelicals as a legion of morals police determined to impose their notion of right behavior on others. To them, Christians are anti-abortion, anti-gay, anti-women—probably anti-sex, for that matter—and most of them homeschool their children to avoid defilement. Christians sometimes help with social problems, say by running soup kitchens and homeless shelters, but otherwise they differ little from Muslim fanatics who want to enforce sharia law on their societies.

A research group based in Phoenix was surprised to encounter the degree of abuse directed toward Christians, antagonism that went far beyond a difference of opinion on issues. According to the company president, "Evangelicals were called illiterate, greedy, psychos, racist, stupid, narrow-minded, bigots, idiots, fanatics, nut cases, screaming loons, delusional, simpletons, pompous, morons, cruel, nitwits, and freaks, and that's just a partial list.... Some people don't have any idea what evangelicals actually are or what they believe—they just know they can't stand evangelicals."

The good news isn't sounding so good these days, at least to some.

MIXED AROMA

In a clever metaphor the apostle Paul writes of "the aroma of Christ" that can have a very different effect depending on the nose: "To the one, we are the smell of death; to the other, the fragrance of life." My assignments as a journalist take me to places where Christians give off a perfumed aroma and also to places where Christians offend the nostrils.

The United States is undergoing a marked change in its attitude toward religion, and Christians here face new challenges. When a blogger named Marc Yoder wrote about "10 Surprising Reasons Our Kids Leave Church," based on interviews in Texas (a comparatively religious state) his post went viral. Instead of a hundred or so hits, his website got more than half a million. "There's no easy way to say this," wrote Yoder, in words that struck a nerve: "The American Evangelical church has lost, is losing and will almost certainly continue to lose our youth."* If we don't adapt we will end up talking to ourselves in ever-dwindling numbers.

What lies behind the downward trend? I got some insight from a friend of mine in Chicago who once worked on the staff of Willow Creek Community Church, one of the nation's largest churches. Daniel Hill took a side job as a barista at a local Starbucks where, he now realizes, his pastoral education truly began.

One of his customer said, when the conversation turned to religion, "When Christians talk to you, they act as if you are a robot. They have an agenda to promote, and if you don't agree with them, they're done with you." Often Hill heard an anything-goes attitude: "I don't personally follow Christianity, but I figure whatever makes you happy, do it." As one person told him, "Look, we all know that 'God' is out there at some level, but no one has a right to tell another person what 'God' looks like for them. Each person is free to express that however they want, but they should keep their opinions to themselves."

During his time at the coffee shop Hill heard two distinct approaches to the faith. "Pre-Christians" seemed open and receptive when the topic of religion came up. They had no real hostility and could imagine themselves connecting with a church someday. In contrast, "post-Christians" harbored bad feelings. Some carried memories of past wounds: a church split, a domineering parent, a youth director or priest guilty of sexual abuse, a nasty divorce which the church handled clumsily. Others had simply absorbed the media's negative stereotypes of rabid fundamentalists and scandal-prone television evangelists.

Listening to Hill's stories, I thought back to C. S. Lewis's analogy of communicating faith in secular Britain. It's the difference between courting a divorcée and a virgin, Lewis told a friend in a letter. A divorcée won't easily fall for sweet nothings

---

* According to Barna surveys, 61 percent of today's youth had been churched at one point during their teen years but are now spiritually disengaged.

from a suitor—she's heard them all before—and has a basic distrust of romance. In modern America, Hill estimates, around three-quarters of young "outsiders" qualify as post-Christian, the divorcées of faith.

Not everyone falls into a neat category, of course, but I found Daniel Hill's perspective helpful. I began to think through my own contacts with people who have no faith commitment. Having lived in Hill's home city of Chicago, I must agree with his assessment of young urban dwellers. No one else in our six-unit condominium went to church, and most of them viewed Christians with suspicion. Some of my book group friends in Colorado also fit the post-Christian category.

On the other hand, large portions of the American South and Midwest remain open to faith and qualify as "pre-Christian." I grew up in the religion-soaked South, and on return visits I'm always struck by the difference in attitudes toward religion there. The Bible Belt largely accepts the framework of the gospel. There is a God (don't our coins affirm "In God We Trust"?); we have sinned (country music spells out the salacious details); and Jesus provides a way to forgive those sins (you can still see "Repent" or "Jesus Saves" slogans on some Southern barns and billboards). Hit the radio's Scan button while driving in the South and there's a good chance you'll hear a testimony from someone recounting their once-wayward life, now transformed by a born-again conversion experience.

On my travels to other places too—Africa, Latin America, parts of Asia—I see the continuing appeal of the basic Christian message. People there associate Christians with missionaries who came to them as pastors, teachers, doctors and nurses, agricultural experts, and relief workers. The gospel answers questions of meaning, holds out the promise of an afterlife, and provides a community of support for those in need. To many in the world it still sounds like good news, a Godspell to break the dark spell that shadows so much of life on earth.

When I return from those trips it comes as a shock when people in my home country speak of Christians more sinisterly. Post-Christians hear the same music as if distorted through cracked speakers. Evangelists who speak of sin come across as shrewish and hectoring: *What gives them the right to judge my behavior, especially when so many of them mess up their own lives?* Doctrines such as the Trinity, the Atonement, Original Sin, and Hell seem baffling, even incomprehensible, and who can legitimately claim truth anyway? People who live in prosperous countries, intent on enjoying this life, pay little heed to the idea of an afterlife. And a string of New Atheists upbraid all religion as bad news, a primary source of fanaticism and wars—one called the atrocities of 9/11 "a faith-based initiative"—and long for the day when the human species will finally outgrow its need for religion.

In Europe, the seat of Christian faith for most of its history, many do not give it a thought. Barely a third of French and British respondents even believe that God exists. While visiting France I spoke to a Campus Crusade worker who had practiced evangelism in Florida before moving to Europe. Carrying a clipboard, he would walk up to strangers and ask, "If you died and God asked why you should be allowed into heaven, what would you say?" That approach got mixed results in Florida, but in France he was met with blank stares; he might as well have been speaking Urdu. Now he leads with the question, "Do you believe in God?" and the typical French response goes something like this: "What a fascinating question! Let me think. I've never really considered it before."

As I travel internationally I feel like a commuter between post-Christian and pre-Christian societies. The cultural divide stands out sharply in the U.S., where Christians remain a force to be reckoned with. Some Christians respond to the divide by making harsh judgments about the people they disagree with—one of the main reasons evangelicals have an unsavory reputation. I cringe when I hear such words, and respond by keeping mostly quiet about my faith. Neither approach is healthy.

Jesus granted his followers the immense privilege of dispensing God's grace to a thirsty world. As one who has drunk deeply of that grace, I want to offer it to a world adrift. How can we communicate truly good news to a culture running away from it?

GOOD NEWS, SQUANDERED

The Quakers have a saying: "An enemy is one whose story we have not heard." To communicate to post-Christians, I must first listen to their stories for clues to how they view the world and how they view people like me. Those conversations are what led to the title of this book. Although God's grace is as amazing as ever, in my divided country it seems in vanishing supply.

I've asked strangers and casual acquaintances, "Why do Christians stir up such negative feelings?" Some bring up past atrocities, such as the widespread belief that the church executed eight or nine million witches (a figure that serious historians believe is exaggerated by 99 percent). I've heard complaints about strict Protestant or Catholic schools and tales of clergy intolerance — didn't John Lennon get kicked out of his boyhood church for laughing at an inappropriate time? Others repeat stories similar to that of Steve Jobs, who left church when the pastor had no answer for his questions about God and the starving children of Africa. The comedian Cathy Ladman expresses a common view: "All religions are the same: religion is basically guilt with different holidays."

Neighborhoods that once welcomed churches now file lawsuits against them, not just because of traffic and parking issues but because "We don't want a church in our community!" Animosity goes public when a prominent sports figure talks freely about faith. A few years ago NFL quarterback Tim Tebow and NBA guard Jeremy Lin attracted praise from Christians who appreciated their clean lifestyles and their willingness to discuss their beliefs. At the same time sports-talk radio, websites, blogs, and late-night comedians mercilessly mocked the two.

To our shame the church, or pockets of it here and there, can give good reason for aversion. When I took a break from writing this chapter I turned on CNN and watched a report on a pastor in North Carolina who proposes that we round up all "lesbians and queers" inside a huge fence, perhaps a hundred miles around, and air-drop food to them. Eventually they'll go extinct, he crows, since they don't reproduce. That same week a congregation in Indiana wildly applauded a seven-year-old boy who sang his composition, "Ain't no homos gonna go to heaven." And after the Sandy Hook school shootings in Connecticut, a prominent evangelical spokesman placed the blame on gays, iPods, evolution, and Supreme Court rulings against school prayer.

Recently I received a letter from an agnostic friend furious about Christians' behavior at her mother's funeral. She described the "fear-mongering come-to-Jesus-now proselytizing from the pulpit" by a pastor from "Grace (ironically) Community Something Megachurch." She added, "The only reason I did not climb over the pews and flee was the respect for my mother's evangelical faith." Several who attended the funeral said to her, "If one person accepted Christ during the service, then your mother's death was worth it."

The 2004 movie *Saved!* gives a glimpse into how the broader culture views Christians. Directed by Brian Dannelly, who as a kid managed to get expelled from both a Catholic elementary school and a Baptist high school, the movie wavers between biting satire and over-the-top comedy. A prissy believer named Hilary Faye leads a singing group, the Christian Jewels, who kidnap potential converts and try to exorcize their demons. The school's sole Jewish student, a rebel, fakes speaking in tongues and rips open her blouse during chapel. The parents of a gay teenager send him to a Christian rehab center—with the incongruous name Mercy House—for a one-year treatment program. Meanwhile Mary, who seduced him in an attempt to cure him of homosexuality, learns she is pregnant. The unfolding plot exposes all the Christians as hypocrites, with Hilary Faye at the top of the list, just above her philandering pastor.

In the final scene the gay character escapes from Mercy House and joins others in Mary's hospital room after she gives birth. Even the judgmental hypocrites begin to soften. The message is clear. Why can't we accept each other's differences—in beliefs, morality, sexual preferences, and everything else? Why can't we all just get along?

Nowadays the principle of tolerance rules above all others, and any religion that claims a corner on truth is suspect. Combine that with Christians' reputation for judging others' behavior, and no wonder opposition heats up. As one critic remarked, "Most people I meet assume that Christian means very conservative, entrenched in their thinking, anti-gay, anti-choice, angry, violent, illogical, empire builders; they want to convert everyone, and they generally cannot live peacefully with anyone who doesn't believe what they believe."

Jesus never commanded us to score well in opinion polls, but as I mull over the list of words people use to describe Christians I wonder how we can act as salt and yeast within a society that views us so negatively.

MODERN SAMARIA

Am I overreacting? I wondered whether negative feelings against religion were a local phenomenon until I came across a poll of eighteen thousand people in twenty-three countries. In preparation for a 2010 debate between Britain's former Prime Minister Tony Blair and the atheist Christopher Hitchens, the Toronto sponsors commissioned a simple survey. Here are the poll results on the question "Is religion a force for good?"

Country	Percentage who answer Yes
Saudi Arabia	92
Indonesia	91
India	69
United States	65
Russia	59
Italy	50
Turkey	43
Canada	36
Australia	32
Great Britain	29
Japan	29
France	24
Belgium	21
Sweden	19

In total, 52 percent of those surveyed judged that religion does more harm than good. Although the poll did not delve into what might lie behind such responses, I could not help noting that with a few exceptions the countries that had the most history with Christianity—especially in Europe—had the least respect for religion as a force for good. In contrast, Russia scored much higher, despite its atheist leaders' attempts to stamp out religion in the last century. I also noted that the poll did not include countries in Africa and South America that are experiencing a resurgence in religious faith.

The United States retains a basic respect for religion though it may be following European trends: surveys show a steady rise in the "nones" (now one-third of those under the age of thirty), that is, those who claim no religion, a category now larger than all Episcopalians, Presbyterians, Methodists, and Lutherans combined.

While pondering the poll results, I recalled an article Tim Stafford wrote for *Christianity Today* a few years back. Using parallels to biblical times, he said that Christians in the U.S. sometimes think we live in Babylon, as refugees stuck in a culture that trumpets values hostile to our faith (think Hollywood movies). Actually, we live in something more like Samaria. In Jesus' day the Samaritans lived just down the road from their cousins the Jews, and despite having much in common the two groups could not get along. Like estranged family members, they nursed grudges. To the Jews, Samaritans were heretics, plain and simple. John's Gospel reports, "Jews do not associate with Samaritans."

Surprisingly, groups that are closest to each other may spark the strongest enmity. The world outside Rwanda and Yugoslavia had trouble just keeping straight the differences between Hutu and Tutsi or Bosniak, Serb, and Croat — even as the groups themselves were slaughtering each other over those differences. And now we look at Middle East violence and struggle to understand the rancor between Shiite and Sunni Muslims. People who are the-same-but-not-quite-the-same can somehow generate more hatred than two groups with more obvious otherness. That was true in Jesus' time. The Pharisees used the "S-word" when insulting Jesus, accusing him of being "a Samaritan and demon-possessed." And when Samaritan villagers did not welcome Jesus, his disciples suggested calling down fire from heaven to destroy them.

"The problem is not that my religion is strange," says Stafford. "The problem is that my religion is familiar. Like Samaritans and Jews, Christians and non-Christians have a partly shared worldview (our Western traditions, which include the Bible), a shared point of origin (Christendom), and well-defined points of contention (the exclusivity of Christ). We are familiar with what each other believes. We're suspicious of one another. So we start off with a grudge."

I think of my friends in the book group, who support such

causes as human rights, education, democracy, and compassion for the weak, most of which stem from Christian roots. Yet they now view Christians as a powerful threat to those causes. Meanwhile, conservative Christians look at secularists and also see a powerful threat. *They're the ones who took prayer out of schools and who denounce religious displays at Christmas. More, they betrayed our Christian heritage by redefining marriage and legalizing abortion, and now they're pushing for assisted suicide.* Both groups, secular and Christian, tend to isolate themselves and judge the other without much dialogue or interaction.

I got a taste of the passionate feelings behind the culture wars when I posted a quote from the late Andy Rooney on my Facebook site. "I've decided I'm against abortion," said Rooney. "I think it's murder. But I have a dilemma in that I much prefer the pro-choice to the pro-life people. I'd much rather eat dinner with a group of the former." A mild firestorm erupted as responders posted comments. Some blasted Rooney for being nothing but a TV celebrity with no real credibility. Others defended pro-life volunteers, drawing a contrast between them and the obnoxious other side. One woman wrote, "What point are you trying to make here? That you, like Rooney, find the company of those who support the murder of innocents to be more superficially pleasing than the company of those who believe in protecting those babies? How fleshly of you.... Your post makes me sick."

In short, the responses underscored Andy Rooney's point. Would I want to eat dinner with the flame-throwers who posted comments on my site? I replied—and here is a recurring theme in this book—that the issue is not whether I agree with someone but rather how I treat someone with whom I profoundly disagree. We Christians are called to use the "weapons of grace," which means treating even our opponents with love and respect.

As usual, Jesus shows the way. When the Pharisees taunted him as "a Samaritan and demon-possessed," he denied the accusation of demon-possession but did not protest the racial slur. He rebuked the disciples for their call for violence against the Samaritans. Pointedly, he made a Samaritan the hero of one of his finest parables. He went out of his way to visit a Samaritan village and commanded his Jewish disciples to take the gospel to other such villages.

Eventually the disciples got the point: when Samaritans became Christ-followers with "great joy" after Jesus' ascension, they received the Holy Spirit through the ministry of Peter and John — the same John who had once called for fire from heaven to destroy them.

SIGNS OF THIRST

Some who spurn faith wear their atheism proudly, as a sign of defiance. (The German writer Heinrich Böll commented, "I don't like these atheists; they are always talking about God.") Others discard faith more wistfully or seek alternatives in New Age or other religions. Still others reject the church but not Jesus. All of them are reacting against a faith that no longer sounds like good news.

The same surveys that track the rise of the "nones," who have no religious affiliation, show that only a small minority of them claim to be atheists. Many still call themselves religious though they have not found a spiritual home. I have tried to listen to the uncommitted, not as opponents but as seekers who are still looking. Why did they leave the church and perhaps the faith? What can we learn from them, and how can we invite them back? Can the good news, once spoiled, ever sound good again?

Jesus "came from the Father, full of grace and truth," wrote John in the preface to his gospel. The church has worked tirelessly on the truth part of that formula: witness the church councils, creeds, volumes of theology, and denominational splits over minor points of doctrine. I yearn for the church to compete just as hard in conveying what Paul calls the "incomparable riches" of God's grace. Often, it seems, we're perceived more as guilt dispensers than as grace dispensers.

John records one close-up encounter between Jesus and a Samaritan woman. Knowing well the antipathy between the two groups, she marveled that a Jewish rabbi would even speak to her. At one point she brought up one of the disputed points of doctrine: Who had the proper place of worship, the Jews or the Samaritans? Jesus deftly sidestepped the question and bore in on a far more important issue: her unquenched thirst. He offered her not judgment but a lasting solution to her guilt over an unsettled life. To her and her alone he openly identified himself as Messiah and chose her as a grace dispenser. Her transformation captured the attention of the whole town, and Jesus stayed for two days among the "heretics," attracting many converts.

That scene of Jesus and the Samaritan woman came up during a day I spent with the author Henri Nouwen at his home in Toronto. He had just returned from San Francisco, where he spent a week in an AIDS clinic visiting patients who, in the days before antiretroviral drugs, faced a certain and agonizing death. "I'm a priest, and as part of my job I listen to people's stories," he told me. "So I went up and down the ward asking the patients, most of them young men, if they wanted to talk."

Nouwen went on to say that his prayers changed after that week. As he listened to accounts of promiscuity and addiction and self-destructive behavior, he heard hints of a thirst for love that had never been quenched. From then on he prayed, "God, help me to see others not as my enemies or as ungodly but rather as *thirsty* people. And give me the courage and compassion to offer your Living Water, which alone quenches deep thirst."

That day with the gentle priest has stayed with me. Now, whenever I encounter strident skeptics who mock my beliefs or people whose behavior I find offensive, I remind myself of Henri

Nouwen's prayer. I ask God to keep me from rushing to judgment or bristling with self-defense. *Let me see them as thirsty people,* I pray, *and teach me how best to present the Living Water.*

Graham Greene wrote a novel, *A Burnt-Out Case,* with autobiographical overtones about a renowned architect of churches who concludes that his works have been defiled by the worshipers who use them. Finding no more meaning in art or pleasure, and distraught over the suicide of his lover, the architect travels to a leprosarium in Congo run by Catholic missionaries and gains new energy as he oversees the building of a hospital for the leprosy patients.

Meanwhile the architect's servant, named Deo Gratias, disappears in the jungle. In a poignant scene, the architect wanders through the dark thicket calling out for his stumped, leprous servant: "Deo Gratias, Deo Gratias!"

He was calling, quite literally, for the grace of God. In different ways we all do in some form, we Christians, pre-Christians, and post-Christians. We thirst.

CHAPTER 2

GRACE ENDANGERED

But you take pleasure in the faces
Of those who know they thirst.

RAINER MARIA RILKE

The British writer Theodore Dalrymple confesses, "It is not as easy as one might suppose to rid oneself of the notion of God." After conceding that he is not a believer, he then proceeds to describe the void. Believing there is no God does not make the thirst go away.

> Few of us, especially as we grow older, are entirely comfortable with the idea that life is full of sound and fury but signifies nothing. However much philosophers tell us that it is illogical to fear death, and that at worst it is only the process of dying that we should fear, people still fear death as much as ever. In like fashion, however many times philosophers say that it is up to us ourselves, and to no one else, to find the meaning of life, we continue to long for a transcendent purpose ... To tell us that we should not feel this longing is a bit like telling someone in the first flush of love that the object of his affections is not worthy of them. The heart hath its reasons that reason knows not of.

For those who tune in, the longings whisper loudly. A teenager sits in his darkened bedroom wondering if anyone cares whether he lives or dies. A woman addicted to pain killers fingers a Styrofoam cup of coffee at a recovery group, wanting something less vague than a "Higher Power." A long-married couple stares out the restaurant window on their anniversary, awkwardly silent because they have nothing more to say. One therapist lists the complaints he hears from clients each day—emptiness, vague depression, a yearning for personal fulfillment, a hunger for spirituality—and diagnoses a "loss of soul," a void that modern culture fails to satisfy with its lure of entertainment and material goods.

I'm convinced that human beings instinctively seek two things. We long for meaning, a sense that our life somehow matters to the world around us. And we long for community, a sense of being loved.

Although Christians and the uncommitted may agree on a diagnosis, we disagree on the cure. Unlike the Samaritan woman, not everyone chooses to sample the Living Water that Jesus promised would quench thirst. To mention one example, the daughter of the famous atheist Bertrand Russell says that her father's "whole life was a search for God.... Somewhere at the back of my father's mind, at the bottom of his heart, in the depths of his soul, there was an empty space that had once been filled by God, and he never found anything else to put in it."

In Bertrand Russell's own words, "There is darkness without and when I die there will be darkness within." What kept the philosopher from faith?

Russell's daughter mentions one reason. "I would have liked to convince my father that I had found what he had been looking for, the ineffable something he had longed for all his life. I would have liked to persuade him that the search for God does not have to be vain. But it was hopeless. He had known too many blind Christians, bleak moralists who sucked the joy from life and persecuted their opponents; he would never have been able to see the truth they were hiding."

Sadly, many spiritual seekers I know tell stories similar to Bertrand Russell's, finding in the church neither a sense of community nor a resolution to their search. Church ends up turning them away from God rather than toward God. It strikes them as boring and formulaic, its community insular, its doctrine intolerant. A neighbor of mine put it well: "I tried religion. I spent eight years in Catholic schools, attended Mass every day and then on Sunday. The whole time I was sitting there I wanted to get out. I'm really supposed to believe that I'll burn in hell forever because I missed a day of Mass or broke a vow during Lent?"

Another acquaintance railed against Christians for fostering a spirit of "us versus them." Christians assume they have the one right answer to life's problems, an attitude that strikes her as arrogant and condescending. To her, church comes across as a private club that values outsiders mainly as potential members. "It seems to completely undermine sincere relationship building if you are looking at people as 'targets' to convert," she said. She went on, passion flaming, until suddenly she caught herself for being too negative and cynical.

"There is so much I am still trying to figure out," she added pensively. "But I do think honest critique is important ... I'm just in the process of figuring out what it means to do it in love." In that comment about herself, this woman may have put her finger on the core problem with Christians communicating faith: we do not always do so in love. That is an indispensable starting point to presenting faith in a grace-full way.

LOVE

"You never really understand a person until you consider things from his point of view ... until you climb into his skin and walk around in it," said Atticus Finch, the fictional lawyer in *To Kill a Mockingbird.* According to the experts, that process is not so simple and actually involves four encounters, not just two.

Imagine that I encounter a Muslim for the very first time. I meet him and he meets me. Lurking like ghosts behind those two encounters, though, are two more: my image of who he is and his image of who I am. I think of terrorists and the Taliban; he thinks of American drone missiles and internet pornography. We both have our vision clouded by preconceptions formed from news stories, Hollywood movies, and all the other stereotypes involved when two races and cultures confront each other.

Something similar happens when I meet an atheist. As soon as I tell him I am a Christian writer and he tells me he is an atheist, the preconceptions kick in. For true dialogue to occur, we must cut through those stereotypes and genuinely consider the other's point of view. Perhaps this is part of what Jesus meant when he said, "Love your neighbor *as yourself.*"

I thought about this process when I came across four common complaints about Christians in a magazine published by *Christianity Today*:

- You don't listen to me.
- You judge me.
- Your faith confuses me.
- You talk about what's wrong instead of making it right.

Reviewing these complaints, it occurs to me that Christians fail to communicate to others because we ignore basic principles in relationship. When we make condescending judgments, or proclaim lofty words that don't translate into action, or simply speak without first listening, we fail to love—and thus deter a thirsty world from Living Water. The good news about God's grace goes unheard.

I doubt God keeps track of how many arguments we win; God may indeed keep track of how well we love. When I ask, "Tell me the first word that comes to your mind when I say *Christian*," not one time has someone suggested the word *love*. Yet without question that is the proper biblical answer. "As I have loved you, so you must love one another," Jesus commanded his disciples at the Last Supper. He said the world will know we are Christians — and, moreover, will know who he is — when his followers are united in love.

God has a large stake in how we love. John adds that through love we make known an invisible God: "No one has ever seen God; but if we love one another, God lives in us and his love is made complete in us." In his famous chapter on love in 1 Corinthians 13, Paul declared that without love all our words and deeds dissonate, like an annoying cymbal or clanging gong — irritating noises that call to mind some of the words people use to describe Christians.

A friend of mine who worked as a consultant in the corporate world reviewed all the courses he had taken — and taught — on principles of good management. It occurred to him that he had never taken a course in how to love, even though the Bible presents it as the primary command in life. At a gathering I attended, he asked us to think about one question: "When have I felt loved?" I came up with a list: when someone listens to me attentively, makes me feel important, encourages me (and sometimes even challenges me), cares for me when I'm hurting, gives me an unexpected gift.

Then he told us that when he guided some of his clients through this same exercise, one female executive in a dysfunctional company decided to put the principles into practice. Although her company discouraged fraternizing, this woman started going down the hall and stopping in offices to visit her employees, with no real agenda. The first person was terrified, thinking she had come into his office to fire him. "No, no" she said, "I just figured that after three years of working together, I should get to know you."

She spent time with all thirteen of her employees until one day her own boss called her in. "I don't know what the hell you're doing," he said, "but this company was almost bankrupt. It turned around, and when I asked our personnel what happened, everybody said you were responsible."

Most conversions come about as an outgrowth of friendship. All the expensive and well-designed programs of evangelism and church growth combined produce only a fraction of the results of simple friendship. In the words of Tim Keller, "Don't think in terms of what used to be called friendship evangelism. Think in terms of friendship. Your evangelism should be organic and natural, not a bunch of bullet points and agenda items that you enter into a conversation hoping to get to so you're almost like a marketer."

Here's a good test of how well we love: Are other people glad to be with us? Somehow Jesus managed to attract the kind of people frowned upon by most religious types, and yet those renegades clearly liked being with Jesus. Think of the prostitute who crashed a dinner party and anointed him with expensive perfume, or of Zacchaeus, a tax collector scorned by his neighbors as a Roman collaborator. Rather than judging them, Jesus loved and honored them, and in the process brought to the surface a thirst that only he could satisfy.

THE STRANGER

There is a natural human tendency to withdraw into an enclave and associate with people just like us, avoiding opposition from those who see the world differently.

I admit, I prefer the ease of a gathering of like-minded friends to the awkwardness of other social encounters. "So, you're a writer ... what kind of books do you write?" The correct answer goes something like this: "I write books of popular theology exploring universal human questions." In many settings if I give that answer eyes will glaze over or open wide in alarm, and the questioner will quickly slide away. Yet these are the very conversations I need: first, to sharpen my own beliefs and, second, to live out my faith. It takes no grace to relate to someone who looks, thinks, and acts just like me.

According to Jonathan Sacks, the former chief rabbi of Great Britain, "The Hebrew Bible [Old Testament] in one verse commands, 'You shall love your neighbor as yourself,' but in no fewer than 36 places commands us to 'love the stranger.'" He adds, "The supreme religious challenge is to see God's image in one who is not in our image."

All too often Christians take the opposite approach. Some demonize opponents, branding them "secular humanists" or "heretics" or "perverts," and then retreat into a fortress mentality. Not long ago the novelist Anne Rice, who had been outspoken about her conversion a few years before, announced, "I quit being a Christian.... I remain committed to Christ ... but not to being 'Christian' or to being part of Christianity. It's simply impossible for me to 'belong' to this quarrelsome, hostile, disputatious, and deservedly infamous group." She cited Christians' antagonism to gay people as a major factor in her decision.

Politics especially encourages adversary relationships — the opposite of love — and Christians who enter the cultural fray are prone to caricature those with whom they disagree as *liberal* or even *immoral*, and to shun them. The radical Southern preacher Will Campbell learned of a church that was suing a nearby topless bar. "Imagine, suing them!" he said. "Shouldn't we want to be close to sinners, befriend them, convert them?"

Love has the power to win over the stranger. A news event in 1995 shocked both sides in the culture wars controversy. Norma Leah McCorvey, the "Jane Roe" of the famous *Roe v. Wade* Supreme Court case of 1973, converted to Christ, got baptized, and joined the pro-life campaign. Most astoundingly, it was the director of the anti-abortion group Operation Rescue who influenced her. As she tells the story, the change occurred when that director stopped treating her like an antagonist. He apologized for publicly calling her "baby killer" and started spending time with her during her smoking breaks in the parking lot that, oddly enough, their offices shared. In time McCorvey accepted an invitation to church from a seven-year-old girl whose mother also worked at Operation Rescue. Pro-abortion forces had dismissed McCorvey—her dubious past of drug-dealing, alcohol, and promiscuity made bad public relations—but Christian leaders took the time to counsel her in the faith while keeping her out of the spotlight for some time.

In a command found in no other religion, Jesus bids us show love not only to strangers and sinners but also to our outright adversaries. "Love your enemies," he said in the Sermon on the Mount, and "pray for those who persecute you." Once while speaking to my church I quoted those words of Jesus and flashed onscreen a photo of a dozen al-Qaeda terrorists. I asked, "What would happen if every church in the United States adopted a member of al-Qaeda, learned to pronounce his name, and prayed for him?"

A short time later I heard from an Army reserve chaplain named Thomas Bruce who took that charge seriously. Just before mobilizing for a year of duty in Iraq he launched the web-based prayer movement Adopt a Terrorist for Prayer. He registered the website as ATFP.org, an ironic echo of the Defense Department's own "Anti-Terrorism Force Protection." On it he posts photos of dangerous terrorists from the FBI's and State Department's most-wanted lists and invites users to "adopt" one to pray for. A thousand people have done so.

Not everyone appreciates Bruce's efforts. One person ridiculed him: "Christians come up with some goofy stuff. This is right up there. Love your enemies, and your enemies will KILL you." Some disagreed with the entire concept: "If you harbor anything but hatred for these terrorists, your morality is simply malfunctioning."

Why would Jesus give such an outrageous command? Perhaps anticipating objections, he provides the answer: "... that you may be children of your Father in heaven. He causes his sun to rise on the evil and the good, and sends rain on the righteous and the unrighteous." Luke's version is even more explicit: "You will be children of the Most High, because he is kind to the ungrateful and wicked." The more we love, and the more *unlikely* people we love, the more we resemble God—who, after all, loves ornery creatures like us.

Martin Luther King Jr. had much opportunity to practice the principle of "Loving Your Enemies." In a sermon by that title, written in jail after he had been arrested during the Montgomery bus boycott, he explained his method:

> To our most bitter opponents we say: "... Do to us what you will, and we shall continue to love you. We cannot in all good conscience obey your unjust laws because non-cooperation with evil is as much a moral obligation as is cooperation with good. Throw us in jail and we shall still love you. Bomb our homes and threaten our children, and we shall still love you. Send your hooded perpetrators of violence into our community at the midnight hour and beat us and leave us half dead, and we shall still love you. But be ye assured that we will wear you down by our capacity to suffer. One day we shall win freedom but not only for ourselves. We shall so appeal to your heart and conscience that we shall win you in the process and our victory will be a double victory."

Having served on the front lines in Iraq, Thomas Bruce has no mushy illusions about terrorists. Nor does he underestimate the power of love for adversaries, citing an example from the book of Acts. A disciple named Stephen was the first fatality of terrorism directed against Jesus' followers. As his enemies hurled stones at him, Stephen prayed, "Lord, do not hold this sin against them." Later Saul, an active participant in the stoning, met Jesus in a vision and repented.

"Can we pray today like Stephen prayed then?" Bruce asks. He adds one more poignant question: "Would Saul, who became the Apostle Paul, have met Jesus if Stephen hadn't prayed for his enemies?"

CULTURED DESPISERS

Opposition takes different forms, and love faces a stern test when we find ourselves the objects of indifference or a sort of snobbish disdain. The New Atheists openly mock Christians and their beliefs, with Richard Dawkins dismissing all religion as "a virus of the mind." Consider the reaction of Virginia Woolf after she learned of the poet T. S. Eliot's conversion to Christianity. She wrote her sister:

> I have had a most shameful and distressing interview with poor dear Tom Eliot, who may be called dead to us all from this day forward. He has become an Anglo-Catholic, believes in God and immortality, and goes to church. I was really shocked. A corpse would seem to me more credible than he is. I mean, there's something obscene in a living person sitting by the fire and believing in God.

Such attitudes should not surprise us: Paul, the first missionary, met contempt in the cultural centers of Athens and Corinth. A few years after Virginia Woolf, the pastor Dietrich Bonhoeffer faced mocking opponents in Nazi Germany, where the nation's educated elite scorned the church as narrow-minded and hypocritical. Writing to fellow pastors, Bonhoeffer advised that in response to cultured despisers who stand against the church, "the quiet service of love is the best spiritual care."

What does love look like in the face of hostile criticism? A gentle answer turns away wrath, the writer of Proverbs tells us. Are we kind to those who are unkind to us, or do we match their criticism and name-calling?

I have seen how the quiet service of love may disarm despisers, in the compelling example of Dr. Francis Collins. No one can dispute Collins's credentials as a scientist: he holds both a PhD and an MD degree and directed the Human Genome Project toward its triumphant goal of mapping all three billion letters of the human genetic code. Collins also identifies himself as a committed Christian and has engaged in cordial public debates with atheists such as Christopher Hitchens and Richard Dawkins (the latter in a *Time* cover story).

Due to his Christian faith, Francis Collins's nomination to head the National Institutes of Health, the nation's largest scientific organization, attracted strident criticism. One scientist accused Collins of suffering from dementia, and another complained, "I don't want American science to be represented by a clown." Skeptics scoffed at his respect for the Bible: When TV host Bill Maher told Richard Dawkins (falsely) that Collins believes in a talking snake, Dawkins replied, "He's not a bright guy."

In time, though, Collins won over most of his critics. As I have watched his career, one thing impresses me more than his many achievements: how he treats his opponents. On periodic visits to Oxford he has tea with Richard Dawkins. Similarly, he met often with the militant atheist Christopher Hitchens, author of *God Is Not Great*. And when Collins learned that Hitchens had esophageal cancer, he called to offer help: "As NIH director I approve many government-funded research grants, and I know about some rather cutting-edge approaches based on cancer genomics." Over the next few months he spent hours with the Hitchens family going over options for treatment.

Christopher Hitchens lived with his cancer for a year and a half, an ordeal that he chronicled in regular columns for *Vanity Fair* magazine. He told of receiving hateful messages from Christians, including one who, believing mistakenly that Hitchens had throat cancer, rejoiced that "he got cancer in the one part of his body he used for blasphemy ... THEN comes the real fun, when he's sent to HELLFIRE forever to be tortured and set afire."

Yet one of Hitchens' last columns paid tribute to Francis Collins, whom he described as "one of the greatest living Americans" and "our most selfless Christian physician." He wrote, "This great humanitarian is also a devotee of the work of C. S. Lewis and in his book *The Language of God* has set out the case for making science compatible with faith.... I know Francis, too, from various public and private debates over religion. He has been kind enough to visit me in his own time and to discuss all sorts of novel treatments, only recently even imaginable, that might apply to my case."

Christopher Hitchens had no deathbed conversion and passed from this life as a convinced atheist. But from one friend, at least, he received spiritual care, "the quiet service of love." Francis Collins fulfilled the command in Hebrews, "See to it that no one misses the grace of God ..." The rest is in God's hands.

HUMILITY

Martin Marty, the prolific Lutheran scholar at the University of Chicago, reported in *The Christian Century* magazine that readers have asked him when he planned to comment on the media's discovery of "the New Atheism." He put together a list of advice, "to myself and anyone else who cares," including the following:

- Keep cool. America has seen cycles like these before and has managed to survive.

- Send cards of thanks. These authors bring up differences in an age of indifference.
- Don't sneer. Many of these authors sneer. Where does that get us?
- Don't sound triumphalist. Some say "we" have "them" outnumbered 97 to three. If true, that represents a comfort margin for believers, but what does it prove?
- Don't argue. No one wins arguments—which are determined by one's knowing the answer—about the existence or nonexistence of God, but everyone can profit from a conversation that tries to pose good questions and respond to them.
- Read better books by these authors, from which you might learn something, as opposed to their sensational polemics on a subject they are not well versed in.
- Agree with the authors that in the name of religion horrible things have been done and are being done, but point out that that's not the whole story of religion. Criticism of religion from within is more searching and matters more.
- Hold up the mirror if you are a believer, and ask whether anything anyone is saying or doing gives legitimate grounds for anti-religion to voice itself and creates a market for books like these.

I am struck by the underlying tone of humility in the comments from Marty, one of America's most distinguished scholars of religion.

Ask uncommitted people to describe Christians and you'll likely hear such words as "smug," "exclusive," and "self-righteous." Christians can come across as superior and judgmental, dismissing others' beliefs while being defensive about their own. When I sense those tendencies in myself, I try to remember how I feel when someone argues that I'm wrong about something—which gives a strong clue to how others must feel when I present my own beliefs insensitively. I've yet to meet someone who found their way to faith by being criticized.

When I graduated from a Christian college, I knew everything: who were the "real Christians" and who were the fakes, which theologians were orthodox and which were heretics, what behavior was spiritual and what was not. Every year since graduation I've gained a better sense of how little I know. I've had to come to terms with my false pride and learn humility—a prerequisite for grace. At the same time I have learned to embrace mystery, an outlook I find in such biblical books as Job, Ecclesiastes, and Psalms. And I'm trying to add, in spirit if not in words, the line, "Of course, I could be wrong."

We Christians do not have all the answers. We stumble along, believing that an invisible God really does exist, that there is more to life than mere sound and fury, that despite all appearances the universe is a product of personal love. Along the way we muddle ethical issues and miss the priorities of God's kingdom. We have little reason for pride.

The priest Henri Nouwen learned humility on a mission trip to South America. He went expecting to pass on his wisdom to the poor and unenlightened. During his six-month stay, Nouwen concluded that a desire to save, whether from sin or poverty or exploitation, is one of the most damaging motives in ministry. "Humility is the real Christian virtue," says Nouwen. "When we come to realize that ... only God saves, then we are free to serve, then we can live truly humble lives." Nouwen changed his approach from "selling pearls," or peddling the good news, to "hunting for the treasure" already present in those he was called to love—a shift from dispensing religion to dispensing grace.

It makes all the difference in the world whether I view my neighbor as a potential convert or as someone whom God already loves.

TWO STORIES

How do we communicate a deeply felt faith with a style of humility? Two stories may show the way.

In his book *Blue Like Jazz* Donald Miller tells of setting up a confession booth at the liberal university he attended in Oregon. He and a group of fellow Christians staffed the booth in the midst of a raucous campus festival notorious for its drunkenness and debauchery. In a surprising twist, though, the Christians used the booth as a way of confessing their own sins to the skeptical students who wandered by. They apologized for the mistakes of the church and for the ways in which they personally had failed to live out what they believed.

As Miller confessed to one startled curiosity-seeker, "Jesus said to feed the poor and to heal the sick. I have never done very much about that. Jesus said to love those who persecute me. I tend to lash out, especially if I feel threatened, you know, if my ego gets threatened. Jesus did not mix his spirituality with politics. I grew up doing that. It got in the way of the central message of Christ. I know that was wrong, and I know that a lot of people will not listen to the words of Christ because people like me, who know him, carry our own agendas into the conversation rather than just relaying the message Christ wanted to get across."

Over the next several hours Miller and his friends spoke to scores of fellow students. "Many people wanted to hug when we were done," he writes. "All of the people who visited the booth were grateful and gracious. I was being changed through the process. I went in with doubts and came out believing ..."

The second story unfolded in the nearby state of Utah. For a number of years Craig Detweiler has been bringing his communications students from Biola University and Pepperdine University to the Sundance Film Festival, the premier showcase for independent films. One year Sundance featured a sold-out showing of a movie scathing in its portrayal of American evangelicals. The film tells the story of a white-bread suburban family killed in a car wreck on the way to a Southern Baptist church meeting. Upon their arrival in heaven a tattooed Jesus dispatches them again to earth, this time stripped of original sin, and they celebrate their new shamelessness by walking around naked and doing things that shock their friends and neighbors. Scandalized, other Christians at a Bible study hatch a plan to give the resurrected family an apple pie laced with poison, sending them promptly back to heaven.

The Sundance audience laughed uproariously throughout the film, relishing the depiction of Christians as repressed, intolerant, even homicidal. The director received a standing ovation and then fielded questions from the audience. Someone asked if any conservative Christians had seen it. "I'm ready for that fight," he declared, prompting more applause.

Without thinking Craig Detweiler stood to his feet with a response. I'll let him relate what happened next:

> I struggled to compose my words. My voice cracked slightly. I eked out, "Jay, thank you for this film. As a native of North Carolina, a fellow filmmaker, and an evangelical Christian ..."
>
> I never use the word *evangelical*. It is so loaded with negative baggage that I usually attempt to distance myself from such associations. But in this instance, it seemed quite right. I was speaking for my community, responding to a particular stance we'd staked out for ourselves. Jay stepped back, ready for that fight. He tensed up, preparing to launch a counterattack. The crowd sensed that things were about to get ugly. My next words caught them off guard:
>
> "Jay, I apologize for anything ever done to you in the name of God."

The entire tenor in the room shifted. Audience members turned around. "Did I hear that correctly?" They craned their necks. "Who said that?" Jay fumbled for words, not knowing how to respond. He was ready to be attacked. He was not prepared for an apology. He offered a modest, "Thank you." The audience was literally disarmed. . . .

Audience members approached me afterward with hugs. A lesbian couple thanked me. Gay men kissed me. One person said, "If that is true, I might consider giving Christianity another chance." Tears were shed far and wide. All it took were two little words: "I apologize."

My students leaped at the occasion, talking to the cast and crew, inviting them to join us for further conversation. Our "enemies" became fast friends, joining us for lunch. The cast came to our class the next day, answering questions for an hour. An actor admitted how scared he was to enter our church meeting place. Onstage, he confided, "Coming into this building, my heart was beating more than at any audition I've ever had." The producer said, "This was the most significant moment of our week." A simple apology set off a series of conversations and exchanges about our faith and how we live it.

Experiences such as these convince me that the approach of admitting our errors, besides being most true to a gospel of grace, is also most effective at expressing who we are. Propaganda turns people off; humbly admitting mistakes disarms. Far from claiming to have it all together, Christians regularly confess that we do not. After all, Jesus said he came for the sick and not the well, for sinners and not for saints. In the words of the old gospel song, "He looked beyond my faults and saw my need." True followers of Jesus distinguish themselves primarily by admitting failure and the need for help.

CHAPTER 3

SOUL THIRST

The soul knows for certain only that it is hungry....
A child does not stop crying if we suggest to it that perhaps
there is no bread. It goes on crying just the same.

SIMONE WEIL

I've referred to my book group friends, who view Christians mainly as a political voting bloc. In ten years of regular meetings only twice have they shown an obvious interest in matters of faith.

One evening Josh told us about his sister, now a Tea Party evangelical living in Virginia. She had been a drug addict, unable to hold a job or keep a marriage together. "Then one day she found Jesus," Josh said. "There's just no other way to put it. She changed from night to day. Her ideas drive me crazy, but I can't deny the change in her life. She had tried every kind of rehab and recovery therapy and nothing else worked."

Later in the evening Josh asked me in private to recommend some books that might explain the Christian faith in a way he could understand. "My sister sends me books that are totally unconvincing," he said. "They seem written for people who already believe them. Would C. S. Lewis be appropriate?" I smiled approvingly and went to my bookshelves to pull out a few.

Another time, quite to my surprise, the Marxist professor asked my advice on versions of the Bible. He had decided to buy one and read it all the way through, Genesis to Revelation. "That's quite a goal," I said. "What prompted it?" I knew he had been battling prostate cancer for several years. Recently, he explained, doctors had informed him he was approaching the end of his life. In the few weeks or months left to him, he wanted to revisit with mature eyes the faith he had abandoned in his youth.

We talked several times before he died. "I agree with you on the questions," he said. "I just can't agree on the answers."

The questions — universals, what we all have in common — are a good place to start in communicating the good news.

LOST AND FOUND

Thomas Merton wrote in his journal. "In fact, spiritual dryness is one of the most acute experiences of longing we can have." I look inward at my own spiritual thirst, and think also of people I know. What are the symptoms? A restless search for pleasure, fear of death, boredom, addiction — any of these can betray a longing that is at root spiritual, the cries and whispers of someone who has lost the way.

How differently will I relate to the uncommitted if I view them not as *evil* or *unsaved* but rather as *lost.* For some that word summons up scenes of revival preachers who fulminate against "the lost." I mean it in a different, more compassionate sense. Several times while hiking in the mountains of Colorado I have missed markers along the trail and have wandered off course. I stare in confusion at my map and compass, trying not to panic. Already I've wasted precious time and energy, and I know the dangers of spending the night unprepared in a high-altitude wilderness. At last I see another hiker and call out. When I reach him, he kindly takes my map and shows me where I am and where I need to go. Anxiety fades as I realize I'm no longer lost. I know the way home.

I must say, though, that I've also found unexpected treasures on those mountain detours, views and discoveries that few other hikers get to experience. Once I know I'm safe, I can look back on my hours of lostness as an adventure, one I can learn from. Strangely enough, some of the scariest times, such as when I "cliff out" and can't find a way down, become the stories I like to swap with fellow climbers.

Barbara Brown Taylor recalls her own wanderings: "In my life, I have lost my way more times than I can count. I have set out to be married and ended up divorced. I have set out to be healthy and ended up sick. I have set out to live in New England and ended up in Georgia. When I was thirty, I set out to be a parish priest, planning to spend the rest of my life caring for souls in any congregation that would have me. Almost thirty years later, I teach school." She concludes:

> While none of these displacements was pleasant at first, I would not give a single one of them back. I have found things while I was lost that I might never have discovered if I had stayed on the path. I have lived through parts of life that no one in her right mind would ever willingly have chosen, finding enough overlooked treasure in them to outweigh my projected wages in the life I had planned. These are just a few of the reasons that I have decided to stop fighting the prospect of getting lost and engage it as a spiritual practice instead. The Bible is a great help to me in this practice, since it reminds me that God does some of God's best work with people who are truly, seriously lost.

In my lifelong study of the Bible I have looked for an overarching theme, a summary statement of what the whole sprawling book is about. I have settled on this: "God gets his family back." From the first book to the last the Bible tells of wayward children

51

and the tortuous lengths to which God will go to bring them home. Indeed, the entire biblical drama ends with a huge family reunion in the book of Revelation.

Many of Jesus' own stories center on the theme of lostness, captured most movingly in the parable of the prodigal son. Jesus' tales of lostness—a coin, a sheep, a son—make two important points. First, the lost are a high priority, worth whatever effort it takes to find them, even if it means leaving the ninety-nine to search for the one. Second, when found, the lost deserve to be celebrated. "This brother of yours was dead and is alive again; he was lost and is found," cried the joyful father, defending his open arms of grace before the resentful older brother.

The stories were a threat to the Pharisees, who were content to shun the lost and associate with other Pharisees, gaining status by following familiar rules. And they are a threat to me for I, too, prefer the comfort of predictable religion to the messy business of seeking the lost. The parable of the prodigal son, especially, tears down my neat categories that separate responsible from irresponsible, obedient from rebellious, moral from immoral. Such is grace.

From a stream that runs outside my Colorado home I have a constant, startling image of God's free gift of grace to the undeserving. Like water, grace always flows downward. The stream that begins as a rivulet in a melting snowfield at the top of a mountain trickles down to form runnels, then lovely alpine lakes, then a roaring river, and finally a wide blue lake. Sometimes I think of the hymn "There's a Wideness in God's Mercy" when I pass that lake.

I have learned a new way of looking at the lost from the theologian Jürgen Moltmann, who came to faith during World War II as a captured German soldier in a British POW camp. Scottish women brought the enemy prisoners home-baked goods and a Bible, and, touched by their gesture, he began to read it. After the war he returned to his homeland where he went on to serve as a pastor and professor in the German church hierarchy. Later, though, he began to question a religious system that stratifies bishops, priests, and laypersons and then sets them all against the unbelievers. Didn't Jesus call his followers brothers and sisters, implying something more like a family than a corporation? Doesn't God reign over all the world, including those outside the fold?

"The church is where Christ is," Moltmann decided. The *manifest* church comprises those who accept Christ and embrace the gospel. "But Christ is also in the place where the poor, the hungry, the sick, and the prisoners are to be found: 'As you did it to one of the least of these my brethren, you did it to me.' That is the *latent* church." You cannot read the Bible without hearing the loud message that God cares for the displaced, the downtrodden, the oppressed, the humble, the needy—in other words, those who know their lostness and who long to be found.*

The Beatitudes spell out that the restless and discontent—the latent church, in Moltmann's phrase—may already be close to God. Think about it. The rich act as though this life will never end; the poor feel hunger pangs for something more. Those who mourn sense the rupture of a world severed from God and thus edge closer to the Father who promises to make all things new. Peacemakers and the merciful, whatever their motivation, strive for harmony, for a human family restored.

The poor in spirit qualify just as much as the economically poor. Christian Wiman, the urbane editor of *Poetry* magazine, uses the same word as Moltmann to describe the stirrings that led him back to faith. He writes, "When I assented to the faith that was *latent* within me—and I phrase it carefully, deliberately, for there was no light, no ministering or avenging angel that tore my life in two; rather it seemed as if the tiniest seed of belief had

---

* H. G. Wells wrote, "Christianity has been denounced by modern writers as a 'slave religion.' It was. It took the slaves and the downtrodden, and it gave them hope and restored their self-respect so that they stood up for righteousness like men and faced persecution and torment."

finally flowered in me, or, more accurately, as if I had happened upon some rare flower deep in the desert and had known, though I was just then discovering it, that it had been blooming impossibly year after parched year in me, surviving all the seasons of my unbelief."

It makes a huge difference whether I treat a nonbeliever as someone who is *wrong* rather than as someone who is on the way but lost. For a helpful model I look to the apostle Paul's speech in the cultural center of Athens, as recorded in Acts 17. Instead of condemning his audience to hell for practicing idolatry, Paul begins by commending their spiritual search, especially their devotion to an "unknown God." God planned creation and human life, Paul told the Athenians, so that we "would seek him and perhaps reach out for him and find him, though he is not far from any one of us." He builds his case from common ground, quoting two of their own writers to affirm basic truths. Demonstrating a humble respect for his audience, Paul circles the themes of lostness and estranged family before presenting a richer understanding of a God who cannot be captured in images of gold, silver, or stone.

There is a time to critique the surrounding culture and a time to listen, in the process perhaps awakening a latent thirst. "I went looking for spirit and found alcohol; I went looking for soul, and I bought some style; I wanted to meet God, but they sold me religion," the rock star Bono sometimes shouts at concerts. In *Yahweh*, a song I heard him perform in a packed arena, he offered God his hands, which clench into fists, his mouth "so quick to criticize," and finally his heart: "Take this heart, and make it break." By the end of the concert he had twenty thousand fans joining him in the chorus to Leonard Cohen's "Hallelujah."

When Bono decided to talk in detail about his faith he chose an unlikely collaborator, a stranger to the faith. In the resulting book, the agnostic French journalist Michka Assayas challenges Bono to explain how he could possibly believe in Christianity in the midst of the very secular world of rock and roll. One by one, Bono answers his questions. He freely admits the flaws of the church yet also claims that following Jesus has satisfied his own search for meaning while giving him causes to pursue beyond celebrity and pleasure.

COMMON GROUND

Dag Hammarskjöld, who served as secretary-general of the United Nations during some of the tensest days of the Cold War, explained that in dealing with adversaries he would begin by searching for the smallest point of common ground. When he found a single point of agreement between two parties, he then worked toward building relationship and trust that could perhaps lead to honest dialogue on harder issues. As a model, he looked to Jesus, who was God's way of sharing the common ground of humanity: "He sat at meat with publicans and sinners, he consorted with harlots."

Communicating faith to skeptics usually works best when it emphasizes how we are alike, not how we are different. I am learning to resist the tendency to see others as opponents or targets and instead look for areas of common ground, places where we can stand together. Many post-Christians, I find, live by what I call "habits of the soul," acting out Christian principles of compassion and justice that persist even in a society moving away from faith. "Like a whispering in dark streets, rumors of God run through your dark blood," wrote the poet Rilke.

Christian apologetics focuses on ideas and truth. Though important, that approach may be overrated since most people don't spend much time consciously reflecting on truth. Rather, they act by instinct. Some of those instincts are very good, and many are a legacy of a Christian past. For example, everyone I know in the medical field accepts the need to treat the "undeserving," such as irresponsible people whose health problems are self-inflicted, even though from a strictly pragmatic approach that treatment makes little sense. (In India I have met Brahmins who would not think of giving aid to the poor or the sick; they believe such charity wrongly rewards people who deserve their plight as punishment for deeds in a former life.)

Or, I think of all that I have in common with my book group friends. We have many of the same interests and share concerns about the state of our society. These folks don't want their kids to waste themselves on methamphetamine, get pregnant out of wedlock, or turn to violent crime. Responsible citizens, they contribute to society both in their careers and in volunteer activities. Working mainly through politics, they advocate on behalf of neglected children and healthcare and environmental causes. I can build bridges by affirming such instincts despite their uncertain source.

In the process the uncommitted challenge me to examine why I uphold these values. I join the Audubon Society and Friends of the Earth because I see the natural world as God's work of art, and want to preserve the magnificent planet on which God placed us. I support Amnesty International and International Justice Mission in their advocacy for political prisoners and the oppressed, because I believe each person on earth expresses the image of God and has ultimate worth. Pure selfishness tempts me to neglect the vulnerable while my faith requires me to care.

To my surprise, many post-Christians cannot explain their good instincts. Sigmund Freud found himself puzzled by his. He admitted that something inside him caused him to act morally, even to practice a traditional sexual morality he did not believe in, though he could not account for that behavior. "Why I — and incidentally my six adult children also — have to be thoroughly decent human beings is quite incomprehensible to me," he said. Like Freud, many moderns act out habits of the soul absorbed from a culture influenced by Christians.

Most people assume life has some meaning, although prominent scientists and philosophers proclaim the opposite. Albert Camus wrote a novel, *The Stranger*, depicting a man named Meursault who lives out his belief that life has no purpose or ultimate destiny. "Do you love me?" his girlfriend asks, and he replies that he probably doesn't and in fact sees no meaning to the question. "Will you marry me?" she presses. He is indifferent, not caring one way or the other. His mother's death draws no emotional reaction either; in fact he goes swimming and watches a comedy at the cinema the next day. Eventually Meursault murders a man for no reason, again showing no emotion. The court sentences him to execution, which he also faces with utter indifference. It matters not at all whether he does something or the opposite. "There is but one truly serious philosophical problem and that is suicide," said the author Camus, and his disturbing novel bears out that philosophy.

Who lives that way, though? Instinctively we do not live with utter indifference. We judge some things more beautiful than others, some people more virtuous than others, some acts more meaningful than others. We fall in love, care for helpless infants, grieve when relatives die, prosecute murderers — in a thousand ways we live as though life has meaning, as if love, beauty, truth, justice, and morality are not just arbitrary concepts but somehow real.

We make choices as if they matter, despite all the modern thinkers who declare just the opposite. That instinct is theological at the core. "Either life is holy with meaning, or life doesn't mean a damn thing," says the author Frederick Buechner.

In crucial areas nonbelievers and Christians occupy a large expanse of common ground. Like Paul speaking to the Athenians, we can affirm the good instincts still present in surrounding culture while gently pointing to their source.

In February 2013, *Christianity Today* published the testimony of Rosaria Champagne Butterfield, who described her younger self as a "leftist lesbian professor" who despised Christians. "I tired of students who seemed to believe that 'knowing Jesus' meant knowing little else. Christians in particular were bad readers, always seizing opportunities to insert a Bible verse into a conversation with the same point as a punctuation mark: to end it rather than deepen it. Stupid. Pointless. Menacing. That's what I thought of Christians and their god Jesus, who in paintings looked as powerful as a Breck Shampoo commercial model."

As a professor of English and women's studies, Butterfield cared deeply about morality, justice, and compassion. For guidance she looked to Freud, Hegel, Marx, and Darwin — and not to Jesus, mainly because of his zealous "band of warriors." While researching the Religious Right and "their politics of hatred against queers like me," she forced herself to read the Bible, the source that in her opinion had led so many people off track. She published a critical article in the local newspaper about Promise Keepers and proceeded to file away the response letters in two boxes, one for hate mail and one for fan mail.

One letter, however, fit neither box. In a kind and inquiring spirit, a Presbyterian pastor from Syracuse, New York, encouraged her to explore further her conclusions. How did she arrive at them? On what basis did she decide on her moral convictions? After first throwing it away, she later fished it out of the recycling bin and stared at it. Eventually she accepted the pastor's invitation to dinner and over the next two years became friends with Ken and his wife Floy. "They entered my world," she recalls. "They met my friends. We did book exchanges. We talked openly about sexuality and politics. They did not act as if such conversations were polluting them. They did not treat me like a blank slate."

Meanwhile, Butterfield continued to read the Bible, many times, in multiple translations. Finally, she found herself in the pew of that pastor's church, feeling conspicuous with her butch haircut. "Then, one ordinary day, I came to Jesus, openhanded and naked. In this war of worldviews, Ken was there. Floy was there. The church that had been praying for me for years was there. Jesus triumphed. And I was a broken mess. Conversion was a train wreck. I did not want to lose everything that I loved. But the voice of God sang a sanguine love song in the rubble of my world."

Rosaria Butterfield, now herself a pastor's wife, still champions morality, justice, and compassion. She came to faith in search of a foundation for what she valued, drawn by the tender care of two Christians who graciously pointed her to that foundation.

The uncommitted share many of our core values, but if we do not live out those values in a compelling way, we will not awaken a thirst for their ultimate Source. Christians can do no better than follow the example set by Jesus, who specialized not in techniques and arguments but in spirit and example. He took skeptics seriously, listening to them and responding forthrightly and yet compassionately. The gospel of Mark adds a telling detail to a scene in which a potential wealthy convert rejects Jesus' message and walks away: "Jesus looked at him and loved him."

I turn again to the conversation between Jesus and a Samaritan woman who had found some solace in an alternative religion. What if Jesus had engaged in an argument with her about their differences over where to worship? Instead he summoned up a thirst already evident in her troubled life of five failed marriages. "Everyone who drinks this water will be thirsty again," he said, referring to the well water she was drawing for him, "but whoever drinks the water I give them will never thirst. Indeed, the water I give them will become in them a spring of water welling up to eternal life."

In that brief exchange Jesus demonstrated a model for relating to a pluralistic culture. We dare not disdain the choices others have made, for that would not show love. Instead, we should tune in to the underlying thirst.

BEAUTY AND PAIN

"If there is no God, never was a God, why do we miss him so much?" asked one agnostic European Jew as he looked back on the horrors of the twentieth century. Certain universal human experiences—beauty, pain, evil, death—bring deep thirst to the surface.

Affliction and beauty pierce the human heart, said Simone Weil. I have seen both act as spurs toward faith, and they work in different ways: where affliction penetrates by force, beauty strikes a chord of response akin to praise or gratitude. When I was lost, spiritually, it was beauty that brought me back to faith—the beauty of nature, of music, of love—by reviving a desire to connect with the Father of all good gifts.

On those unplanned detours in the mountains, sometimes I'll turn a corner and find an extravagance of wildflowers that takes my breath away. Hiking in the splendidly named Oh Be Joyful Valley, my wife and I lay down in a field of alpine wildflowers with hummingbirds whistling around us in a setting as pristine as the Garden of Eden. Such sights give me another startling image of grace, for God has lavished this planet with beauty that shines forth whether noticed or not. Nature goes on, beauty goes on, whether or not anyone is there to observe it.

I thank God that during two decades in Colorado I've had opportunities to observe. Once while mountain biking I disturbed a herd of elk and came across a baby elk still glistening from birth, eyes large with fear, motionless as a rock. Another time, descending a canyon trail, I saw two bighorn sheep stand on their hind legs and head-butt each other with a sound that cracked like thunder. On another hike, early in the morning we surprised a flock of mountain bluebirds, who darted up and caught the sunlight with an explosion of color like silent fireworks. You only get these sights in the wilderness, and then you realize you may be the only persons on earth graced with that particular glimpse of God's creation.

I agree with George MacDonald, who wrote,

One of my greatest difficulties in consenting to think of religion was that I thought I should have to give up my beautiful thoughts and my love for the things God has made. But I find that the happiness springing from all things not in themselves sinful is much increased by religion. God is the God of the Beautiful — Religion is the love of the Beautiful, and Heaven is the Home of the Beautiful — Nature is tenfold brighter in the Sun of Righteousness, and my love of Nature is more intense since I became a Christian.*

It baffles me that places of natural beauty do not necessarily foster religious faith — how can Oregon and Washington have such low church attendance? Nature was one of the keys that brought me back to God, for I wanted to know the Artist responsible for both the beauty and the whimsy that I found there. When I feel grief over a friend's illness or death, and my world lurches to a stop, instinctively I want to take a long hike as a reminder that the larger world moves on, fiercely beautiful, regardless of any crisis great or small. Wasn't that God's message to Job?

Pain works at a different level than beauty. It distills life, adds urgency. Christian Wiman, the *Poetry* editor, found the mantra "spiritual but not religious" of scant comfort when he faced the all-too-specific terror of incurable cancer. Needing something

---

* MacDonald embodied a gracious Christianity, and his work deeply influenced the writers C. S. Lewis, J. R. R. Tolkien, G. K. Chesterton, Oswald Chambers, W. H. Auden, Madeleine L'Engle, and J. K. Rowling. In his lifetime he befriended a wide variety of Christians and nonbelievers, including Lewis Carroll, Alfred Lord Tennyson, Charles Dickens, Anthony Trollope, Henry Wadsworth Longfellow, John Ruskin, and Walt Whitman. Even the skeptic Mark Twain, who initially disliked MacDonald, became his friend, and the two often discussed writing a novel together.

firmer on which to stand, he found his way back to a more solid faith: "Definite beliefs enable us to withstand the storms of suffering that come into every life, and that tends to destroy any spiritual disposition that does not have deep roots."

The poet Matthew Arnold wrote of the ebbing of the Sea of Faith in modern times, a retreat that leaves the world with "neither joy, nor love, nor light / Nor certitude, nor peace, nor help for pain." That last void, *nor help for pain*, may edge individuals back toward faith, even in modern societies with their many allurements to pleasure. Sexy advertisements and a shallow celebrity culture somehow lose their appeal when your three-year-old child is dying in a hospital — or when you are. Where else can one turn but to God when all of life seems frozen in a perpetual winter?

Mortimer Adler, a philosopher and editor of *Great Books of the Western World*, first came to embrace theism, a belief in God. Though attracted to the writings of Thomas Aquinas, for decades he resisted calling himself a Christian, a hesitation no doubt influenced by his Jewish heritage. Then in 1984, after a trip to Mexico, he fell ill from a virus that incapacitated him for months. Bedbound, he sank into depression and sometimes would unaccountably burst into tears. During this period an Episcopal priest visited him faithfully and prayed with him.

Adler himself knew only one prayer, the Lord's Prayer, and he repeated it over and over, clinging to every word: *Our Father, who art in heaven, hallowed be your name* ... As he lay awake in the hospital one night, he realized he had crossed a bridge without knowing it, a leap of faith to a personal God who hears our prayers. He rang for the night nurse and scratched out a note which included these words: "Dear God, yes, I do believe, not just in the God my reason so stoutly affirms, but the God to whom Father Howell is now praying, and on whose grace and love I now joyfully rely." Affliction had shown him the way.

EVIL

In a small book written in tribute after his son's death in a climbing accident, Nicholas Wolterstorff mused, "When we have overcome absence with phone calls, winglessness with airplanes, summer heat with air-conditioning—when we have overcome all these and much more besides, then there will abide two things with which we must cope: the evil in our hearts and death." Evil and death pose universal questions to which Christians can offer comfort and perhaps a new perspective.

Years ago in Chicago I had a conversation with a kindly pastor that brought me face-to-face with evil. I had read in a church newsletter article that during World War II this pastor had participated in the liberation of the Dachau concentration camp. I asked him about the experience. For the next twenty minutes he recalled the sights, the sounds, and especially the smells that greeted his unit as they marched through the gates of Dachau just outside Munich. Nothing prepared them, and nothing could possibly prepare them, for what they found inside.

"A buddy and I were assigned to one boxcar," he told me. "Inside were human bodies, stacked in neat rows, exactly like firewood. Most were corpses, but a few still had a faint pulse. The Germans, ever meticulous, had planned out the rows—alternating the heads and feet, and accommodating different sizes and shapes of bodies. Our job was like moving furniture. We would pick up each body—so light!—and carry it to a designated area. I spent two hours in the boxcar, two hours that for me included every known emotion: rage, pity, shame, revulsion—every negative emotion, I should say. They came in waves, all but the rage. It stayed, fueling our work."

He then told me about a fellow soldier named Chuck, who agreed to escort twelve SS officers in charge of Dachau to an interrogation center nearby. Chuck came from Cicero, a tough area of Chicago, and claimed to have worked for Al Capone before the war. A few minutes later the crew working in the boxcar heard the rattly burp of a machine gun in three long bursts of fire. Soon Chuck came strolling out, smoke still curling from the tip of his weapon. "They all tried to run away," he said with a leer.

I interrupted the pastor's story to ask if anyone reported what Chuck did or took disciplinary action. He laughed and gave me a get-serious-this-is-war look. "No, and that's what got to me. It was on that day that I felt called by God to become a pastor. First, there was the horror of the corpses in the boxcar. I could not absorb such a scene. I did not even know such Absolute Evil existed. But when I saw it, I knew beyond doubt that I must spend my life serving whatever opposed such Evil—serving God.

"Then came the incident with Chuck. I had a nauseating fear that the captain might call on me to escort the next group of SS guards, and an even more dread fear that if he did, I might do the same as Chuck. The beast that was within those guards was also within me."

The reality of human evil keeps intruding on secular sensibilities. How did the most sophisticated nation in Europe descend to the depths of the Holocaust? How could trained physicians in Nazi Germany agree to grotesque experiments on concentration camp inmates? In recent years I have spent time at the scene of infamous crimes: in the former Yugoslavia, where more than a hundred thousand people died, many of them massacred in ways not so different from what happened in Germany; at Virginia Tech and Newtown, Connecticut, where disturbed young men slaughtered students at random. As I listened to heartbroken families whose lives were changed forever by senseless violence, the media explanations for such events—ancient grudges, mental illness—did not seem adequate. Like the pastor in Chicago, I came face-to-face with Evil.

I have spent much of my writing career exploring the question of suffering and evil. Why doesn't God act the way we want a God to act, intervening more often, stopping such atrocities? And why don't we act the way God wants us to act? According to the Bible, the two are related. We live on a planet that has been invaded by evil forces, and God's followers are called to be part of the solution.

As the pastor in Chicago told me, "Without being melodramatic, I sometimes wonder what might have happened if a skilled, sensitive person had befriended the young, impressionable Adolf Hitler as he wandered the streets of Vienna in his confused state. The world might have been spared all that bloodshed — spared Dachau. I never know who might be sitting in that chair you're occupying right now.

"And even if I end up spending my life with 'nobodies' ... I learned in the boxcar that there's no such thing. Those survivors with a pulse were as close to no-bodies as you can get: mere skeletons wrapped in papery skin. But I would have done anything to keep those poor, ragged people alive. Our medics stayed up all night to save them; some in our company lost their lives to liberate them. There are no 'nobodies.' I learned that day in Dachau what 'the image of God' in a human being is all about."

Evil offers convincing proof of the "lostness" of the human race. It may also give rise to longings that lead to faith, a thirst for a better world than this one. And the sense that something is wrong comes to a head when we confront death.

DEATH

The soldiers who liberated Dachau reacted with shock and revulsion, the normal response of a person confronted with a human corpse. People go to great lengths to identify and honor the dead. Why? Not infrequently I come across dead foxes on the road and dead deer or elk in the woods behind my home, sights that cause momentary sadness but nothing like my reaction if I came across a human body. Christians believe we react in such a way not only because one of our species has died but because something sets humans apart from other species. Our inbuilt response hints at the sacredness of human life—"There are no 'nobodies,'" in the pastor's words.

Our ancestors feared God; we moderns fear death. When my wife worked as a hospice chaplain, she met with any willing patients regardless of their faith backgrounds. All of them had terminal conditions, and few at that hospice lived longer than a few weeks. Some wanted nothing to do with a chaplain, although she found that they were a distinct minority. Questions that most of us set aside or ignore during normal life force their way to the surface when death stares us in the face.

Partly through Janet's influence, a friend named Susan began a study course in hospital chaplaincy. As she was setting down some of her reflections in journal form, Susan realized that her own theology had been both tested and formed by spending time with others of a different, or no, faith. She realized that because of her confidence that God is "the God of all comfort" she can enter a room offering genuine compassion and comfort to those who do not believe the same. "God seems to be teaching me to widen my heart while keeping my eyes on him," she says. Her reflections offer a model of presenting faith to post-Christians, especially at a time of crisis.

When she enters a room Susan assumes that, bidden or not, God is already present. "We love because he first loved us," she says, quoting John, "and I picture God pouring from his pitcher into me so that I can pour out to others, and then be replenished with God's love. I enter with a smile, feeling privileged to share the sacred ground on which someone clings to life. If I forget that God goes ahead of me, and think instead that I am *bringing* God into the room, I can have an air of smugness. I feel pressure to say the right thing, try to impress the patient and staff—in short, I take myself too seriously. I need the constant reminder that God precedes me in that room, and that the person in the bed has a story that I can learn from."

Susan says it helps to picture the roles reversed: herself in the bed, imagining a stranger entering the room with a serious look—furrowed brow, hands clasped—and with advice to impart. She encountered a chaplain like that when her own daughter lay in the hospital after a serious accident, and felt no comfort. Rather, she wants someone who shows attentive respect, who has good eye contact and conveys a sense of ease, not cockiness. As a Christian chaplain, she has learned to let the patient decide what direction the conversation should go. That conversation may lead to prayer, but even then Susan must be careful that her prayers express love and compassion, not a veiled message.

She recalls, "I have been with Muslims and New Age believers who seem to be waiting for me to convert them. When I don't, they draw near. Ironically, the more I don't push my faith, the more people can seem interested in what I believe." The same principle applies outside a hospital room too.

CHAPTER 4

RECLAIMING
THE GOOD NEWS

*Between the time a gift comes to us
and the time we pass it along, we suffer gratitude.*

LEWIS HYDE

When I was in high school my church youth group watched a movie about a boy who knew he should tell his best friend about his faith. He kept putting off the conversation until suddenly it was too late: the friend died in a fiery auto accident, its flames a preview of what awaited him in hell. For days afterward I would wake up sweating, thinking of my own friends and their fate, tormented by guilt because I had not "witnessed" to them about what I believed. Later came scary books like *The Late Great Planet Earth* and the *Left Behind* series, portraying in graphic detail what might someday happen to the unraptured.

Sheer adrenaline may prod a person to a point of spiritual crisis, but I wonder about the long-term effects of an appeal based on guilt, fear, and shame. Over time these techniques may well produce a counterreaction. I've found that skeptics and post-Christians are largely immune to such an approach. They need the opposite: a dose of grace that contrasts with the harsh, unforgiving world around them (including, in some cases, their encounters with judgmental Christians).

In the movie *A Beautiful Mind*, Alicia Nash tells how she copes with her husband's schizophrenia: "I look at him and I force myself to see the man that I married, and he becomes that man. He's transformed into someone that I love. And I am transformed into someone that loves him." In other words, she looks at him with eyes of grace. We do that intuitively with people we love, such as a parent with Alzheimer's disease: we see behind the ravaged person they are now to the healthy person they once were.

Jesus had the uncanny ability to look at *everyone* with grace-filled eyes, seeing not only the beauty of who they were but also the sacred potential of what they could become. We his followers have the same challenge: "So from now on we regard no one from a worldly point of view," Paul told the Corinthians. Evidently we are not doing likewise since many people think of faith, especially evangelical faith, as bad news. They believe Christians view them through eyes of judgment, not eyes of grace.

Somehow we need to reclaim the "goodnewsness" of the gospel, and the best place to start is to rediscover the good news ourselves.

A DIFFERENT SOUND

Frederick Buechner writes, "Turn around and believe that the good news that we are loved is gooder than we ever dared hope, and that to believe in that good news, to live out of it and toward it, to be in love with that good news, is of all glad things in this world the gladdest thing of all."

It has taken me years to rediscover the good news. I have written elsewhere about the "toxic" churches of my youth that for a time poisoned my attitude toward faith. And as a writer I have met my share of cranks and hypocrites in the church. To be fair, however, I have also encountered many humble "saints" who

faithfully serve God. What is a saint? I like Reynolds Price's definition: someone who, however flawed, "leads us by example, almost
never by words, to imagine the hardest thing of all: the seamless
love of God for all creation, including ourselves."

It strikes me as genuinely good news that we are creations of
a loving God who wants us to thrive, not random byproducts of
a meaningless universe. That God entered our world and demonstrated in person that nothing—not even death—can separate us
from God's love. That the story of Jesus has this main theme: "For
God so *loved* the world that he gave …" That human existence
will not end with the imminent warming of our atmosphere or
the gradual cooling of our sun, and my particular destiny will not
end with death. That God will balance the scales of human history
not by karma but by grace, in such a way that no one will be able
to accuse God of unfairness.

Mark Rutland whimsically recalls a survey in which Americans were asked what words they would most like to hear. He
predicted the first choice: "I love you." Number two was "I forgive
you." The third choice took him by surprise: "Supper's ready." It
dawned on Rutland that these three statements provide a neat
summary of the gospel story. We are loved by God, forgiven by
God, and invited to the banquet table. In the midst of a planet
marked by brokenness—violence, natural disasters, ruptured relationships—the gospel is truly good news. Like an iPod listener
dancing in a subway station full of glum commuters, a Christian
hears a different sound, of joy and laughter on the other side of
pain and death.

Sometimes I get a clearer picture of the good news when I
travel to other countries, especially those without much Christian
influence. A few years ago I visited Kazakhstan, a large, under-
populated country that tends to attract the wrong kind of public-
ity. Sasha Baron Cohen made it a laughingstock in his 2006 spoof
film *Borat: Cultural Learnings of America for Make Benefit Glorious*

Nation of Kazakhstan. More soberly, it made the news in 2013 as the home of the Boston Marathon bombers.

I spent a long weekend with Kazakh staff members of Campus Crusade (now "Cru"). To be honest, I have always shied away from that organization and its slick presentation of the gospel. I keep wanting to add some realism to its programmed approach. God loves you (*Yes, but God is invisible and you'll encounter times that severely call that love into question*) and has a wonderful plan for your life (*a plan that, in truth, includes self-sacrifice, hardship, and discipline*). During my time with the Kazakhs, however, I heard story after story of young people encountering the gospel as good news. Almost every one followed a plot line similar to this:

"I entered university just as the Soviet Union collapsed. Until then we had lived under Communism, bordered on one side by Russia and the other by China. My father was an alcoholic, and home life was terrible, sometimes abusive. Suddenly no one believed the Communist propaganda anymore. In fact, no one knew what to believe. The economy was in shambles. I had no idea what to do with my life, what to look forward to.

"Then someone approached me, struck up a conversation, and told me there is a God who loves me and has a wonderful plan for my life. I had never given much thought to the existence of God. It made sense, though, and as we became friends this person introduced me to Jesus, and my life completely changed. I found a purpose for living and gained a loving community around me. Now I spend my time sharing this good news with others."

I heard enough of these stories that I could not dismiss them and had to confront my own snobbishness about formulaic ways to present the good news. ("I like my way of doing it better than your way of not doing it," said the evangelist Dwight L. Moody to a critic of his methods.) In a nominally Muslim country, emerging from the dreary years of Communism, the gospel of Jesus sounded like a clear bell announcing the dawn of a new day.

After returning from Kazakhstan I looked at the earliest record of Jesus' followers proclaiming his message, the dozen or so speeches in the book of Acts. Unlike the scary movies and sermons from my youth, not one of them focuses on personal salvation as a way of escaping hell in the afterlife. Rather, they present how the good news about eternity should transform *this* life. The Christian sees the world as a transitional home badly in need of rehab, and we are active agents in that project.

In the same vein, after the resurrection Jesus did not highlight his "just returned from another world!" experience; instead, he commanded his followers to get to work now by making disciples and tending his flock. As Eugene Peterson paraphrases John 3:17, "God didn't go to all the trouble of sending his Son merely to point an accusing finger, telling the world how bad it was. He came to help, to put the world right again."

To use Jesus' favorite image, we serve a shadow *kingdom* that operates amid the very earthly powers that tried to eliminate its founder. Early Christians lived by different rules than the surrounding culture, first attracting the attention of outsiders and ultimately winning them over. Here is one report from a sympathizer in the Roman Empire:

> They marry, like everyone else, and they have children, but they do not destroy their offspring. They share a common table, but not a common bed. They exist in the flesh, but they do not live by the flesh. They pass their days on earth, but they are citizens of heaven. They obey the prescribed laws, all the while surpassing the laws by their lives. They love all men and are persecuted by all. They are unknown and condemned. They are put to death and restored to life. They are poor, yet make many rich. They lack everything, yet they overflow in everything. . . .
>
> They are assailed by the Jews as barbarians; they are

persecuted by the Greeks; yet those who hate them are unable to give any reason for their hatred.

Christians are amphibious creatures, "in the world ... not of the world," in Jesus' words. And in a modern society that runs by competition, self-indulgence, and power, we should stand out by following a notably different script.

GRACE ON TAP

Living "in the world," we can look for natural opportunities to dispense grace—not just words—to those around us. Gabe Lyons recommends inviting community leaders, whether Christian or not, into church to tell how best to engage with the neighborhood and its problems. As he notes, African American churches have historically done that, finding ways to honor teachers, firefighters, social workers, and politicians, all of whom serve without much recognition.

A pastor friend of mine in Chicago operates an internet wedding site. Couples who don't know a pastor, and thus look for one on the internet, contact him. He insists on counseling sessions before agreeing to perform the ceremony, and he always asks two questions: "Why do you want to get married?" (almost all of them are already living together) and "Why do you want a pastor involved?" Remarkable conversations unfold as the parties struggle aloud with their answers. As one said, "Well, if there is a God, marriage is so important that we think God ought to be involved somehow."

Kathleen Norris writes about a "cocaine whore" in rural Montana who would sleep with anyone who could provide her with booze or cocaine, or merely show her the slightest bit of attention. She found Alcoholics Anonymous first, then God, and then church. Soon she was signing up for every Bible study and volunteering for every church-ministry project, as well as for committees that others had to be begged to join. "Salvation took such hold in her that, as the pastor put it, he began to wonder if Christians don't underrate promiscuity. Because she was still a promiscuous person, still loving without much discrimination. The difference was that she was no longer self-destructive but a bearer of new life to others." The twelfth step in AA's guide to recovery—helping others in need—is an act of gratitude. We respond to healing grace by giving it away.

Pastors in both places, Chicago and Montana, began with a good thing, love, and gently pointed toward something even better. Romantic love may lead the way to the Source of all love; passion rightly channeled brings life, not ruin.

I know a former Southern Baptist pastor in North Carolina who, against all odds, now runs a private cigar club. He explains, "I learned from my years in the ministry that when men go deep in conversation and get honest with each other, there's usually a cigar involved. That's when they talk about what really counts— sitting on a patio after a golf match or relaxing together on a deck when their wives are inside the house. So in our club we have volunteers available who strike up friendships and know how to respond when the men want to talk about their failing marriages or job layoffs or rebellious teenagers."

Once, while speaking on the topic of grace in Toronto, I asked the audience about their own experiences conveying grace to others. One woman shocked us all: "I feel called to minister to telephone marketers. You know, the kind who call at inconvenient hours and deliver their spiel before you can say a word." Immediately I flashed back to the times I have responded rudely or simply hung up. "All day long these sales callers hear people curse at them and slam the phone down," she continued. "I listen attentively to their pitch, then I try to respond kindly, though I almost never buy what they're selling. Instead, I ask about their personal life and whether they have any concerns I can pray for. Often they ask me to pray with them over the phone, and sometimes they are in tears. They're people, after all, probably underpaid, and they're surprised when someone treats them with common courtesy."

Hearing such stories, I am aware how often I miss possible hinge moments in my own interactions with people. I marvel at the Toronto woman's gracious response and think of the times I get irritated with marketers and with employees on computer help lines who don't speak good English. I catch myself treating store cashiers and Starbucks baristas as if they were machines, not persons. I get a wedding invitation and groan at the hassle of having to shop for a gift and dress up. I rush away after a golf match rather than relaxing on the patio with my partners. Subtly or not so subtly, I let the other person know that I've been interrupted and need to get back to work. In the process, I miss golden opportunities to dispense grace.

What would it take for church to become known as a place where grace is "on tap"? All too often outsiders view us as a kind of elite club of the righteous. An alcoholic friend once made this point by comparing church with AA, which had become for him a substitute church. "When I show up late to church, people turn and look at me. Some scowl, some smile a self-satisfied smile—*See, that person's not as responsible as I am.* In AA, if I show up late the meeting comes to a halt and everyone jumps up to greet me. They realize that my desperate need for them won out over my desperate need for alcohol."

One gray fall day in Denver I visited an urban church that makes grace the center point of ministry. This congregation addresses the contentious gay issue not by writing position papers but simply by welcoming all who come. Their bulletin expresses it this way:

> Married, divorced or single here, it's one family that
>   mingles here.
> Conservative or liberal here, we've all gotta give a
>   little here.

Big or small here, there's room for us all here.
Doubt or believe here, we all can receive here.
Gay or straight here, there's no hate here.
Woman or man here, everyone can serve here.
Whatever your race here, for all of us grace here.
In imitation of the ridiculous love Almighty God has for
each of us and all of us,
let us live and love without labels.

From there I went to a barbecue fundraiser for a nonprofit
organization that provides food for Denver's hungry population.
A number of sponsoring churches had sent representatives, and I
agreed to say a few words and give away some books. The organiz-
ers hoped for a turnout of three hundred, but a cold, drizzly rain
kept attendance down to less than half that. The Denver Broncos
football team was playing that day, and it occurred to me, as I
looked out over the sparse crowd huddled under umbrellas, that
sixty thousand screaming fans in a stadium had gladly paid to sit
through miserable weather for three hours. Instead, a cause like
hunger attracted a small group of churchgoers, idealistic college
students, and street people who always seem to know where food
is being served.

In the sermon I had heard at church that morning, the guest
preacher mentioned she had puzzled over the story of the widow
who gave all she had, no more than a few pennies. Why did Jesus
merely use her as an object lesson, contrasting her with the rich
people who proudly made large contributions? Why didn't he do
something to address her state, perhaps by proposing a poverty
program? The preacher told us her conclusion: "God leaves the
justice issue up to us." I had heard Gary Haugen, founder of the
International Justice Mission, say something similar: "God has a
plan to fight injustice, and that plan is us—his people. There is
no Plan B."

I pondered that statement as I stood in the rain and watched a small crowd of volunteers assemble food parcels while a soul sister belted out, "His eye is on the sparrow." For whatever reason, God seems to leave a lot of issues up to us. And the church totters on; we are, after all, the chosen channel for God's good news.

SHARING GOD'S WISDOM

Theologian Miroslav Volf describes evangelism as "sharing God's wisdom." The God who created human beings knows what kind of life works best for us. Some things are obvious—don't steal, don't lie, don't murder—and human society clearly works better that way. Some things are counterintuitive: care for the vulnerable, find your life by serving others, forgive when wronged, love your enemies. Yet that way of life ultimately proves most satisfying, for in following it we become the persons God intended us to be.

As my aging body needs attention and repair, I have increasing appreciation for one of the titles given to Jesus: the Great Physician. A doctor cannot heal unless the patient presents a complaint. (The great tragedy of leprosy, diabetes, and other pain-numbing conditions is that the affected person cannot sense that something is wrong and so doesn't seek help.) No one, not even God, can help a person who sees no need for healing. "Do you want to get well?" Jesus asked those who came to him with a physical ailment, a question that applies to those who suffer spiritually as well.

Each time I visit my doctor for a checkup he goes through a list of questions that in any other context would seem intrusive. Do I drink alcohol? How much? What about coffee? Do I smoke? Use drugs? Am I sexually active? Do I exercise regularly? I take no offense at his prying into my personal life because I know we have the same interests at heart: my health.*

---

* According to the World Health Organization, some 70 percent of illnesses are lifestyle-related and nearly half of all deaths result from human-caused risk factors. If we could eliminate such factors as poor nutrition, unsafe sex, tobacco, alcohol, poor sanitation, indoor air pollution, and obesity we could add up to sixteen years to the average life span.

When I'm recovering from an injury, my doctor gets even bossier. "I don't want you jogging or playing golf for a month," he told me after surgeries on my foot and knee. "Whatever you do, don't drive!" he ordered while I was wearing a brace for a broken neck. I accepted his counsel willingly because I recognized he was prescribing what was best for me and not just depriving me of pleasure.

The oft-misunderstood Christian notion of sin makes many people uncomfortable. Indeed, it establishes a clear line of accountability—but to a God who loves me and has my best interests at heart. Again the parallel to a doctor applies. Coming from a strict church background, I missed this good-news aspect of God's wisdom. I thought of God as a cosmic policeman enforcing arbitrary rules rather than as a doctor who wants me to thrive. My conversations with the uncommitted convince me that many people have a similarly erroneous concept of sin. At the heart of sin lies a lack of trust that God intends the best for us.

Ignatius of Loyola defined *sin* as refusing to believe that God wants my happiness and fulfillment. Human rebellion began in the Garden of Eden when God said in effect, "Trust me. I know what is best for you." Adam and Eve failed the test, and we have paid the consequences ever since. Today, some likewise insist that we humans should decide for ourselves what is best. A damaged human making that judgment is like an alcoholic deciding whether or not to drink. For our own well-being we need to trust God for basic guidance about how to live.

As pastor of a thriving church in Manhattan, Tim Keller often converses about faith with skeptics and post-Christians, and he has learned to present sin not so much as "doing bad things" as "making good things into ultimate things." Says Keller,

Instead of telling them they are sinning because they are sleeping with their girlfriends or boyfriends, I tell them that they are sinning because they are looking to their romances to give their lives meaning, to justify and save them, to give them what they should be looking for from God. This idolatry leads to anxiety, obsessiveness, envy, and resentment. I have found that when you describe their lives in terms of idolatry, postmodern people do not give much resistance. Then Christ and his salvation can be presented not (at this point) so much as their only hope for forgiveness, but as their only hope for freedom.

Unless we love natural goods — sex, alcohol, food, money, success, power — in the way God intended, we become their slaves, as any addict can attest. Jesus demonstrated in person how to live freely and fully, and not surprisingly he upset the religious establishment in the process. I cannot imagine anyone following Jesus around for two or three years and commenting, "My, think of all he missed out on." More than likely they would say, "Think of all I am missing out on."

Eugene Peterson points out that "the root meaning in Hebrew of *salvation* is to be broad, to become spacious, to enlarge. It carries the sense of deliverance from an existence that has become compressed, confined and cramped." God wants to set us free, to make it possible for us to live open and loving lives with God and our neighbors. "I run in the path of your commands, for you have set my heart free," wrote the psalmist.

We need not hide, like Adam and Eve in the garden. We have been forgiven and transformed so that, according to Peter, we actually "participate in the divine nature, having escaped the corruption in the world caused by evil desires."

When I leave the doctor's office after an annual checkup I have a clearer picture of my ideal health, which will include exercise, proper diet, and careful attention to some nagging ailments. From time spent with God, I have a clearer picture of spiritual health too—not an anxious, furrowed-brow perfectionism or an uptight legalism, but a relaxed confidence in God's love and a trust that God has my very best interests at heart.

Perhaps the most powerful thing Christians can do to communicate to a skeptical world is to live fulfilled lives, exhibiting proof that Jesus' way truly leads to a life most abundant and most thirst-satisfying. The fruits of the Spirit—love, joy, peace, patience, kindness, goodness, faithfulness, gentleness, and self-control—flow out of a healthy soul and in the process may attract those who have found such qualities elusive or unattainable.

WALKING THE TALK

I must, however, insert a caution about a pitfall that can cancel out any words we say and undermine how others perceive the good news we claim to represent. Unless Christians demonstrate truth with our lives, what we say about what we believe will sound like empty advertising slogans. Stanley Hauerwas, named "America's best theologian" by *Time* magazine, summed up the problem: "I have come to think that the challenge confronting Christians is not that we do not believe what we say, though that can be a problem, but that what we say we believe does not seem to make any difference for either the church or the world."

When a poll of college students asked, "Write the first thing that comes to mind when you hear the word 'Christianity,'" the most common answer was, "People who don't practice what they preach." Surveys by the Barna Group alarmingly confirm that judgment:

> When asked to identify their activities over the last thirty days, born-again believers were just as likely to bet or gamble, to visit a pornographic website, to take something that did not belong to them, to consult a medium or psychic, to physically fight or abuse someone, to have

consumed enough alcohol to be considered legally drunk, to have used an illegal, nonprescription drug, to have said something to someone that was not true, to have gotten back at someone for something he or she did, and to have said mean things behind another person's back....

Among young outsiders, *84 percent* say they personally know at least one committed Christian. Yet just *15 percent* thought the lifestyles of those Christ followers were significantly different from the norm.

Adults fare little better. A few years ago Ronald Sider wrote a seminal book, *The Scandal of the Evangelical Conscience*, lamenting how far short we fall in distinguishing ourselves from the rest of the culture. Divorce rates among Christians mirror the rest of society's, as do the rates of physical and sexual abuse; sexual promiscuity among Christian teenagers is only marginally lower; only 9 percent of evangelicals fully tithe their money; evangelicals are among the most racist of any groups surveyed by George Gallup; Catholics have more abortions than the national average. "The astonishing quality of the early believers' lives attracted people to Christ," Sider commented in an interview. "Today our hypocrisy drives unbelievers away."

Fortunately, the gospel has within it a self-correcting principle, and every so often prophetic individuals — Benedict of Nursia, Ignatius of Loyola, Francis of Assisi, Martin Luther, John Wesley, Mother Teresa — rise up to call the church back to its mission. A core minority of religious Americans, whom sociologists label "the devoutest of the devout," do maintain low rates of abortion, divorce, and out-of-wedlock childbearing; they also volunteer for and support organizations that care for the needy. Alas, the media prefer to spotlight the hypocrisies and moral failures of prominent figures.

I find it encouraging that in our own time a younger generation looks to those with a radical bent—people like Francis Chan, David Platt, Jonathan Wilson-Hargrove, and Shane Claiborne—for spiritual leadership. As Claiborne says, "I am convinced that if we lose kids to the culture of drugs and materialism, of violence and war, it's because we don't dare them, not because we don't entertain them. It's because we make the gospel too easy, not because we make it too difficult. Kids want to do something heroic with their lives, which is why they play video games and join the army. But what do they do with a church that teaches them to tiptoe through life so they can arrive safely at death?"

On my travels I have met Christian radicals who respond to that call: they combat sexual trafficking, assist victims of disaster, dig wells, produce bicycle ambulances for places where no roads exist, run homes for AIDS orphans. Closer to home, David Platt dared members of his Alabama church to move into a disadvantaged—and dangerous—part of Birmingham, and forty families did so. Similar intentional communities have taken root in major cities and even in rural Georgia. Ironically, most radicals I know don't see themselves as radicals at all. They see themselves as simply following Jesus.

Dorothy Day used to say that we should live in such a way that our lives wouldn't make much sense if the gospel were not true. Not everyone feels called to radical service, of course. Yet ordinary Christians must live in a way that differs from the surrounding culture or our message will never get a hearing.

Herein lies the most solemn challenge facing Christians who want to communicate their faith: if we do not live in a way that draws others to the faith rather than repels them, none of our words will matter. Secular culture masterfully promises more than it can deliver. Growing up in a sheltered environment, I have to fight a tendency to think that I am missing out on something. Lust seems so much sexier than fidelity. Selfishness strokes my ego: why should I care about the poor when I can insulate myself from them? It takes active faith to follow Jesus' counter-culture way.

Along the way, however, I have come to know some of "the devoutest of the devout," and without exception they strike me as *more* alive, not less. Around them, I too want a drink of Living Water that satisfies. And as I stumblingly try to follow the way that Jesus sets out, I realize the good-news truth of God's wisdom and gain a glimpse of what God designed me to be.

To early Christians in the Roman Empire, who were facing active hostility and persecution, Peter gave this advice, a model of how to share God's wisdom: "Live such good lives among the pagans that, though they accuse you of doing wrong, they may see your good deeds and glorify God on the day he visits us.... Always be prepared to give an answer to everyone who asks you to give the reason for the hope that you have. But do this with gentleness and respect, keeping a clear conscience, so that those who speak maliciously against your good behavior in Christ may be ashamed of their slander."

CREATIVE GRACE

Jesus once asked his disciples, "For who is greater, the one who is at the table or the one who serves?" In that society, rife with slaves and servants, the question probably sounded rhetorical, if not ridiculous. No one envied a servant. Yet Jesus went on to say, "But I am among you as one who serves." By serving others we follow Jesus, building up his kingdom step-by-step.

N. T. Wright spells out some specifics: "What you do in the present—by painting, preaching, singing, sewing, praying, teaching, building hospitals, digging wells, campaigning for justice, writing poems, caring for the needy, loving your neighbour as yourself—will last into God's future. These activities are not simply ways of making the present life a little less beastly, a little more bearable, until the day when we leave it behind altogether. They are part of what we may call building for God's Kingdom." They are also, I would add, central to our mission of showing the world grace.

The church I attended in Chicago, located near a slum housing project, began as an outreach project of a large, traditional church. In time, though, the mother church cut off all funding. They learned that our inner-city tutoring program was teaching kids to read without using the Bible exclusively. Worse, the mission church had installed a pool table in the basement for kids to use! The mother church had missed the whole concept of grace. Grace dispensers give out of their own bounty, in *gratitude* (a word with the same root as *grace*) for what we have received from God. We serve others not with some hidden scheme of making converts, rather to contribute to the common good, to help humans flourish as God intended.

Michael Cheshire, a friend of mine in a neighboring town, had the vision of starting a church. He sensed a problem, though. In his words, "I have found that the longer I have been a Christian, the fewer non-Christians I know. It's not that I don't like them; church has just become the place we all find our friends, mates, and social interaction.... Inevitably, people ask what I do for a living. The moment they know I'm a pastor, they look at me like I'm going to take up an offering."

Michael's solution? "We decided to attend to our community instead of asking our community to attend the church." His staff started showing up at local community events such as sports contests and town hall meetings. They entered a float in the local Christmas parade. They rented a football field and inaugurated a Free Movie Night on summer Fridays, complete with popcorn machines and a giant screen. They opened a burger joint, which soon became a hangout for local youth; it gives free meals to those who can't afford to pay. When they found out how difficult it was for immigrants to get a driver's license, they formed a drivers school and set their fees at half the going rate.

My own church in Colorado started a ministry called Hands of the Carpenter, recruiting volunteers to do painting, carpentry, and house repairs for widows and single mothers. Soon they learned of another need and opened Hands Automotive to offer free oil changes, inspections, and car washes to the same constituency. They fund the work by charging normal rates to those who can afford it.

I heard from a church in Minneapolis that monitors parking meters. Volunteers patrol the streets, add money to the meters with expired time, and put cards on the windshields that read, "Your meter looked hungry so we fed it. If we can help you in any other way, please give us a call." In Cincinnati, college students sign up every Christmas to wrap presents at a local mall — no charge. "People just could not understand why I would want to wrap their presents," one wrote me. "I tell them, 'We just want to show God's love in a practical way.'"

In one of the boldest ventures in creative grace, a pastor started a community called Miracle Village in which half the residents are registered sex offenders. Florida's state laws require sex offenders to live more than a thousand feet from a school, day care center, park, or playground, and some municipalities have lengthened the distance to half a mile and added swimming pools, bus stops, and libraries to the list. As a result, sex offenders, one of the most despised categories of criminals, are pushed out of cities and have few places to live. A pastor named Dick Witherow opened Miracle Village as part of his Matthew 25 Ministries. Staff members closely supervise the residents, many of them on parole, and conduct services in the church at the heart of Miracle Village. The ministry also provides anger-management and Bible study classes.

I have seen scores of such ministries around the world that embody grace.* One that will always stand out in memory is

---

* Two books describe specific examples of churches that excel in dispensing grace: *Kingdom Calling* by Amy Sherman and *Ministries of Mercy* by Timothy J. Keller.

a restaurant called Agua Viva in Lima, Peru, that I came across serendipitously. Just off a main street known for peddlers and pickpockets, I entered a beautiful colonial courtyard, vintage 1820, in a high-ceilinged room trimmed with mahogany. The manager rustled across the room in a batik sarong to greet me and my companions, her Spanish tinged with a melodious French accent. The food was gourmet style, among the best meals I've ever eaten, yet at a very modest price. Waitresses glided in and out of the room, each in native costume from their African and Asian homelands. The manager explained they are Christians — not nuns, exactly, but an order of committed lay workers.

Only a few clues betray the restaurant's spiritual roots. The inside cover of the menu proclaims "Jesus lives! For this we are happy." And at a certain time each evening the waitresses appear together to sing a vespers hymn for their patrons. Besides these clues, said the manager, the work itself should stand as a witness. "Don't ask us how our prayer life is going; look at our food. Is your plate clean and artfully arranged? Does your server treat you with kindness and love? Do you experience serenity here? If so, then we are serving God."

The restaurant keeps its prices low because the women, who have taken a vow of poverty, do all the work. They cook, wait on tables, scrub floors, worship, all to the glory of God. During the day, mothers from the slums of Lima fill the same elegant room. The Missionary Workers lead training classes on basic hygiene, child-raising, and physical and spiritual health. Once off duty, the restaurant staff devote themselves to the poor, carrying out services funded by profits from the restaurant.

Some of Agua Viva's wealthy patrons know of the outreach programs, and some do not. The Missionary Workers rarely talk about their work unless asked. But these sample comments in a guest book show that their unique two-edged mission is having an impact:

- "I thank the Missionary Workers for being a living reminder of simplicity and joy in the heart of Christianity. Thank you for having helped me cross to the side of Salvation."
- "Continue to make us thirst for this Living Water whose transparent brilliance shines out through your faces."
- "You are a most eloquent living evidence for nonbelievers. You are a gift of God; the Holy Spirit breathes here. Through good cooking, God is transmitted too. Thank you for your ray of sunshine in a cloudy sky."

The same order operates restaurants in Belgium, Vietnam, Upper Volta, the Philippines, and Argentina. All have the same name: *L'Eau Vive* in French, *Agua Viva* in Spanish. The English translation: Living Water.

PART TWO

GRACE DISPENSERS

While discussing the growing antipathy toward Christians, a friend remarked to me, "There are three kinds of Christians that outsiders to the faith still respect: pilgrims, activists, and artists. The uncommitted will listen to them far sooner than to an evangelist or apologist." Although nonbelievers do not oppose a spiritual search, they will listen only to those Christians who present themselves as fellow-pilgrims on the way rather than as part of a superior class who has already arrived. Activists express their faith in the most persuasive way of all, by their deeds. And art succeeds when it speaks most authentically to the human condition; when believers do so with skill, again the world takes note.

CHAPTER 5

PILGRIMS

Jesus came announcing the Kingdom of God,
but what appeared was the church.

WILHELM DILTHEY

Gina Welch is a young, citified Jewish writer who grew up in Berkeley, California, and graduated from Yale. In a desire to know more about evangelicals, whom she kept running into after a move to Virginia, she decided to attend the late Jerry Falwell's church in Lynchburg. As a bonus, she hoped the resulting clash of cultures might provide the grist for a book. She came with a clear bias against Falwell: "I considered him a homophobe, a fearmonger, a manipulator, and a misogynist — an alien creature from the most extreme backwater of evangelical culture." (Note: Falwell used the word *fundamentalist*, not *evangelical* to describe himself, a distinction lost on most in secular culture.)

As for Welch herself, "I cuss, I drink, and I am not a virgin. I have never believed in God." A neophyte, Welch didn't know you could just show up at church. She thought you had to qualify somehow, like pledging a sorority, so she signed up for a Connections class offered to anyone interested in membership. Soon she found herself immersed in an exotic subculture with its own rules: no swearing, drinking, smoking, plunging necklines, spaghetti straps, facial piercings, short skirts, or R-rated movies.

At first the lingo confused her, with the leaders using such insider phrases as *feed my lambs*, *soul-winning*, and *spiritual gifts*. Over the next months she played by the rules (mostly) and faked her way into a singles ministry called EPIC: Experiencing Personal Intimacy with Christ. She attended worship services, learning over time to appreciate the rousing praise music that had seemed jarring and distasteful at first. With some misgivings she went forward one Sunday to get baptized and even volunteered for a mission trip to Alaska, all as part of her undercover journalism and without revealing her true identity.

COMING CLEAN

Gina Welch accepted at face value the transformed lives of those she met, such as recovering addicts now serving on the staff of a rescue mission and couples who adopt children as part of their pro-life commitment. She liked the sense of calmness that prayer produces and the informal way that evangelicals talk to God. The friendliness, optimism, and, yes, happiness of the people she got to know surprised and impressed her.

Christian theology proved more of a barrier. The Trinity baffled her, as did the Atonement: How could Jesus taking on our sins satisfy an angry God? She listened to her mission teammates explain the gospel in Children's Church. "The message—it's okay that you do bad things, because everyone does bad things, and everyone can be forgiven, but you should try to be as good as you can be anyway—was a nice one. But the phrasing of it—Jesus loves you in spite of the fact that you're a dirty rotten sinner— how could that provide children with solace?"

In a poignant passage, Welch describes the effect of hearing a sermon on Psalm 139. "God-love, the love in the psalm, the love in *Jesus loves you*—that was Mobius strip love, love with no beginning or end, love that was both calm and complete, unflinching in the face of anything you could reveal about yourself. Who wouldn't want that? I certainly did, especially in that moment—knowing the secrets in my own heart, knowing that soon they'd be revealed." She ends the moment of longing and vulnerability with this line: "But wanting it still didn't make me believe it."

After an abrupt withdrawal and almost two years of no contacts with her friends at Thomas Road Baptist Church, she returned and met separately with her mentor Pastor Ray and with a former friend named Alice, telling them at last of her scheme to write a book about evangelicals. She admitted the deception and the questionable ethics of what she had done. She had ended the project after the trip to Alaska in part because she felt uncomfortably close to the people she was deceiving and in part because she knew it was wrong to feign belief in something that others stake their lives on. They took her confession well. Pastor Ray even prayed for her and for the book, which would be published the following year as *In the Land of Believers: An Outsider's Extraordinary Journey into the Heart of the Evangelical Church*.

Welch reflects on her friendship with Alice, "I loved having that sense of community and also that serious, regular self-inquiry. Our relationship had changed me; feeling so happy in our friendship had made me think differently about Christians. But just like her, I couldn't imagine ever believing anything other than what I believed. I had no choice in that."

Setting aside the dubious ethics behind *In the Land of Believers*, Welch's account offers a fascinating glimpse into a subculture that is rarely examined so respectfully from the outside. As I read her book I recalled my own days growing up in that same subculture, the opposite background from the author's. I knew virtually no one but fundamentalists. I too had to learn the Christian phrases that soon became clichés, went forward again and again wondering if this time it was genuine, practiced praying aloud in a way that sounded spiritual, worried over my lack of emotion during such solemn events as baptism and the Lord's Supper.

Those who grow up in the church and those who approach it as a journalistic exercise face the same danger: it can become learned behavior that belies reality rather than expresses it.

Through the grace of God, and after a period in which I tossed aside the subculture like a smothering and unwelcome costume, I found that the words and practices I learned in church can convey truth as well as hypocrisy. I must, however, disagree with Welch's conclusion about not having a choice in what we believe. Surely we do have some choice, and Welch made one in turning away from what she encountered at one particular church. She has no doubt moved on to other writing projects, and I imagine the words she heard while sitting in a pew in Lynchburg will gradually fade from memory. Perhaps her experience of being loved, even by those she deceived, will not.

Though Welch ends up dismissing the church, her story shows what best communicates to outsiders. The politics of Thomas Road Baptist Church, she found repellent. Their theology mystified her. Despite these barriers, the power of supportive community exerted its own pull. As she writes, "what I envied most about Christians was not the God thing—it was having a community gathering each week, a touchstone for people who share values, a safe place to be frank about your life struggles, a place to be reminded of your moral compass. Having a place to guard against loneliness, to feel there are others like you."

The church, especially in small groups and mission teams, offers a place where we can talk openly about what matters most, something that doesn't easily happen at the workplace or at cocktail parties.

PILGRIMS PROGRESSING

Gina Welch began her experiment with a typical skeptic's attitude, viewing serious Christians as holier-than-thou fanatics to be avoided at all costs. She sees them differently now. To her surprise, the folks at Thomas Road treated her with grace, not condescension or judgment, even after she came clean about her deception. For a period of time she felt like one traveler among others, trying to find her way.

I have visited churches where authority figures make sweeping promises about a higher plane of living, or about prosperity and good health, as if superior faith will elevate you into a privileged class. That message may get results for a while — until reality sets in. And the approach has far less effect in a cynical post-Christian environment, among spiritual "divorcées." Welch shows what does communicate: as she stuck it out and got to know Christians, they seemed less like a private club of the righteous and more like ordinary pilgrims, with the same struggles as everybody else. A pilgrim is a fellow-traveler on the spiritual journey, not a professional guide.

Tellingly, the one sermon that stood out to Welch centered on what she calls God's "Mobius strip love ... unflinching in the face of anything you could reveal about yourself." A jaded world identifies with pilgrims because we're all human and we all mess up. We get sick, lose loved ones, settle for an unfulfilling job, battle temptation, yell at our children, hurt those we care about, make bad choices. Followers of Jesus have no claim on moral superiority; to the contrary, we come to God out of need and must constantly cry out for help.

Yet Christians also rely on a Higher Power who wants us to succeed and desires the best for us. The Spirit of God stands by to help us resist temptation and then offers forgiveness and a remedy for those times when we fail. Gina Welch could disbelieve the doctrine, but she could not easily refute the testimonies of changed lives, the power of story.

John Bunyan wrote *The Pilgrim's Progress* from a prison cell, and the allegory struck such a chord that for two hundred years no book except the Bible sold more copies in English. "Christian," the main character, consistently chose the wrong road and the wrong friends. Each time he fell down, though, he let God pick him up and dust him off. Like most of us, he progressed not by always making right decisions but by responding appropriately to wrong ones. The author knew grace: Bunyan titled his own spiritual biography *Grace Abounding to the Chief of Sinners*.

The church is, above all, a place to receive grace: it brings forgiven people together with the aim of equipping us to dispense grace to others. On his trip to South America, Henri Nouwen learned the paradoxical truth that "we minister above all with our weakness." Too often, he observed, Christians operate out of the desire to be in control, to tell others what to do and how to think. But Jesus called us to be servants, and servants empty themselves of privilege and any sense of superiority.

Consistently, I have found, the uncommitted respond best to someone who leads from weakness rather than one who appears to have it all together. I saw this truth lived out most profoundly in my friend Brennan Manning, who died as I was writing this book. Brennan piped a one-note tune, the melody of grace, and his own life embodied that theme. Our backgrounds could hardly have been more dissimilar — Southern fundamentalist versus Northeastern Catholic — and yet by different routes we both stumbled upon an artesian well of grace and gulped it ever after.

One autumn afternoon Brennan and I hiked on a carpet of golden aspen leaves along a mountain stream, and I heard the details of his life: his loveless childhood, his marathon search for God, his marriage and divorce, his lies and cover-ups, his continuing struggles with alcoholism. His was a life of failure punctuated by grace.

Brennan Manning began speaking mostly to evangelical Protestant audiences after his status as a divorced "inactive priest" made him unwelcome in many Catholic gatherings. A small, trim man with a head of snow-white hair, he would usually start his talks slowly, until something akin to possession would take over, and with a strong voice and the poetic rhythm of a rap artist he would launch into a riff about the grace of God, such as this one:

> Why is Brennan Manning lovable in the eyes of God? Because on February 8th of 1956, in a shattering, life-changing experience, I committed my life to Jesus. Does God love me because ever since I was ordained a priest in 1963, I roamed the country and lately all over the world proclaiming the Good News of the gospel of grace? Does God love me because I tithe to the poor? Does he love me because back in New Orleans I work on skid row with alcoholics, addicts, and those who suffer with AIDS? Does God love me because I spend two hours every day in prayer? If I believe that stuff I'm a Pharisee! Then I feel I'm entitled to be comfortably close to Christ because of my good works. The gospel of grace says, "Brennan, you're lovable for one reason only—because God loves you. Period."

Rising in eloquence, he held audiences spellbound. One university chaplain told me that no speaker had ever had more impact on his fickle students than this aging, alcoholic failed-priest from New Jersey. Despite all his faults, or perhaps because of them, in his listeners he summoned up thirst along with the stunning wild revelation that they too were loved by God—the same Mobius strip love that so appealed to Gina Welch. Using the power of his own story toward semi-transformation, Brennan invited fellow pilgrims to join him on the venture.

EARLY DEPARTURE

The image of a pilgrim fits well with skeptics' high regard for authenticity. Like Gina Welch, most people draw conclusions about the Christian faith by observing the lives of ordinary believers, not by studying doctrine. And that introduces its own set of problems, which I only hinted at in the last chapter and now must face into.

As John Bunyan's classic book makes clear, pilgrims easily stray off course. Jesus-followers don't always follow Jesus. Prone to dead ends and detours, we sometimes travel a very different path than the one Jesus laid down. A character in the movie *Hannah and Her Sisters* summed up the problem rather harshly: "If Jesus came back and saw what was going on in his name, he'd never stop throwing up."

I have often puzzled over why God entrusted flawed human beings with the task of conveying the good news. To put it bluntly, Why did Jesus leave us alone? Did he really consider that small band of unreliable disciples capable of fulfilling the mission of the kingdom of God? And what about today? The church that we know — nearing extinction in the Middle East, scorned in secular Europe, a tiny minority in much of Asia, fractious everywhere — what chance does it stand in changing the world for good?

For an answer to these questions I must go back to when Jesus turned over the mission to his followers. Perhaps another look at familiar scenes can shed light on what God had in mind by setting loose a bunch of scattered pilgrims on a path so sinuous and fraught with danger. Though they may seem like a diversion, the next few pages explore what for me is the heart of the underlying issue.

Jesus' story reaches a climax with the resurrection: almost overnight the disheartened disciples morph into bold street preachers once they realize their leader has conquered death. That, at least, is the story often repeated. Read the accounts closely, though, and you'll find the plot a bit more twisted. Matthew remarks that "some doubted" even after seeing the resurrected Jesus in person. John includes a scene from Galilee, several days' walk from Jerusalem, where six of the eleven remaining disciples have now gone fishing, apparently resuming their former careers in spite of Jesus' return to life.

For six weeks, in fact, the disciples wander around dazed and confused, like survivors of catastrophe, sometimes retreating to familiar haunts once shared with their beloved leader, sometimes clustering behind locked doors. Then in the book of Acts the scene shifts back to Jerusalem when Jesus appears once more and hope flutters anew. *Maybe now is the time when he'll unleash the power long promised by the prophets!* Instead, Jesus issues a directive that has become known as the Great Commission, sending them to "the ends of the earth." As the disciples stand there trying to absorb it all, he floats upward like a balloon into the sky, never to be seen again.

I imagine Luke smiling as he records it years later, that comic scene of eleven earnest partisans arching their necks to stare at clouds as angels ask the obvious question, "Why do you stand here looking into the sky?" Luke omits the implication: *Didn't he tell you to get moving? Well, do it!*

While researching a book on Jesus I decided that the ascension represents my greatest struggle of faith — not whether it happened, but why. After all, the ascension turned loose that company of motley pilgrims collectively known as the church.

If Jesus had not ascended, had stayed behind in some capacity as Super-pope, there would be no need for a book like this one. Grace would be overflowing, not vanishing. Christians would not have to repent for tragic mistakes such as the Crusades and the Inquisition and anti-Jewish pogroms, for Jesus could have stopped such misguided endeavors in their tracks. When moral questions arose, such as slavery, end-of-life issues, or gay rights, the church could appeal directly to Jesus for a ruling that would settle the matter once and for all. Instead, as if aping the disciples, all too often we stare slack-jawed at the sky or muddle along in confusion.

Why did Jesus turn over his holy mission to the likes of us? The answer, as I understand the Bible's plot, leads me to one of the great mysteries of Christian doctrine.

THREE AND ONE

For this quick summary of the Trinity I apologize in advance to professional theologians. I know that all three persons of the Godhead are present from the beginning to the end. I find it helpful, though, to consider the Bible as something like a three-act play, with each act illuminating what went before.

God the Father dominates Act One. Again and again God intervenes: to punish Adam and Eve and then Cain, to choose Noah and then Abraham and later Moses and David, to free a tribe from slavery, to reward and chasten kings, to dispatch prophets with words of reproof and hope.

Act Two spotlights God the Son, the main subject of all four Gospels. For Jews raised on stories of an unapproachable God, the notion that an itinerant teacher from Galilee—from *Galilee!*—could make such outlandish claims as "Anyone who has seen me has seen the Father" was too much to swallow and led to their fateful rejection of him. Even Jesus' select disciples abandoned hope, though later they would see his shocking death as part of the plot anticipated well in advance.

Pentecost introduces Act Three, with emphasis on a Spirit who takes up residence in human agents. "It is for your good that I am going away," Jesus assured his anxious disciples just before his arrest. "When the Advocate comes, whom I will send to you from the Father—the Spirit of truth who goes out from the Father—he will testify about me. And you also must testify . . ."

Viewed through the lens of that three-act plot, my own questions appear in a different light. Why didn't God stop events like the Holocaust? Why doesn't God intervene more often, more decisively? I now see these as Old Testament-style questions more appropriate to Act One, when God the Father was apt to micro-manage human history (or at least the Israelites' history).

Jesus' disciples asked similar questions. If Jesus had the power to heal the sick, raise the dead, and even quiet a storm, why not use that power on a much broader scale? They missed the point that he had turned down shortcuts at the beginning of his ministry when he declined Satan's offer of a magic solution to the world's problems.

"Lord, are you at this time going to restore the kingdom to Israel?" were the disciples' last words to Jesus, and it was left to the angels to provide an indirect answer: "Why do you stand here looking into the sky?" *Get moving—you're the main actors now.*

Though in three years Jesus managed to change history forever, while on earth he affected only a few thousand people in a region the size of a small New England state. He did nothing for the needs of China or Australia or South America or even Europe. All that would come later, through the work of his followers. As Jesus told them, in words that barely sank in at the time, "Whoever believes in me will do the works I have been doing, and they will do even greater things than these, because I am going to the Father."

We bumbling pilgrims are "the Jesus left behind" after the ascension, the heirs of God's Spirit. Paul takes the concept further, calling us the body of Christ and God's temple—meaning the actual presence of God in the world. We are the reason Jesus came, to set in motion a kingdom without borders that eventually would indeed reach Europe and China and Australia and the Americas. Where is God in the world today? Everywhere. Act Three, in the riskiest plot twist of all, has turned God loose, in us and through us.

The Victorian writer Henry Drummond gave his own capsule summary of Act Three: "The Holy Spirit is just what Christ would have been had He been here. He ministers comfort just as Christ would have done—only without the inconveniences of circumstance, without the restriction of space, without the limitations of time." Drummond goes on to explain that the Spirit does such work primarily through ordinary people, those who take up Jesus' mission. Our job, in short, is to show the world another way to live.

Anne Lamott gives a more contemporary version of Henry Drummond's line of thought: "Again and again I tell God I need help, and God says, 'Well isn't that fabulous? Because I need help too. So you go get that old woman over there some water, and I'll figure out what we're going to do about *your* stuff.'"

PARENTAL PRIDE

Apparently, God prefers to act through agents. Meteors, glaciers, floods, tectonic-plate movements, volcanic eruptions, genes and DNA strands—all these played a part in forming the planet we inhabit. Next, God assigned stewardship of that planet to the one species made in God's image. Then Jesus delegated to human agents—*us*—the task of spreading the good-news message of God's love, a message that includes not just words but practical deeds. Eugene Peterson paraphrases Paul's charge to the Philippians: "Go out into the world uncorrupted, a breath of fresh air in this squalid and polluted society. Provide people with a glimpse of good living and of the living God."

The theory is one thing, and how we carry it out quite another. Skeptics look at the disunity of the church, at the wars of religion, at the slowness to address injustices like slavery and apartheid, and find many reasons to doubt a God of love and justice. They may unfairly overlook many Christian contributions, yet the doubts do not easily go away. God has assigned notoriously fallible human beings the holy task of bringing good news and liberation to the world.

In contrast to the pyrotechnics of Old Testament times and the miracles of Jesus, the era of Spirit seems almost anticlimactic. Miracles may occur now and then, but for the most part ordinary pilgrims do God's work by preaching, caring for widows and orphans, challenging society's wrongs, and marshaling the faithful to show the world a better way to live. God must have known the risk involved in entrusting feckless human beings with such a mission.

In my career in Christian journalism I've met my share of characters who seem more suitable for Worldwide Wrestling than for spiritual leadership. Yet I must acknowledge that some of the oddest characters I've met, the larger-than-life ones with a surplus of ego and a deficiency of sophistication, are those who have accomplished most in the work of the kingdom: organizing relief work, feeding the hungry, proclaiming the good news. That pattern simply replicates what the Bible shows so clearly. God used Jacob with his slippery ethics, David with his moral lapses, Jeremiah with his morosity, Saul of Tarsus with his abusive past, Peter with his bodacious failures.

Thinking back over the Christian personalities I've known, as well as those featured in both Old and New Testaments, I've come up with the following principle: God uses the talent pool available. None lived without sin and embarrassing failures. Yet somehow God used them to advance the cause of the kingdom.

I look at the people sitting in chairs in my local church, which meets in a school cafeteria. A window-washer who lifts weights and plays the drums. A woman recovering from traumatic brain injury, who recently lost her husband and cries at the drop of a hat. A lawyer married to a lawyer. A single mother whose car keeps breaking down. Then, even more incredulously, I look in the mirror. The burden of the kingdom of God rests on the backs of ordinary pilgrims, not angels or spiritual giants.

Why choose a plan with the odds stacked against it? It's like turning over a Fortune 500 company to a gang of six-year-olds. I find a simple answer in the Bible's overarching theme that God is love. That quality, more than anything else, makes clear the reason behind all creation. Love cannot really exist without an object to receive it.

Early in her career Mother Teresa of Calcutta was struck by Jesus' words on the cross: "I thirst." For her they came to symbolize not just physical thirst but God's own thirst to draw humanity close. She made "I thirst" the motto for the Sisters of Charity, ordering those words to be displayed in every chapel of the society. "We carry in our body and soul the love of an infinite thirsty God," she wrote one sister. "God thirsts. God thirsts for us and humanity thirsts for God." God thirsts not out of need but out of desire, for God's essence is love.

In several of his letters Paul speaks of our adoption as sons and daughters of God, and perhaps the image of a loving parent comes closest to expressing God's love in a way we can grasp. A father sits on uncomfortable bleachers and watches his son make moves like Beckham on a soccer field; a mother fields a phone call announcing that her daughter has been accepted into medical school. How do they respond? *That kid's trying to show me up—I'll break his kneecaps. That girl thinks she's so smart—I'll teach her, I'll unplug her computer.* Of course not. "Did you see that goal? That's my boy out there! That's my son!" "Did you hear? She made it! She's going to be a doctor!"

In some incomprehensible way, we ordinary pilgrims have the capacity to bring parental pride to the God of the universe. The notion fills me with awe and wonder—and sometimes regret. At the end of the day I ask myself, "What did I do to bring God pleasure today?" I review my interactions with neighbors, the way I handled an unwelcome phone call, my use of money and time. Did I "please God in every way" as Paul prayed for the Colossians?

PILGRIM COMMUNITY

We live out our pilgrim faith not alone, but in community with others, and the New Testament describes a new community—

the kingdom of God — that should attract, rather than repel, the world around us. What does a healthy community of pilgrims look like in our day?

One year I decided to go through the listings in the local phone book under "Churches" and systematically visit a different one each Sunday. Even though I live in a small town, I found representatives of most denominations as well as several unaffiliated churches — a total of twenty-four congregations if I skipped cults and certain fringe groups. On Sundays I felt some of the same discomfort Gina Welch describes in her memoir, stepping into a subculture without really knowing the rules and expectations. Sometimes I would ask myself, Why in the world would anyone want to go to this church?

Some churches made me feel welcome right away. In others, I felt like an intruder. I flashed back to my first visit to a meeting of the Audubon Society. There, people who knew each other stood around discussing obscure bird calls and the technical specifications of binoculars, using an insiders' lingo that I could barely follow. Everyone else shared a community that seemed to exclude me.

I once read a description of church as a place where "a nice, pleasant, bland person stands in front of other nice, pleasant, bland people urging them to be nicer, more pleasant and more bland." With an intuition difficult to explain I could usually sense the "aliveness" of a congregation within five minutes. Were people conversing in the foyer? Did I hear the sound of laughter? What activities and issues did the bulletin board highlight? The aliveness factor had little to do with theology. In two of the most conservative churches members slumped in their seats and glumly went through the motions while the pastors acted as if their main goal was to get to the benediction.

A very liberal church — it had rewritten hymns and even the Lord's Prayer to make them politically correct — showed the most energy in community and global outreach programs. The church, said Archbishop William Temple, is "the only cooperative society in the world that exists for the benefit of its nonmembers." Some churches, especially those located in urban areas, focus on the nonmembers in immediate neighborhoods. Others adopt sister churches in different countries and send mission teams abroad. In my church tour, the saddest groups were those whose vision did not extend beyond their own facility and parking lot.

After visiting all twenty-four churches I came away with a clearer picture of the qualities to look for in a healthy congregation of pilgrims. They all seemed to center on our charge to, in Peter's words, "serve others, *faithfully administering God's grace* in its various forms."

Barbara Brown Taylor, an Episcopal priest, decided to leave her clergy position in part because of the church's failure to administer that grace:

> One thing that had always troubled me was the way people disappeared from church when their lives were breaking down. Separation and divorce were the most common explanations for long absences, but so were depression, alcoholism, job loss, and mortal illness. One new widow told me that she could not come to church because she started crying the moment she sat down in a pew. A young man freshly diagnosed with AIDS said that he stayed away because he was too frightened to answer questions and too angry to sing hymns. I understood their reasoning, but I was sorry that church did not strike these wounded souls as a place they could bring the dark fruits of their equally dark nights.

As I read accounts of the New Testament church, no characteristic stands out more sharply than diversity, the primary testing ground of grace. Beginning with Pentecost—a gathering of people from many countries—the Christian church dismantled the barriers of gender, race, and social class that had marked Jewish congregations. Paul, who had given thanks daily that he was not born a woman, slave, or Gentile, marveled over the radical change: "There is neither Jew nor Gentile, neither slave nor free, nor is there male and female, for you are all one in Christ Jesus."

Diversity complicates life, and perhaps for this reason we tend to surround ourselves with people of similar age, economic class, and outlook. Church offers a place where infants and grandparents, unemployed and executives, immigrants and blue bloods can all come together. One morning I sat sandwiched between an elderly man hooked up to a puffing oxygen tank on one side, while on the other side a breastfeeding baby grunted loudly and contentedly throughout the service. Where else can we go to find that mixture? When I walk into a new church, the more its members resemble each other, and resemble me, the more uncomfortable I feel.

Diversity, however, only succeeds in a group of people who share a common vision. In his prayer in John 17, Jesus stressed one request above all others: "That they may be one." Paul's letters repeatedly call for unity and an end to divisions. The existence of so many denominations worldwide shows how poorly Christians have fulfilled that goal. Major church splits have occurred over such issues as what kind of bread to use in the Eucharist and whether to make the sign of the cross with two or three fingers. We have not, in fact, been faithful stewards of God's grace.

Ideally, the church should be a place that reminds us of lasting truths: that God intends the best for us, that sin and failure are inevitable but forgiveness is guaranteed, that a supportive community bears burdens and comforts the needy. A pastor friend of mine did a series of sermons on the phrase "one another." He found twenty-nine uses of that word in the New Testament which, taken together, show what a true community would look like. They include the following:

Love one another
Forgive one another
Pray for one another
Bear one another's burdens
Be devoted to one another
Regard one another as more important than yourself
Do not speak against one another
Do not judge one another
Show tolerance for one another
Be kind to one another
Speak truth to one another
Build up one another
Comfort one another
Care for one another
Stimulate one another to love and good deeds

I wonder how different the church would look to a watching world, not to mention how different history would look, if Christians everywhere followed that model.

In my visits I never found a perfect church. Nor should we expect to, if the New Testament gives any indication. Some nearly put me to sleep while others tried so hard to be avant-garde that I forgot why I had come. When tempted to judge, I simply reminded myself that the church traces back to God's own bold "experiment": to allow ordinary people like us to embody God's presence on earth, as pilgrims.

Though pilgrims may falter or stray from the path, one thing matters above all: the destination. Fix your eyes on Jesus, says the book of Hebrews. He is the pioneer and perfecter of faith who endured great travail, "for the joy set before him."

In an allusion to John Bunyan's *Pilgrim's Progress*, the philosopher John Hick describes two travelers who take a journey together. Their lives have much in common since they both face the same hardships and enjoy the same pleasures. One traveler, however, believes he is on the way to the Celestial City while the other sees it as a simple expedition with no real goal in mind. As a result they experience the journey very differently.

Writes Hick, "One sees the pleasures that travel brings as foretastes of the greater joy awaiting him, and its pains as being worth enduring for the sake of that final happiness. The other takes the good and the bad as they come, making the best of a journey that ultimately has no point.... The journey will prove either to have been 'Pilgrim's Progress' or 'Just one damn thing after another.'"

CHAPTER 6

ACTIVISTS

We lead our lives well when we love God with
our whole being and when we love our neighbors
as we (properly) love ourselves.

MIROSLAV VOLF

For all of its helpful insights, John Bunyan's allegory gives an incomplete picture of what we should be about. The pilgrim in his story wanders through life seeking an escape from the world. Instead, true pilgrims are called to engage with the world by actively attending to its ills.

I once heard Bono of the band U2 describe his mission of mercy to an orphanage in Ethiopia. For a month he and his wife Ali held babies, helped nurse them back to health, and then donated money to equip the orphanage. While there Bono also wrote and performed for the older orphans songs about eating healthy vegetables and the need to wash your hands.

Bono said that after his return to Ireland his prayers changed, taking on an angry, defiant tone. "God, don't you care about those children in Africa? They did nothing wrong and yet because of AIDS there may soon be fifteen million parentless babies on that continent. Don't you care?!"

Gradually Bono heard in reply that, yes, God cares. In fact, where did he think the idea of a mission trip to Africa came from? The questions he had hurled at God came sailing back to him as a kind of rebuke. *Get moving. Do something.* The role of leading a global campaign against AIDS held little appeal for Bono at first—"I'm a rock star, not a social worker!"—but eventually he could not ignore what unmistakably felt like a calling.

Over the next few years politicians as varied as Bill Clinton and Senator Strom Thurmond, and then Tony Blair and Kofi Annan and George W. Bush, found a musician dressed all in black and wearing his signature sunglasses camped outside their offices waiting to see them. In a time of economic cutbacks, somehow Bono managed to persuade those leaders to ante up fifteen billion dollars to combat AIDS.

With government support assured, Bono next went on a bus tour of the United States, speaking to large churches and Christian colleges because he believed that Christians were key to addressing this particular global problem. He invited other pilgrims to participate in what God wanted accomplished in the world, and many did.

CHANGE AGENTS

Jesus set out his platform in his very first public talk: "The Spirit of the Lord is on me, because he has anointed me to proclaim good news to the poor. He has sent me to proclaim freedom for the prisoners and recovery of sight for the blind, to set the oppressed free." Those of us who follow Jesus necessarily adopt that same agenda. As a result, many of the questions that we throw at God return to us like a boomerang.

Consider, for example, the excellent question, "Why doesn't God do something about global hunger?" The angels' words after Jesus' ascension echo through the centuries: "Why do you stand here looking into the sky?" We, Jesus' followers, are the agents assigned to carry out God's will on earth. Too easily we expect

God to do something *for* us when instead God wants to do it *through* us.

The Christian activist, however, must walk a tightrope: how to confront the world's problems without commingling with the very powers that created those problems. We must live "in the world … not of the world" as Jesus said in his final meal with the disciples. Throughout history Christians have sought the right balance, sometimes veering too close to the surrounding culture and sometimes withdrawing to the point of irrelevance.

I have learned much on this issue from the theologian Miroslav Volf, a Croatian who lived through the Balkan War of the 1990s and went on to teach at Fuller Seminary and Yale Divinity School. The son of a Pentecostal pastor, Volf grew up feeling like "a minority of the minorities," a member of a fringe group in a region with a troubled religious past. During his early years, then-Yugoslavia was officially atheist: Volf's father served time in a Communist labor camp, and Miroslav himself underwent extensive police interrogation. When communism fell, he watched as the country broke apart along religious lines and the bloody civil war began.

People of faith face two opposite dangers, Volf concluded. Some withdraw from the culture around them, in the process forfeiting any potential influence. The Pentecostals of his youth did so, emphasizing their private and church lives and preparing for the afterlife. They were barely "in the world" at all. Yet Jesus had given clear instructions to his disciples in a commissioning prayer: "As you sent me into the world, I have sent them into the world."

During the war Volf saw just the opposite, an "of the world" approach, as religious groups aligned themselves with those in power. Croat Catholics, Serb Orthodox, and Bosniak Muslims carved up his country and began an ethnic cleansing campaign against minority groups. Church history includes many disturbing examples of this approach. In the Americas, pastors and priests blessed the conquerors who exploited native tribes. In Africa, missionaries often worked hand in hand with colonial powers. (Bishop Desmond Tutu remarks, "When the missionaries came to Africa they had the Bible and we had the land. They said 'Let us pray.' We closed our eyes. When we opened them we had the Bible and they had the land.")

Volf proposes a different model for people of faith. Leading with what we believe, he says, tends to provoke opposition — witness the tragic history of the Balkans. By emphasizing doctrine, we set ourselves apart from "the other" and may be tempted to impose our beliefs by force. Instead, guided by the Golden Rule we should concentrate on living out our beliefs, progressing from *hand* to *heart* to *head*. Practical acts of mercy (extending a hand) will express our love (the heart), which in turn may attract others to the source of that love (head beliefs).*

I believe Volf may also have framed the best way of communicating our faith in modern times, especially to post-Christians. Protestants, notably those who would welcome the label *evangelical*, have traditionally stressed "proclaiming the word" in a direct appeal to the mind. We preach sermons, write books on apologetics, conduct city-wide evangelistic campaigns. For those alienated from the church, that approach no longer has the same drawing power. And for the truly needy, words alone don't satisfy; "A hungry person has no ears," as one relief worker told me.

A skeptical world judges the truth of what we say by the proof of how we live. Today's activists may be the best evangelists.

PITFALLS AND DETOURS

Even acts of mercy must be done with care. Soho Machida, a Zen Buddhist monk from Japan who teaches at Princeton University,

---

* Albanian evangelicals, about 1 percent of the population, followed that pattern admirably during the Balkan war, caring for 20 percent of the refugees expelled from Kosovo, many of them Muslim.

gives an outsider's view of Christians. "No other religion has ever produced figures like Albert Schweitzer or Mother Teresa, whose lives have become monuments to humankind's goodwill," he says with appreciation. "Christianity has contributed immeasurably to a wider recognition of human rights around the world. There are also many impressive stories about patients with fatal diseases or prison inmates who recover their hope for life through converting to Christianity."

Machida admires the Christian emphasis on transforming the world, in contrast to some Asian religions that teach a passive acceptance of fate. Then he adds this cautionary note about believers: "If they have the slightest consciousness of themselves as the superior helping the inferior, or the faithful saving the unfaithful, they immediately lose their Christian dignity." Some Christians, he observes, convey a spirit of superiority toward others and may even project hostility toward the rest of society.

I will focus on evangelicals, the branch of the faith I know best. Again and again I hear a similar complaint about evangelicals who are doing good deeds. A friend of mine in Chicago who runs a shelter for addicts and homeless people, and is tantalizingly hard to place on any theological map, once told me, "I love evangelicals. They make our best volunteers. They truly care about people's needs, and you can get them to do anything." He paused a second before adding with a sly smile, "The challenge is, you've got to soften their judgmental attitudes before they can be effective."

When I read feature stories in *Time* and *Newsweek* about evangelicals I often wince because, like my Chicago friend, the media look upon evangelicals as intolerant and judgmental. They miss the vibrancy and enthusiasm, the good-newsness that the word represents in much of the world and that I have seen firsthand. In the United States everything eventually boils down to politics, an adversary sport, and Americans tend to view evangelicals as "of the world"—a monolithic voting bloc obsessed with a few moral issues.

I once conducted an informal survey among airline seatmates and other strangers willing to strike up a conversation. "When I say the word evangelical, what comes to mind?" I would ask. In response I would usually hear the word *against*: evangelicals are against abortion, against pornography, against gay rights, against universal health care, against evolution, against immigration. Outsiders regard evangelicals as moralists who want to impose their "head" beliefs on a diverse society. As Miroslav Volf noted, when a religion — any religion — tries to force itself on others who do not share its beliefs, it creates a backlash and stirs up opposition.

In recent times leading evangelicals in the U.S. have turned to politics as a way to express their activism and advance their agenda. Yet, looking at history, I cannot avoid the impression that evangelicals have had a spotty record in politics. Evangelicals led the fight for women's suffrage and the abolition of slavery — and also led the fight against both movements. African American pastors, many of them evangelicals, spearheaded the civil rights movement even as white evangelicals in the South largely opposed it. In the 1980s, Jerry Falwell urged American Christians to buy gold Krugerrands and to promote U.S. investment in South Africa in an effort to shore up the white regime. Currently, evangelicals take a prominent role in supporting pro-life legislation while also championing the death penalty, gun rights, and military ventures.

In sum, evangelicals have taken political stances that sometimes appear impulsive, sometimes heroic, and often contradictory. Is it any wonder that the rest of the world views us with suspicion and that the good-news message gets lost?

(To further muddy the waters, many evangelicals in places like Europe and New Zealand align themselves with liberal political parties, believing their faith enjoins them to back social programs for the poor and to oppose war. And in China many Christians see no contradiction in their support for the world's largest Communist government. Until recently Kerala, the state in India with the highest proportion of Christians, voted with the Communist Party.)

Kevin Roose, a student at Brown University, decided to investigate evangelicals and so he enrolled for a semester at Liberty University. As he explains in *The Unlikely Disciple*, "My social circle at Brown included atheists, agnostics, lapsed Catholics, Buddhists, Wiccans, and more non-observant Jews than you can shake a shofar at, but exactly zero born-again Christians. The evangelical world, in my mind, was a cloistered, slightly frightening community whose values and customs I wasn't supposed to understand. So I ignored it."

After he spent time at Liberty, however, Kevin's opinions changed. The media stereotypes did not always apply. "This is not a group of angry zealots. I knew I'd see a different side of Liberty students once I resolved to blend in among them, but I thought it would be a harsher side. I had this secular/liberal paranoia that when evangelical students were among themselves, they spent their time huddled in dark rooms, organizing anti-abortion protests and plotting theocratic takeovers. But that's not true at all."

Roose learned that, contrary to the media stereotype, many evangelicals are uninvolved in politics. In fact, American evangelicals spend twelve times as much on foreign missions and international relief efforts as they do on political action.

DEFYING THE STEREOTYPE

For several decades now I have reported on the evangelical subculture. Along the way I have met evangelicals, often unheralded and out of the spotlight, who serve as frontline activists of a different sort. Not primarily political activists, these are reformers on the ground who work to serve the common good. While researching the book *What Good Is God?* I observed some of them extending a hand of mercy on several continents.

In South Africa I spent time with Ray McCauley, a larger-than-life character who in younger days competed against Arnold Schwarzenegger in the Mr. Universe contest. Ray founded a church in Johannesburg based on the charismatic "name it and claim it" philosophy, a church that ultimately grew into the largest in South Africa, with thirty-five thousand members. As the apartheid government began to crumble, Ray's racial attitudes, politics, and rigid theology began to soften. Some white members grew disgruntled over the new approach and left; gradually the church's makeup changed in a way that reflected the racial spectrum of the nation. Today the church's programs include AIDS outreach, a housing project, and a rehabilitation farm for addicts.

At the other end of the country, in Cape Town, I met Joanna Flanders-Thomas, a dynamic woman of mixed race. As a student she had agitated against the apartheid government. After that nationwide victory she turned to a local problem, the most violent prison in South Africa, where Nelson Mandela had spent eight years of confinement. Joanna started visiting prisoners daily, bringing them a simple gospel message of forgiveness and reconciliation. She earned their trust, got them to talk about their abusive childhoods, and showed them a better way of resolving conflicts. The year before her visits began, the prison recorded 279 acts of violence against inmates and guards; the next year there were two.

A few months later I traveled to Nepal, the world's only Hindu kingdom, a dirt-poor country where the caste system prevails. There I met with health workers from fifteen nations, mostly European, who serve under an evangelical mission specializing in leprosy work. Most major advances in leprosy treatment have come through Christian missionaries — mainly because, as my Chicago friend put it, "You can get them to do anything." I met well-trained surgeons, nurses, and physical therapists who devote their lives to caring for leprosy victims, many of them from the lowest caste. In their leisure time some of these missionaries climb the high mountains in Nepal, others focus on bird life, and at least one French doctor studies Himalayan moths. Several had run the Kathmandu marathon, and two had taken a madcap motorcycle ride across mountains and rivers into neighboring Tibet. None fit the image of "uptight, right-wing evangelicals," yet all would claim the word *evangelical.*

The United Nations estimates that three million women and children are trafficked worldwide each year. I attended a conference of several dozen Christian organizations that work to liberate women from prostitution, which in poor nations constitutes a modern form of slavery. Delegates from forty nations brought along some of the women they've rescued, who told wrenching stories of abuse and credited the ministries with setting them free and helping them find new careers. One organization alone shelters five hundred young women freed from sex slavery in the brothels of Mumbai, India.

Also in India, Christians have led the way in embracing the Dalits (formerly Untouchables) and other low castes by building schools and clinics to serve them. Millions from the lower castes have subsequently left the Hindu faith, which excludes them from its temples, and found a home among Christians.

Thanks to such activity, in other countries the word *evangelical* has a very different connotation than in the U.S. In the Middle East, for example, the media focus on clashes between Muslims and Christians, yet a friend of mine who heads a ministry there says, "Evangelicals in the Middle East are thought of as the people with Good News, the very definition of the word 'evangelical.' They have been at the forefront of development, job training, human rights, and religious freedom. They have also been out front in medicine and medical education at all levels and are known to care for the poor." Hospitals and schools founded by missionaries rank among the finest in the Arabian Gulf states.

LIVING UP TO OUR NAME

Some of my friends believe we should abandon the word *evangelical*. I prefer that we keep the name and live up to its true meaning (the Greek word *euangelion* means "glad tidings" or "good news").

On a visit to Brazil I met a fellow American who had accompanied a local pastor to a barrio in São Paulo. He began to feel anxious as he noticed the minions of a drug lord patrolling the neighborhood with automatic weapons. The street narrowed to a dirt path. Plastic water pipes dangled overhead, open sewage ran through the alleys, and a snarl of wires tapped power from high-voltage lines. Anxiety turned to fear as he noticed that people inside the tin shacks were glowering at him, a suspicious gringo invading their turf. Was he a narc? An undercover cop? Then the drug lord noticed on the back of his T-shirt the logo of a local Pentecostal church. He broke out in a big smile. "O, evangélicos!" he called out, and the scowls abruptly changed to smiles. Over the years that church had extended practical help to the barrio, and now the foreign visitors were gladly welcomed.

More recently I spoke at a Christian gathering with the strange name Wild Goose Festival, described to me as "a sort of left-wing-Christian-hippie-activist-Woodstock." More than two thousand attended, camping out on soggy, rain-soaked grounds to listen to musical groups and speakers who exhorted them to live out their faith. Some booths promoted human rights: "Who Would Jesus Torture?" read one large banner. Another poster quoted Shane Claiborne: "How can I worship a homeless person on Sunday and ignore one on Monday?" Some sought to end "hobophobia" by offering both dignity and practical help to the homeless. A veteran of the civil rights movement, leaning on a cane, boomed out a sermon in a rhetorical style reminiscent of Martin Luther King Jr.; he had just spent time in jail for leading a protest against a reactionary state legislature.

Activists I have met from both sides of the political spectrum have one thing in common, the belief that in ministering to the vulnerable they are following Jesus. Christians once divided over their understanding of our role in the world: more liberal Christians emphasized human needs whereas conservatives focused on evangelism. Evangelicals have since learned that the two prongs of conversion and social change actually work together.

Studies in Latin America document how personal transformation can lead to social improvement. A man steps forward to receive Christ at an evangelistic meeting. He joins a local church that counsels him to stop getting drunk on weekends. With their support and help, he does so. He starts showing up at work on Monday mornings and eventually gets promoted to a foreman's position. Bolstered by his faith and a renewed sense of self-worth, he stops beating his wife and becomes a better father to his children. For her part, his newly empowered wife takes a job that enables her to afford education for their children. Multiply that by several score converted villagers, and soon the economy of the entire neighborhood rises.

Moreover, conservative Christians have come to accept that Jesus' gospel applies to the whole person and not just the soul. Didn't Jesus inaugurate his own ministry with a declaration of good news for the poor, the oppressed, the prisoners, and the blind? Today, doctors on Mercy Ships perform free surgeries for the blind in underserved countries, and Habitat for Humanity pursues its lofty goal of suitable housing for the poor. In a reprise of the settlement movement a century ago, evangelicals are moving into major cities to help stabilize low-income neighborhoods. They staff homeless shelters, addiction programs, and pregnancy centers because they believe such activism helps further God's kingdom, a down-to-earth response to Jesus' prayer that God's will be done here "as it is in heaven."*

---

* Books such as *Evangelicals You Don't Know* by Tom Krattenmaker and *Kingdom Calling* by Amy L. Sherman give many more examples.

WORDLESS HOPE

In countries such as Pakistan and Afghanistan, Christians must keep silent about their faith. Sometimes, as happened to medical workers in Afghanistan in 2010 and 2014, they are martyred for it. Activists are facing new challenges for which there is no guidebook, feeling their way through uncharted territory. Nowadays aid groups in sensitive countries must sign a code of conduct that prohibits them from using aid "to further a particular political or religious standpoint." Christians sharing food and medicines is one thing; ideas are an entirely different matter.

During one of the periodic droughts that devastate East Africa, I visited a sprawling refugee camp in a Somali desert to see what evangelical relief work looks like in a "closed" country. I wanted to know why workers volunteer for such hardship tasks. What motivates them, and what impact do they have?

Early on, World Concern was nearly overwhelmed by the chaos at their assigned site in remote Somalia. Medical supplies ordered months before had not yet arrived and food had run out. Sixty thousand refugees were ready to mutiny. An old man rushed up to the relief workers, shaking a stick and screaming, "We don't need a clinic! We need food. Can't you see our babies are starving?" At least thirty babies were dying each day in the makeshift camp.

Medically, the camp was hell on earth. Dysentery, whooping cough, measles, diphtheria, and tuberculosis were breaking out, their symptoms complicated by the malnutrition. It took only six months for the seven relief workers to move the refugee camp from a flashpoint of catastrophe into the orderly community that I visited. Except for a break during the heat of the afternoon, relief workers staffed clinics and food distribution stations from seven in the morning until seven at night.

At night the workers gathered around a campfire, reviewed the day, and reminisced about their home countries and their experiences in other crisis zones. In different ways I kept asking my underlying question: Why do people sign up for a daily regimen of low-paid work under the broiling sun with so few amenities of modern life?

Dr. John Wilson, a soft-spoken, silver-haired pediatrician from North Carolina, mentioned a sense of duty. "Sometimes I feel like Jonah out here—I came because I thought I should, whether or not I felt like it. My father was a missionary doctor in Korea, beginning in 1907, the only doctor serving five million people. Professionally, I've tried a little of everything: a busy private practice, teaching at a university, working with coal miners. Over the years I've come to believe I ought to tithe not just my money but also my time to God."

Dr. Wilson added that practicing medicine in undeveloped areas has its own attractions. "After seeing hundreds of children who may have nothing more than a runny nose or a sore throat, it does something to me to come over here and have a part in saving lives." The doctor who preceded Wilson once performed an appendectomy by flashlight inside a tent during a driving rainstorm, using tablespoons as retractors and dish towels as sponges. Health workers have the chance to practice pure medicine, with no insurance payments to pursue, no profits to maximize, and no malpractice suits to worry about.

Dr. Wilson's age (he has since retired) was an exception among the relief workers in Somalia. The vast majority were in their early twenties: idealistic, fresh-faced youth who could be posing for a Peace Corps poster. Lois, a twenty-one-year-old blonde who wore her hair in pigtails, shrugged off the hardships of life in a camp. "I think of my nursing school classmates," she told me. "At graduation we all compared assignments: a new hospital in Canada, an Air Force position in Greece, a famous teaching hospital in San Diego, a private school in Minneapolis. I remember the expressions on my friends' faces when I said I would be doing relief work in a war-stricken Muslim country on the horn of Africa. 'That's really an insane thing to do!' one girl said."

Lois continued, "I often think back to that graduation day as I sit in a folding chair at night. Here in the desert, under an equatorial sky free of pollution, the Milky Way gleams, splitting the heavens like a highway of light. I sit alone, listen to the soft gurgle of the Juba River, and think of my friends back home. In some ways, I guess coming here does look like an insane thing to do. Yet I have never felt more satisfied and fulfilled in my life. Most of my friends from nursing school are grinding out the three-to-eleven shift at some hospital. They're the ones who are losing out. I'm having the adventure of a lifetime. How could anyone feel sorry for me?

"A spirit of hope now infects every person in this camp, all because donors in the West and relief workers here sacrificially gave of themselves. I can't verbalize the source of my hope here because the government forbids talking about the Christian faith. But I can demonstrate by my presence and my spirit that there is hope, a concept difficult for some Muslims to grasp because their religion is so fatalistic. To me, it speaks loudly that more than twenty Christian relief agencies, including World Concern, have selflessly brought healing to a Muslim nation.

"Perhaps one day I'll be back in America working the night shift at a comfortable suburban hospital. Then I'll probably struggle with new issues, such as how to be selfless and grateful in a land of plenty. But I know that I'll always be thankful my career as a nurse began here, where my presence can make a life-or-death difference. In fact, I almost feel sorry for people who never have the chance to serve God like this. I believe I am beginning to learn what Jesus meant when he said, 'If you lose your life, you will find it.'"

FAITHFUL PRESENCE

In 2010 sociologist James Davison Hunter published a book with the title *To Change the World*. He begins by citing the mission statements of many Christian organizations: to redeem culture, transform society, and "change the world for Christ." Looking at the evidence, he ruefully concludes that is not happening, at least not in the way the sloganeers envision.

The gospel has indeed transformed some pagan cultures in history, and in parts of the world it continues to have an impact on whole societies. Nevertheless, when the faith runs into fierce resistance, such as in Islamic countries, it may succumb or fade into insignificance. Think of the churches mentioned in the New Testament, now archeological ruins in Turkey, Syria, and Iraq. And there is no indication that the modern works of mercy dispensed in places like Somalia or tsunami-affected areas of Indonesia have dampened opposition to Christianity. The doctors and nurses I interviewed in Somalia spoke of a lasting impact on their own faith, not on the faith of those they helped.

In Western countries, as I have indicated, fervent faith may provoke a different kind of opposition, from skeptics and post-Christians. Hunter suggests abandoning talk of redeeming culture and transforming the world, because such language implies conquest and takeover. Instead, Hunter proposes a different goal, to maintain "a faithful presence within" the surrounding culture, best demonstrated by an example of sacrificial love. He quotes the well-known pastor Rick Warren, who says in *The Purpose Driven Life*, "I'm looking for a second reformation. The first reformation of the church 500 years ago was about beliefs. This one is going to be about deeds. It is not going to be about what the church believes, but about what the church is doing."

Increasingly, evangelicals are beginning to speak of "the common good," a phrase borrowed from Catholics. The church works best not as a power center, rather as a countercultural community — in the world but not of it — that shows others how to live the most fulfilled and meaningful life on earth. In modern society that means rejecting the false gods of independence, success, and pleasure and replacing them with love for God and neighbor. As the relief workers in Somalia testified, what seems at first sacrificial may actually bring the greatest satisfaction.

A Harvard student told me of attending a university gathering at which Mother Teresa spoke. One by one the world's luminaries come to that school, often failing to impress the cynical students. This time a wrinkled and withered woman in a nun's habit, so diminutive that she had to stand on a box to reach the microphone, didn't even try to win over her audience. Gently but firmly she informed them that they lived in a culture of death, that they were surrounded by false gods of material wealth and sexual pleasure, and that most of them would probably forfeit their lives in search of success. When she finished, the Harvard students, despite having just received a sound scolding, stood to their feet and gave her a prolonged ovation.

By the very example of her life Mother Teresa had shown them another way, as if switching on a light to expose a room full of junk. Albanian by birth, she had left a career teaching geography at an elite Catholic girls' school in Calcutta to work instead among the poor and dying, almost all of them Hindus. She lived out a faithful presence in an alien culture, serving the common good and gaining the world's respect in the process.

Gabe Lyons, a product of the evangelical subculture and himself a graduate of Liberty University, recalls a time when Christians focused on "caring for those who believe like we believe.... But the common good requires us to care for all people—loving our neighbor no matter what they believe." Lyons is merely echoing what the New Testament says about a hostile environment. According to the book of Hebrews, we are "foreigners and strangers on earth," and Peter urges that "Each one should use whatever gift he has received to serve others, faithfully administering God's grace in its various forms."

I have seen Christians around the world practicing those various forms of grace-dispensing. Some, like the relief workers I visited in Somalia, do it on the frontlines of disaster and injustice. Others do it in less spectacular ways, by taking in foster children, volunteering for soup kitchens and homeless shelters, or simply contributing money toward relief work elsewhere. In Miroslav Volf's formula, extending the hand of mercy expresses the heart of love, which may attract others to the source of that love.

A VISIBLE APOLOGETIC

John Marks, a producer for television's *60 Minutes*, went on a two-year quest to investigate evangelicals, the group he had grown up among and later rejected. He wrote a book about his findings, *Reasons to Believe: One Man's Journey Among the Evangelicals and the Faith He Left Behind.* The church's response to Hurricane Katrina turned the corner for him and became a strong reason to believe. One Baptist church in Baton Rouge fed sixteen thousand people a day for weeks; another housed seven hundred homeless evacuees. Still another church served as a distribution point for fifty-six churches, and churches in surrounding states sent regular teams to help rebuild homes for years after the hurricane, long after federal assistance had dried up.

Most impressively to Marks, all these church efforts crossed racial lines and barriers in the Deep South. As one worker told him, "We had whites, blacks, Hispanics, Vietnamese, good old Cajun.... We just tried to say, hey, let's help people. This is our state. We'll let everybody else sort out that other stuff. We've got to cook some rice."

Marks concludes,

I would argue that this was a watershed moment in the history of American Christianity ... nothing spoke more eloquently to believers, and to nonbelievers who were paying attention, than the success of a population of believing

127

volunteers measured against the massive and near-total collapse of secular government efforts. The storm laid bare an unmistakable truth. More and more Christians have decided that the only way to reconquer America is through service. The faith no longer travels by the word. It moves by the deed.

Jesus mentioned good deeds as a sort of visible apologetic: "Let your light shine before others, that they may see your good deeds and glorify your Father in heaven." Sometimes, though not always, outsiders take notice. Joe Klein, the political editor of *Time* magazine, while volunteering to repair tornado-ravaged homes in Oklahoma, observed the many church groups from around the country and commented in a cover story, "Funny how you don't see secular humanists giving out hot meals."

Deeds also impressed another New York journalist, Nicholas Kristof. Winner of two Pulitzer Prizes and a regular columnist for the *New York Times*, Kristof wrote an op-ed tribute to John Stott, the British vicar who had an admirably simple lifestyle, donating the royalties from his books of theology to a charity promoting scholarship in the developing world. Through his work with the Lausanne Conferences, Stott did more than any single person to lead evangelicals toward a holistic approach to the faith.

Kristof openly acknowledges that "nearly all of us in the news business are completely out of touch with a group that includes 46 percent of Americans," the proportion who described themselves in a Gallup poll as evangelical or born-again Christians. He admits the common media stereotype: "The entire evangelical movement often has been pilloried among progressives as reactionary, myopic, anti-intellectual and, if anything, immoral."

In his tribute, Kristof gives a strong counterpoint, using John Stott as a model: "Yet that casual dismissal is profoundly unfair of the movement as a whole. It reflects a kind of reverse intolerance, sometimes a reverse bigotry, directed at tens of millions of people who have actually become increasingly engaged in issues of global poverty and justice."

Mr. Stott didn't preach fire and brimstone on a Christian television network. He was a humble scholar whose 50-odd books counseled Christians to emulate the life of Jesus—especially his concern for the poor and oppressed—and confront social ills like racial oppression and environmental pollution.

Evangelicals are disproportionately likely to donate 10 percent of their incomes to charities, mostly church-related. More important, go to the front lines, at home or abroad, in the battles against hunger, malaria, prison rape, obstetric fistula, human trafficking or genocide, and some of the bravest people you meet are evangelical Christians (or conservative Catholics, similar in many ways) who truly live their faith.

I'm not particularly religious myself, but I stand in awe of those I've seen risking their lives in this way—and it sickens me to see that faith mocked at New York cocktail parties.

Jesus taught us to pray that God's will be done "on earth as it is in heaven." A skeptic may scoff at such a mirage, yet imagine for a moment a world with no homelessness or poverty, no divorces or unwanted children, no discrimination, no violence, no sexual abuse, no theft or cheating, no addictions, no abuse of the environment, a world in which governments rule with justice and financial institutions operate with integrity and politicians work together for the common good. That is what Jesus' followers should strive for.

Christians are not mere wayfarers en route to the next life, but rather pioneer settlers of God's kingdom in advance, a sign of what will follow. By living out lives of grace in a spoiled environment, we point forward to a time of restoration. One Harlem preacher likens us to the pink plastic spoons at Baskin Robbins: we give the world a foretaste of what lies ahead, the vision of the biblical prophets. In a world gone astray we should be actively demonstrating here and now God's will for the planet.

CHAPTER 7

ARTISTS

The Lord who created must wish us to create
And employ our creation again in His service

T. S. ELIOT

Much as I admire activists, I am not one. Most days I sit alone in my home office staring at a computer screen while pressing plastic keys that make an insect-click sound.

This used to bother me. I once wrote an article titled "They Also Serve Who Only Sit and Click," comparing my routine with my social worker wife's. At dinner each evening she would recount her visits to bed-bound senior citizens and the meals she organized for the homeless. "What about your day?" she would ask, and usually I had to rack my brain to come up with something worth mentioning. Not much happens in a writer's day: the mailman comes, I get a letter from a reader, I find a good adverb.

When I travel on assignment I meet the kind of people mentioned in the last chapter, activists who roll up their sleeves and tackle major problems. They lift my faith and remind me of the important work of the kingdom. Once again, though, I play a vicarious role by writing about them. While they work on the frontlines, I spend my time moving electrons around on a computer screen, ordering them into words and sentences in hopes that someday they will connect with someone.

131

On a trip to Lebanon in 1998 I met a woman who said she had read my book *Disappointment with God* during the Lebanese civil war. She kept it in a basement bomb shelter. When the artillery fire intensified around her high-rise apartment building, she would make her way down the darkened stairway, light a candle or a kerosene lantern, and read my book. I cannot describe how humbling it was for me to hear that when Christians were dying because of their faith, when the most beautiful city of the Middle East was being reduced to rubble, at that moment words I wrote from my apartment in Chicago somehow brought her comfort.

On the same trip another woman told me that my book about grace helped her have a better attitude toward the Palestinian guerrillas who had confiscated her apartment and forced her out. "What really upset me was that they made me keep paying the utility bills!" she said. I hung my head, for when I wrote that book I was thinking of neighbors who play loud music or let their dogs run loose, not guerrillas who move in uninvited. So often I feel a disconnect between what I write about in seclusion and the ways in which others apply those words in the real world. Only with difficulty (and age) have I learned to accept a role behind the frontlines, truly believing that we also serve who only sit and click.

Most of my writing centers on topics of interest to readers who share my faith. I have friends, though, who labor for years over a novel or a film that they hope will influence the broader culture, and then abandon it because they cannot find a willing film distributor or book publisher. *Have I wasted my time?* they wonder. To make a living by creating, whether it involves books or films or visual arts, is a lonely enterprise fraught with risk.

Yet in modern times, and especially for post-Christians, the creative arts may be the most compelling path to faith. Communicating at a more subtle level, they cut through defenses and awaken thirst. Someone who would never think of attending church will visit an art museum or watch a movie or play. To mention just one example, Peter Hitchens, brother of the atheist Christopher, credits a five-hundred-year-old painting of *The Last Judgment* with stirring his return to faith. Staring at the painting, its naked figures stripped of their time-bound fashions, gave him a sudden sense of religion being a thing of the present and not just the past. He felt a proper and holy fear of a world beyond that sits in judgment on this one.

One year I attended a musical called *The Mysteries* in London's West End. A South African troupe had taken the form of the old medieval mystery plays and culturally adapted it. The play began, like the Bible, with Adam and Eve, a male and a female actor standing stark naked on a blank stage. Then came Noah, Abraham, Joseph, Moses, David and many others acting out the plot of the biblical story, all the way to Jesus. The actors sang in five different languages, accompanied by musicians who beat on tires, oil drums, and garbage can lids rather than musical instruments. In their version, Afrikaner policemen, not Roman soldiers, were the ones who crucified Jesus. At the end of the play the secular and sophisticated London audience leaped to their feet after the joyous resurrection scene. The cycle was complete, I thought as I looked around at theatergoers waving handkerchiefs and shouting "Bravo!" British missionaries had carried the gospel to South Africa. Now Africans were bringing it back, wrapped in their own cultural terms, to people who had mostly forgotten it.

The arts have become a pulpit for culture at large, one too often neglected by people of faith. N. T. Wright says that the arts "are highways into the center of a reality which cannot be glimpsed, let alone grasped, any other way." Joseph Ratzinger, who later became Pope Benedict XVI, goes further: "The only really effective apologia for Christianity comes down to two arguments, namely, the saints the Church has produced and the art which has grown in her womb."

GOADS

I was contemplating the role of artists when I came across a passage in the book of Ecclesiastes that applies to my own profession of writing. I sat up and took note. "He pondered and searched out and set in order many proverbs. The Teacher searched to find just the right words ..." Clearly, the Teacher of long ago knew something of what I do when I undertake to compose or rearrange words.

In a jumble of mixed metaphors the Teacher adds, "The words of the wise are like goads, their collected sayings like firmly embedded nails — given by one Shepherd." In typical contrapuntal style he later gives this tweak, "Be warned, my son, of anything in addition to them. Of making many books there is no end, and much study wearies the body."

For writers and others who seek to impart wisdom, says the Teacher, there is a time to be a goad and a time to be a firmly embedded nail.

A goad, such as a farmer uses on oxen, prods to action. Goads cause enough discomfort to get animals — or people — to do something they otherwise might not do. History has seen many examples of the creative arts used as goads, and they often rattle the governing powers.

Victor Jara was a Chilean musician whose blend of folk music and political activism kindled the hopes of the poor. The day after a right-wing coup led by Augusto Pinochet, the general's minions arrested Jara and broke the bones in his guitar-playing hands. As he lay on the ground, they taunted him to play some of his songs about love and peace. This goad the new regime could not tolerate, and three days later soldiers riddled his body with forty-four bullets.

The visual arts, too, get under the skin of authoritarian regimes. According to Pablo Picasso, a fascist officer barked at him, "Did you do that?" and pointed to a photo of the huge painting *Guernica*, which graphically depicts the bombing of civilians.

"No, you did," the artist replied. He sent the painting into protective exile, where it stayed until democracy returned to Spain four decades later.

It occurs to me that the prophets of the Bible served as goads. Speaking sometimes in peasant language and sometimes in magnificent poetry, their words all reduce to a one-line message: Repent and change your ways, or else judgment will come.

Harriet Beecher Stowe, a radical Christian, sought to communicate the anti-slavery message to many who had blocked their ears to sermons and jeremiads. Choosing another form, she wrote the novel *Uncle Tom's Cabin*, which sold two hundred thousand copies its first year and as much as any other force goaded a nation toward change. When Stowe met President Abraham Lincoln in 1862, he allegedly exclaimed, "So you are the little woman who wrote the book that started this great war!"

Not so long ago the world experienced a seismic realignment. Within the span of one year, 600 million people gained freedom, with hardly a shot being fired. How did it happen? It will take historians years to sort out all the reasons for communism's collapse. As one who lived through the 1960s — a decade when barricades went up in the streets of Paris, when leftists and not rightists were bombing public buildings in America, and when university intellectuals were swallowing Marxism whole — I trace the fault line back to a lone Russian, his courage hardened to steel in the Gulag, who dared proclaim, "It is a lie." The massive documentation assembled by Alexander Solzhenitsyn bore witness to a contrary truth, and one by one the elite of Europe abandoned the illusion of Marxist utopia.

Many Christians in the creative arts strive to be goads in the flank of society. I applaud them, and sometimes join them. As the above examples show, we should not underestimate the power of the arts in promoting change. Even so, I have come to see the limitations of a goading art. The prophets take up so many pages of the Old Testament because with a few exceptions they were spectacularly ineffective. There was Nathan, of course, who through the sheer power of story stabbed King David to the heart. And there was Jonah, the reluctant goad who much to his own dismay sparked a revival in Nineveh. But few of the other prophets had much impact. Jeremiah 36 records an all-too-typical response: the offended king simply cut up Jeremiah's scroll and burned it.

Solzhenitsyn paid tribute to his colleagues who died unknown in the Gulag, their works memorized and taken to the grave with them, or furtively scrawled down but now lost, buried in tundra caches that will never be discovered. Six hundred million may have found a new measure of freedom in 1989, but one billion Chinese experienced a crackdown that same year after the Tiananmen Square protests. Goads have limited reach.

NAILS

There is a time to be a goad and a time to be a firmly embedded nail. While a goad prods to immediate action, a nail sinks deeper, a lasting marker of "the permanent things," to borrow T. S. Eliot's phrase.

Toward the end of his life, Paul Gauguin painted a huge paneled triptych. In a remarkably unsubtle move he scrawled these words in French across a corner of the painting: "Who are we? Why are we here? Where are we going?" — questions he had learned as a boy in a Catholic catechism class for which he still had no answers. The painting, set in Tahiti, depicts birth, young adulthood, and an old woman who is facing death and "the Beyond" (also labeled by Gauguin). Soon after completing the work, and convinced he could never surpass it, the artist attempted suicide.

That triptych, now hanging in the Boston Museum of Art, poses a grand summation of the questions that haunt modernity. Loren Eiseley, a rare individual who made art out of science, gives the bleak answer to Gauguin's questions as offered by secular science:

In a universe whose size is beyond human imagining, where our world floats like a dust mote in the void of night, men have grown inconceivably lonely. We scan the time scale and the mechanisms of life itself for portents and signs of the invisible. As the only thinking mammals on the planet—perhaps the only thinking animals in the entire sidereal universe—the burden of consciousness has grown heavy upon us. We watch the stars, but the signs are uncertain.... Nevertheless, in the nature of life and in the principles of evolution we have had our answer. Of men elsewhere, and beyond, there will be none forever.

We resemble the frogs at a marsh croaking, "We're here, we're here, we're here!" Eiseley goes on to say. We do not know why we croak or whether anyone is listening. Like frogs, we croak by dumb instinct.

Civilization once looked to art as the means of passing wisdom from one generation to the next. Writing itself was invented in part to convey the sacred: permanent things deserved a permanent place, hence the hieroglyphs on Egyptian tombs. But a modern civilization that no longer believes in permanent things, one that accepts no certain narrative of meaning, resorts to deconstruction, not construction.

The editor of the *New Yorker*, David Remnick, contrasts contemporary writers in Russia with the long tradition of the Great Russian Writer, figures like Tolstoy, Gogol, and even Solzhenitsyn, who represented both sagacity and idealism. Nowadays the liberated writers, free to join the decadent chorus of modernity, are dismantling that tradition brick by brick. Remnick cites a story that begins with an iconic scene familiar to all Russians, an old man relating to a young boy his memories of the Nazi siege of Leningrad. The story ends, however, with the old man raping the boy. No memory is safe from assault.

As voices such as T. S. Eliot, Walker Percy, and Flannery O'Connor have reminded us, in the modern world Christians stand virtually alone in seeing the need for (or even believing in) firmly embedded nails. On the barren landscape of Western civilization, Christians still cling to a view that ascribes meaning and worth to individual human beings. The novelist Reynolds Price says there is one sentence above all that people crave from stories: *The Maker of all things loves and wants me.* Christians still believe in that truth.

"The Catholic writer," O'Connor remarked, "insofar as he [or she] has the mind of the Church, will feel life from the standpoint of the central Christian mystery: that it has, for all its horror, been found by God to be worth dying for." Modern humanity does not perceive the world as worth God dying for. We Christians must demonstrate it. Perhaps the mysterious power of art—its lasting worth as well as its echo of original Creation—can serve as a rumor of transcendence, a pointer to a grand Artist. We are "sub-creators" in J. R. R. Tolkien's words: "... the refracted light through whom is splintered from a single White to many hues."

I have a hunch that as history looks back on the twentieth century, that most chaotic of centuries, some Christian artists will endure for having hammered in a few firmly embedded nails. This world bears the stamp of genius, the stain of ruin, and the hint of redeemability; that triune intuition of Christian faith gives a template of meaning that at least attempts an answer to Gauguin's questions. Who else is even presenting a template?

Fray Luis Ponce de León, one of the masters in literature from Spain's Golden Age, barely survived the Inquisition. Having offended authorities by translating the Song of Songs into Spanish and criticizing the church's Latin text, Fray Luis was dragged from his classroom in the midst of a lecture at the university in Salamanca. Four years of imprisonment and torture followed, until religious hysteria faded and the stooped, nearly broken professor was allowed to return to the classroom. He shuffled in, opened his notes, and uttered what became a legendary phrase in Spain: *Como decíamos ayer*. "As we were saying yesterday," he began, resuming his lecture where he had left off.

Similar words can be heard in parts of Russia and Eastern Europe today. An ideology that tried harder than any other to kill off God, instead ended up committing suicide. The West too may find that prosperity and self-indulgence are not sufficient to satisfy human needs. Sometime in the future, as civilization continues to implode, like a dying star, into an intellectual and moral vacuum, other voices may take up Fray Luis's refrain. *Como decíamos ayer*.

ART POWER

Which modern writers will endure? Surely the poets T. S. Eliot and W. H. Auden will make the list. Solzhenitsyn may, albeit more for the raw force of his words than for their craft. Perhaps J. R. R. Tolkien will also be read a century from now, his imagined world still refracting light to this one. (In separate polls at the turn of the century, both British readers and Amazon.com customers ranked Tolkien's *The Lord of the Rings* as the best book of the millennium.)

One of those artists, T. S. Eliot, makes an interesting study. Faced with the political crises of communism and Nazism, he wrote little poetry for twenty years, concerning himself instead with the more pressing matters of politics, economics, and schemes to improve society. In short, he turned away from firmly embedded nails and toward goads. Yet who reads those obscure works today? I found them only in the rare book room of a university library. Eliot's poetry, to which he ultimately returned, far outlasted his utilitarian prose. Perhaps the best way to convey the values we cherish is not to talk about them all the time, or to try and legislate them, but rather to create literature and art in which they fit as firmly embedded nails.

Music too may express the permanent things. Much like Gauguin, the composer Gustav Mahler was haunted by existential questions. "Whence do we come?" he asked in a letter. "Whither does our road take us? Why am I made to feel that I am free while yet I am constrained within my character, as in a prison? What is the object of toil and sorrow? How am I to understand the cruelty and malice in the creations of a kind God? Will the meaning of life be finally revealed by death?"

Mahler's friend Anton Bruckner showed no such angst. He sought instead to express through music his conviction that God is good and that everything we do should honor God. While laboring on his tenth symphony he remarked to Mahler, "Now I have to work very hard.... Otherwise I will not pass before God, before whom I shall soon stand. He will say 'Why else have I given you talent ... than that you should sing my praise and glory? But you have accomplished much too little.'" In the university classroom Bruckner would abruptly stop his lectures when church bells sounded and, ignoring his mocking students, would kneel on the floor and pray.

Sacred music called the classical composers to their highest artistic achievements. Of his hundreds of works Beethoven wrote only two masses, yet he judged one of them, *Missa Solemnis*, his greatest composition. In their oratorios Handel and Mendelssohn served almost as evangelists, presenting biblical stories and themes in colorfully staged epics. Mozart and Haydn drifted toward religious themes mainly for economic reasons, as commissions for church events made it worthwhile. Even so, Mozart was so obsessed with the *Requiem Mass* he was striving to finish before his death that his doctor tried to take the manuscript away from him to enforce rest.

Even now the doctrinal creeds adopted by early councils of the church are repeated, in the works by Mozart and Haydn and Beethoven, by skilled professionals in every major city in the world. Hardened music critics are still susceptible to their power. Reviewing a recording of Brahms's *German Requiem*, Heuwell Tircuit of the *San Francisco Chronicle* wrote, "The performance is divine (in several senses). It constitutes an overpowering experience, one which is not only technically and stylistically perfect, but moving in an uncanny/religious way. When the chorus sings of 'The living Christ,' even an atheist can believe in Him."*

Sacred music has flowed from the pens of composers whose lives were decidedly irreligious. Johannes Brahms, raised in brothels and not a pious man, composed the *German Requiem*, which enfolds phrases from Luther's Bible in music so fitting it seems as if the words were created just for his melodic setting. The inspiration must be found in the Christian themes themselves. Worthy music may originate from small thoughts—occasionally a good piece surfaces from all the drivel extolling teenage love, for instance—but give Beethoven a concept like "God of God, Light of Light, Very God of Very God," or assign Handel the surrealistic setting of "Worthy Is the Lamb" in Revelation 5, and you can understand what has fueled much great music through the centuries. (On the occasion of its twenty-fifth anniversary the United Nations commissioned a piece entitled "To Posterity," the best generic theme they could agree on.)

When the shackles of communism fell from Czechoslovakia in 1989, the nation celebrated with a concert at St. Vitus Cathedral in Prague. Jubilant citizens joined together with heroes of the resistance, among them the dissident playwright Václav Havel, to listen to Antonín Dvořák's *Mass* and *Te Deum*. The words of that ancient liturgy played by the Czech Philharmonic seemed the most appropriate way to honor the great gift of freedom. The archbishop of

---

* When Yo-Yo Ma visited an ailing Steve Jobs and played Bach on his Stradivarius cello, Jobs teared up and said, "Your playing is the best argument I've ever heard for the existence of God, because I don't really believe a human alone can do this."

Prague, ninety years old, who had survived both Nazi and Communist oppression, sat side by side with Havel, a former prisoner who had just been elected president of the newly independent nation.

THE TEMPTATION OF PROPAGANDA

I could give many more examples of the power of art in communicating faith. At the same time, I cannot help wondering how much difference Christians are making through the arts in the U.S. today. All the words pouring forth in our magazines and books — are they having a perceptible effect on a culture that tilts away from faith? Do we not end up talking mostly to each other?

A journalist in the New York media told me that editors had no qualms about assigning a Jewish person to a Jewish story, a Buddhist to a Buddhist story, or a Catholic to a Catholic story, but would never assign an evangelical to an evangelical story. Why not? "They're the ones with an agenda."

Evangelicals have done much breast-beating in recent years over their lack of influence. By way of contrast, James Davison Hunter (the sociologist who discounts evangelicals' success in their stated goal "to change the world") points to two minorities who have had an impact on culture far beyond what their numbers would indicate. For both groups the arts are key. American Jews comprise less than 4 percent of the overall population and yet have an inordinate influence in Hollywood, the New York media, literature, visual arts, and music. Similarly, through their access to the entertainment media, the gay and lesbian minority has helped change popular attitudes, especially through such mainstream TV programs as *Ellen*, *Modern Family*, and *Will and Grace*.

Using those models, Hunter suggests a more strategic way of penetrating the cultural elite. Some Christian artists are doing just that. Spurred on by organizations such as the International Arts Movement, they share a vision of restoring the church's place as a nourishing environment for creativity.

One reason we make so little difference, I believe, is that the institutional church, like government, distrusts artists and wants to control them. English Puritans objected to Handel's *Messiah* because it was performed in secular theaters and employed non-Christian musicians and soloists. The same church that commissioned Michelangelo to paint the Sistine Chapel later hired a man dubbed "the Trouserer" to clothe the nude figures.

By imposing limits on our artists, we build walls around the subculture. The Christian soldiers of political correctness march onward: articles on abortion published in *Christianity Today* thirty years ago could never be published today; a writer who dabbles in fantasy literature is branded New Age; a novel that contains a single curse word gets pulled from shelves; Christian leaders jeopardize their careers by speaking favorably of Barack Obama; Tony Campolo loses lecture engagements because of his wife's views on homosexuality.

I remember one vivid scene from Solzhenitsyn's memoir, *The Oak and the Calf*. For a brief period even the Communist government of the Soviet Union acknowledged the worth of Solzhenitsyn and thought he might be a goad they could control. Inviting the former prisoner to join their salons, they urged him to write moral and uplifting literature and avoid all "pessimism, denigration, surreptitious sniping." I laughed aloud when I read that scene.

Every power, whether Christian or secular, prefers moral, uplifting literature—as long as they get to define what constitutes moral and uplifting.* The advice Solzhenitsyn got from Communist opinion makers bears striking resemblance to what I sometimes hear from evangelical publishers, who in their concern to give readers a feel-good takeaway do not seem to grasp that both goads and nails are worthless unless they are pointed and sharp.

---

* When Jan Morris was stationed as a foreign correspondent in Sudan after World War II, the Minister of National Guidance ordered her to report "thrilling, attractive and good news, corresponding, where possible, with the truth."

We cannot expect art always to uplift and inspire. In the words of Alan Paton, literature "will illuminate the road, but it will not lead the way with a lamp. It will expose the crevasse, but not provide the bridge. It will lance the boil, but not purify the blood. It cannot be expected to do more than this; and if we ask it to do more, we are asking too much."

A literary agent who works with a variety of artists told me, "Our main barrier comes from the church itself. So many Christians view art as a way to disguise the message they really want to get across. They look at artists as an inferior kind of preacher or apologist."

The more she talked, the more passionate she got. "A lot of Christians are afraid to listen to artists because they are troubled by their lifestyles or what they choose to focus on. Instead of having empathy and compassion—of all people, Christians know the bleakness of life if you believe God is imaginary or uninvolved—they square off in a contest of who is right or wrong about the way life works."

I asked her if she could give specific advice on how the church, once a dominant force in encouraging artistic expression, needs to change. This is how she responded:

- We treat art as consumable commodities for scratching our shopping itch and decorating our homes with, instead of icons for looking at the world and for shaping our inner lives.
- We lack an understanding of the artist as different from the teacher or the pastor or the apologist.
- We should cultivate a respect for the uniqueness of an artist's voice and vision, and a recognition of why we need a whole culture of individual artists who are speaking truth and beauty and prophetic warning into our lives and culture.

- We must be willing to let our artists be human beings instead of spiritual heroes and to let mystery and uncertainty exist side by side with clarity and conviction.

Religious art has gained a reputation for erring on the side of propaganda. As a result, novels and especially films with an explicitly Christian theme provoke mild condescension if not ridicule in some circles. Much of this secular resistance is hypocritical, for Christians are not the only propagandists at work. I could name many baldly propagandistic works from the fields of science and politics: the New Atheists do not strive for objectivity; Michael Moore unashamedly makes documentaries with a targeted message; and one of the most successful movies of all time, *Avatar*, is hardly subtle. Clearly, some kinds of propaganda find wider acceptance than others.

The word *propaganda* originally had no negative connotation. It was coined by a pope who formed the *Sacra Congregatio de Propaganda Fide* ("Sacred Congregation for the Propagation of the Faith") in the seventeenth century in order to spread the faith. As a Christian writer, I admit that I do strive for propaganda in this sense. When I write, I want readers to consider a viewpoint I hold to be true, and I assume the same applies for those who write from the perspective of other religions or no religion at all. In doing so, I want to express my viewpoint in a way that communicates grace, which means compassion and empathy for those I write about as well as respect for those who reject what I believe.

Somewhere in the magnetic field between propaganda and art, the artist of faith must work. One force tempts us to loudly proclaim a message we truly believe while another tempts us to alter the message for the sake of aesthetics. Apparent success often lies with the extremes: for example, a writer may prosper in the religious subculture by erring on the side of propaganda—but ever so slowly the fissure between the Christian and secular worlds will widen and we will find ourselves writing and selling books to ourselves alone.

The poet and novelist May Sarton wrote about art as a gift, in words that apply equally to grace: "There is only one real deprivation, I decided this morning, and that is not to be able to give one's gift to those one loves most.... The gift turned inward, unable to be given, becomes a heavy burden, even sometimes a kind of poison. It is as though the flow of life were backed up."

SCRIBBLES IN THE SAND

There is a time to be a goad and a time to be a nail. Lest the aspiring writer inflate with his or her own significance, however, the Teacher of Ecclesiastes adds with a sigh, "Of making many books there is no end ..."

Even the sharpest goads and the sturdiest nails get lost amid the burdensome accumulation of words and images. I have that sense every time I enter a bookstore or browse Amazon.com to scan through the dozens of new titles that have appeared in the previous week. The "self-help" section promises me a hundred new ways to save my marriage, shrink my waistline, succeed in business. If these work, why are there so many divorces, obese people, and business failures?

Of making many books there is no end. As one who makes a living by writing, I confess that a kind of pride stalks all creativity. Art is a blatant act of ego. I write this sentence with the chutzpah to believe it merits your time to read it. I, a person you have probably never met, hereby ask you to consider my words and thoughts without the prospect of reciprocation. As a witty friend said to me, "Everyone is entitled to my opinion." The Teacher brings me back to earth.

In a striking meditation on John 8, the Irish poet and Nobel laureate Seamus Heaney suggests another metaphor of art: scribbles in the sand. Jesus spoke with such economy and precision that most of his words can serve as both goad and nail. The Gospels record only one time, though, when Jesus wrote. It happened at the tense moment when Pharisees brought to him a woman caught in the act of adultery, demanding that Jesus pronounce the death penalty. Jesus said nothing but stooped and drew in the sand.

In that scene Seamus Heaney finds a metaphor for poetry:

> The drawing of those characters [in the sand] is like poetry, a break with the usual life but not an absconding from it. Poetry, like the writing, is arbitrary and marks time in every possible sense of that phrase. It does not say to the accusing crowd or to the helpless accused, "Now a solution will take place," it does not propose to be instrumental or effective. Instead, in the rift between what is going to happen and whatever we would wish to happen, poetry holds attention for a space....

For both poetry and prose there is a time to spur to action, a time to instruct with wisdom — and also a time merely to open up a space, to suspend the relentless passage of time.

God's Son, who had participated in the design of all creation, left behind no visual images for us to admire from his sojourn on earth. He chose as his one artistic medium not plates of gold or scraps of papyrus, which could be preserved and revered as relics, but rather a palette of Palestinian sand. The next rainstorm that came along obliterated every trace of Jesus' only written words.

Jesus aimed to transform lives, to write his words on his followers' hearts. Following in those footsteps, the apostle Paul would later say to the Corinthians, "You yourselves are our letter, written on our hearts, known and read by everyone." Both Jesus and Paul knew that the souls of individual human beings will long outlive their creations. We deceive ourselves with delusory talk about the "permanence of art"; of the seven wonders of the ancient world, six did not survive into the Middle Ages.

I have told you about my wife, who worked as a social worker among the elderly and as a hospice chaplain. Many days as I sat at home and grappled with adjectives and adverbs, she ministered to the dying. She counseled their families, listened to their grief, offered words of comfort. She touched their souls. Compared with such acts, my own profession shrinks. I am, as Seamus Heaney noted, scribbling in the sand: filling spaces, marking time. Walt Whitman learned that truth as he interrupted his writing to care for wounded soldiers in the Civil War. "Such work blesses him that works as much as the object of it," he wrote a friend. It taught him the difference between the important and the trivial.

Although art nourishes the soul and may be an essential part of our humanity, it represents only one offering among many. Modern society elevates art, investing billions in fine art auctions, museums, and entertaining movies, because it has dethroned so much else.

In a moment of despair one of the twentieth century's finest poets wrote this glum assessment of his craft: "Political social history would be no different if Dante, Michelangelo, Byron had never lived. Nothing I wrote against Hitler prevented one Jew from being killed. In the end, art is small beer." Auden exaggerates, nevertheless I accept his corrective to the usual arrogance of art. There is a time for goads and a time for nails; there is also a time to recognize that artists are scribbling in the sand, filling the interstices of life, their creations soon to be stepped on and washed away by raindrops.

While fully aware of its limited role, I remain convinced that we need art now more than ever—the kind of art that humbly creates spaces in our lives. Compared with any other time in history, we moderns scream and shout at each other, and the entertainment media fill screens with images crude and grotesque. The world today contains little subtlety, no silence, few spaces. The year he lived in Bolivia, the priest Henri Nouwen saw a popular movie just before Advent. It overwhelmed him. "The movie was so filled with images of greed and lust, manipulation and exploitation, fearful and painful sensations, that it filled all the empty spaces that could have been blessed by the spirit of Advent," he said.

Spaces need filling. I know of a man who learned he was going blind. As his sight began to fail, he booked a plane to Amsterdam and spent a week in the Van Gogh museum. He wanted these images to soak into his brain as his last visual memories.

For those of us who attempt art at any level and who also believe in transcendence, here is a place to start. Some are called to be prophetic goads, and some giants may hammer in firmly embedded nails. But the rest of us can aspire, with no tinge of shame, to scribbling in the sand.

As a counterbalance to the seven deadly sins, the church in the Middle Ages came up with seven works of mercy: to feed the hungry; give drink to the thirsty; clothe the naked; house the homeless; visit the sick; ransom the captive; bury the dead. Later the church added a supplemental list of *spiritual* works of mercy: to instruct the ignorant; counsel the doubtful; admonish sinners; bear wrongs patiently; forgive offences willingly; comfort the afflicted; pray for the living and the dead. I find solace in that amended list, for those of us who work with words, music, painting, or other arts can also extend a form of mercy, dispense a kind of grace.

Michelangelo, arguably the greatest artist who has ever lived, later confessed that his work had crowded out his own faith. As his life drew to a close, he penned these lines in a sonnet:

So now, from this mad passion
which made me take art for an idol and a king

I have learnt the burden of error that it bore...
The world's frivolities have robbed me of the time
That I was given for reflecting upon God.

Perhaps. But Michelangelo and others like him have through their efforts — sometimes as goads, sometimes as nails, sometimes as scribblers in the sand — helped turn us from the world's frivolities and given us space for such reflection.

I will never forget standing on a balcony just under the dome that Michelangelo designed over St. Peter's Basilica, listening to a German choir sing a cappella. Some of the words were in Latin, some in German, it did not matter. Inside that magnificent sheltering dome with its perfect acoustics, I was virtually suspended in their music. I had the feeling that if I lifted my legs off the ground, the sound itself would support me. My other memories of Italy involve pollution, long lines, traffic gridlock, and snarling motorbikes. But for this one moment I had inhabited a glorious space not on earth, a moment of time not in time. Art had done its work.

PART THREE

IS IT REALLY GOOD NEWS?

Playing off a short story by H. G. Wells, Simone Weil drew an analogy to a land of blind people in which scientists could devise a complete system of physics leaving out the concept of light. Weightless, pressureless, undetectable by the senses – why believe in light? To the blind, it need not exist. Occasionally, however, questions might arise among the blind. What makes plants grow upwards, defying the law of gravity? What ripens fruits and seeds? What warms the night into day? Light in a country of the blind, says Weil, parallels the role of God on earth. Some of us sense traces of the supernatural, yet how do we prove it to people who can't detect it?

CHAPTER 8

DOES FAITH MATTER?

I want my attorney, my tailor, my servants,
even my wife to believe in God because then
I shall be robbed and cuckolded less often.

VOLTAIRE

A monologue has been floating around in cyberspace, sometimes credited to George Carlin, sometimes to a Columbine High School student, and sometimes to the Dalai Lama. "The Paradox of Our Time," it turns out, actually originated with Dr. Bob Moorehead, a retired pastor near Seattle.

> We have taller buildings but shorter tempers; wider freeways but narrower viewpoints; we spend more but have less; we buy more but enjoy it less; we have bigger houses and smaller families; more conveniences, yet less time; we have more degrees but less sense; more knowledge but less judgment; more experts, yet more problems; we have more gadgets but less satisfaction; more medicine, yet less wellness; we take more vitamins but see fewer results. We drink too much; smoke too much; spend too recklessly; laugh too little; drive too fast, get too angry quickly; stay up too late; get up too tired; read too seldom; watch TV too much and pray too seldom.

We have multiplied our possessions, but reduced our values; we fly in faster planes to arrive there quicker, to do less and return sooner; we sign more contracts only to realize fewer profits; we talk too much; love too seldom, and lie too often. We've learned how to make a living, but not a life; we've added years to life, not life to years.

Moorehead's comments have struck a chord with internet readers. He diagnoses a low-grade discontent, a sense that for all their wonders science and technology have not slaked human thirst. To quote Al Gore, "The accumulation of material goods is at an all-time high, but so is the number of people who feel an emptiness in their lives." And though I don't want to sound like an old-timer clucking about the decline of civilization, cultural trends in the U.S. reveal a society that indeed has been sliding in the wrong direction. According to a Gallup poll, 73 percent of Americans say moral values are worsening while only 14 percent judge them improving.

In my own lifetime the divorce rate has doubled, the rates of teen suicide and violent crime have both tripled, and births out of wedlock have sextupled. With less than 5 percent of the world's population, the U.S. has almost a quarter of the world's prisoners (about the same number as Russia and China combined). We have become accustomed to homeless people sleeping in parks and under bridges, something virtually unknown in my childhood. The leading causes of death are self-inflicted, the side-effects of tobacco, obesity, alcohol, sexually transmitted diseases, drugs, and violence. Meanwhile politicians in Washington argue more yet pass fewer bills than at any time in history, reflecting the nation's polarization.

My secular friends look at these facts and conclude we must work harder to educate children and put new social systems in place. I look at the same facts and doubt politicians' ability to solve our problems. We need more than new systems; we need a transformation, the kind of personal and societal renewal in which the church could play a crucial role.

Unfortunately, most of my secular friends would agree with Bill Gates, who considers religion a waste of time: "There's a lot more I could be doing on Sunday morning," he told an interviewer. They view the church not as a change agent that can affect all of society but as a place where like-minded people go to feel better about themselves. That image of the church stands in sharp contrast to the vision of Jesus, who said little about how believers should behave when we gather together and much about how we can affect the world around us.

Faith is not simply a private matter, or something we practice once a week at church. Rather, it should have a contagious effect on the broader world. Jesus used these images to illustrate his kingdom: a sprinkle of yeast causing the whole loaf to rise, a pinch of salt preserving a slab of meat, the smallest seed in the garden growing into a great tree in which birds of the air come to nest.

AN ONGOING CYCLE

Two books by sociologist Rodney Stark, *The Rise of Christianity* and *The Triumph of Christianity*, spell out how early believers in the Roman Empire took Jesus' agenda to heart. The Christians organized relief projects for the poor and ransomed their friends from barbarian captors. Some voluntarily freed their own slaves. When plague hit, Christians tended the sick—including their nonbelieving neighbors—whereas the pagans forsook them as soon as the first symptoms appeared. (Many church leaders died, in fact, after contracting the illnesses of those they were nursing.) When Romans abandoned their unwanted babies to exposure and wild animals, Christians organized platoons of wet nurses to keep them alive for adoption by church families.

In the waning days of the empire, the watching world sat up

and paid attention. People flocked to the churches, which stood out as caring communities. A fourth-century Roman emperor known as Julian the Apostate complained bitterly about Christians of his time: "These impious Galileans not only feed their own poor, but ours also.... Whilst the pagan priests neglect the poor, the hated Galileans devote themselves to works of charity." His campaign against the Christians failed, and the gospel continued to spread while Roman power ebbed.

Sadly, as Christians flourished and became the dominant cultural force, their contrast with the rest of society faded. Forsaking their pilgrim calling, they put down roots and joined the establishment. Church leaders set up a hierarchy much like the state's, complete with elaborate costumes and all the trappings of power. In a tragic turnabout, they switched roles: no longer persecuted, they began persecuting others as heretics.

A similar cycle has recurred throughout church history. Christians present an attractive counterculture until they become the dominant culture. Then they divert from their mission, join the power structure, and in the process turn society against them. Rejected, they retreat into a minority subculture, only to start the cycle all over again. Traveling internationally, I see different stages in the cycle taking place right now.

One year I visited Brazil and the Philippines, countries where the church is experiencing strong growth. Such nations are enjoying a kind of honeymoon stage in which the gospel still sounds like good news. Poor villagers who have never heard terms like "social justice" or "liberation theology" rise in economic well-being as the newly converted start acting like responsible citizens. I met Brazilians who adopt and care for prisoners—voluntarily, not under anyone's organized program. In the Philippines I met a woman who took literally New Testament commands to look after orphans: she had invited *thirty-four* street children to live in her home and was sponsoring them in school. Like the early Roman

Christians, these believers present an attractive counterculture to their neighbors.

Other nations, such as those in Western Europe, have moved into a decidedly post-Christian stage. Church steeples pierce the skies of Europe, but mostly tourists bother to go inside the old buildings. In what was once the heart of the faith, many leaders view Christianity as passé or irrelevant. Yet the small minority of Christians thrive in a different way. I see healthy signs of creativity and unity among Christians in places like Great Britain and New Zealand. With no social advantage to belief, churches attract people who are serious about their faith—which plants the seed for future growth.

In other regions, encounters with Christians stir up actual hostility. Here is how a magazine editor characterized for me the Christians he meets in an area that has been post-Christian for more than a millennium:

> From my experience of observing many expatriates in the Middle East from various religions, I've come to the sad conclusion that Christians could be the most difficult people to get along with anywhere. They seem to fall into three categories: 1) those who prefer to live in a Christian ghetto where preferably like-minded folks are their friends; 2) those who follow Western Christian church models as their only preference, with a rigid theology that makes them quite religious and judgmental with those who innovate; 3) those who are certain they are in "full-time ministry," convinced they are the true servants of the Most High while the ordinary 9-to-5 plebeians are lower on the spiritual totem pole.

The editor was speaking of Christians who come to the Middle East on business or, in some cases, as covert missionaries.

The traits he finds off-putting—isolation, a judgmental spirit, superiority—mirror complaints I hear from skeptics in my own country.

The United States strikes me as somewhere between the extremes, neither honeymoon nor post-Christian. Nearly half of us attend church, and Christians have an active presence on university campuses and in every major profession. Even so, churches and parachurch agencies may operate more like industries than living organisms. We hire others to take care of the orphans and visit the prisoners; we pay professionals to lead the worship.

Pondering these various stages, I have to fight a feeling of resignation. What will keep the U.S. from following the path of Europe, with the church gradually losing influence and drifting to the margins? And how will believers respond as the culture grows increasingly post-Christian? Will we hunker down and become isolated and self-serving? Or will we, like the early Roman Christians, find ingenious ways to minister to a global power in decline?

G. K. Chesterton names five moments in history, such as the fall of the Roman Empire and the period of Islamic conquest, when Christianity faced apparent doom. Each time, a fresh spirit of renewal emerged from the crisis and the faith revived. As Chesterton puts it, when "the Faith has to all appearance gone to the dogs ... it was the dog that died." He adds, "Christianity has died many times and risen again; for it had a God who knew the way out of the grave." Perhaps a new era emphasizing deeds and not words will usher in that renewal now.

REVERSING THE TREND

As a child in Sunday School I used to sing this song:

> One door and only one
> And yet its sides are two.
> I'm on the inside,
> On which side are you?

The song captured our church's identity. We saw ourselves as a tiny minority who possessed The Truth. A long list of rules and beliefs set us apart from those outside the door. It never occurred to me that my faith had something to contribute to the "outsiders." My main obligation was to get them to join us on the correct side of the door. Now, however, I see that the kingdom of God largely exists for the sake of outsiders, as a tangible expression of God's love for all.

We can learn from a time in the Old Testament when God's people faced an analogous situation. Babylon had destroyed Jerusalem and taken captive tens of thousands of its citizens, who now lived as a beleaguered minority in a "post-Israel" society. How should they respond to this new reality? Speaking on God's behalf, the prophet Jeremiah counseled them to build houses, settle down, plant gardens, marry, and bear children. "Also, seek the peace and prosperity of the city to which I have carried you into exile. Pray to the LORD for it, because if it prospers, you too will prosper."

I have mentioned three ways — pilgrim, activist, and artist — in which we can do just that, demonstrating by our example how a person and a society can best thrive. Instead of fighting a rearguard action against secular opponents, we can communicate our good-news message by living it out among the uncommitted. Our faith does, after all, have many benefits to offer the world, as some unlikely spokesmen have recently begun to acknowledge.

The contemporary German philosopher Jürgen Habermas remarked, "Democracy requires of its citizens qualities that it cannot provide." While authoritarian governments may enforce morality from the top down, free societies must depend on citizens who act responsibly. How can a democracy foster qualities like compassion and honesty? An agnostic, Habermas went further in words that stunned some of his colleagues, saying that the Western legacy of conscience, human rights, and democracy is "the direct heir of the Judaic ethic of justice and the Christian ethic of love." He added, "We continue to draw on the substance of this heritage. Everything else is just idle postmodern talk."

Another philosopher, Alain de Botton, urges fellow atheists to borrow from religion. He admires the success of churches in promoting morality, and cites research showing that belief in God can offer comfort during hard times. De Botton is not proposing a religious revival—he would scoff at such a prospect—but rather challenging fellow atheists to learn from churches that nurture a spirit of community. Modern educators and artists, he complains, no longer impart the practical wisdom that people badly need.

Such thinkers are struggling with the age-old question, "How can we get people to be good?" They agree that Christianity has produced some benefits over the centuries, giving us a foundation for human rights and care for the vulnerable. But where can religious skeptics look for moral guidance and hope today? I wish they could see in the followers of Jesus a possible cure to the societal ills we all agree on. What would that take?

We have grown so used to signs of cultural decline that it is hard to imagine movement in another direction. I came across one example from the Jewish historian Gertrude Himmelfarb, who has spent much of her career exploring just such a renewal in nineteenth-century Britain.

Himmelfarb's book *The De-Moralization of Society* opens with a scene involving Margaret Thatcher, the Iron Lady of British politics. When an interviewer accused Mrs. Thatcher of advocating Victorian values she responded, "Oh, exactly. Very much so. Those were the values when our country became great." Her election opponents gleefully pounced on the quote and Victorian values became a staple of newspaper headlines. Thatcher did not back down, insisting that they included such things as family commitment, hard work, thrift, cleanliness, self-reliance, and neighborliness.

Statistics from the Victorian era show a reverse image of current trends. Literacy increased and poverty decreased. The rates of illegitimate births and crime plummeted. At the end of the nineteenth century, illegitimacy rates in the slums of London stood at 3 percent, compared to 70 percent in underprivileged U.S. neighborhoods today. The crime rate in England dropped by half during the Victorian era.

What caused the turnaround? Like many other historians, Himmelfarb credits a campaign led by evangelical Christians. Methodists pressed for reforms in the labor movement, housing, prisons, public education, sanitation, and health. Their founder John Wesley taught that the gospel of Christ involved more than saving souls. It should have an impact on all of society, and his followers worked to accomplish just that. They were dispensing grace to the broader world, and in the process their spirit helped change a nation, saving it from the revolutionary chaos that had spread across Europe.

Himmelfarb's portrait of Victorian values runs counter to the stuffy image that phrase conjures up today—which, she argues, is part of the problem. The United States has taken such a turn against public morality that a recent surgeon general hesitated to disapprove of promiscuous sex among *pre-teens*. "Everyone has different moral standards," said the surgeon general. "You can't impose your standards on someone else." Himmelfarb sharply disagrees: "We are now confronting the consequences of this policy of moral neutrality."

Values are one thing but the question remains, Do such values need a *religious* foundation? Skeptics such as Jürgen Habermas have reluctantly concluded that they do. When George Orwell pondered the loss of religious faith in Europe (which he had once applauded), he rued the results: "For two hundred years we had sawed and sawed and sawed at the branch we were sitting on. And in the end, much more suddenly than anyone had foreseen, our efforts were rewarded, and down we came. But unfortunately there had been a little mistake. The thing at the bottom was not a bed of roses after all, it was a cesspool full of barbed wire.... It appears that amputation of the soul *isn't* just a simple surgical job, like having your appendix out. The wound has a tendency to go septic."

The poet W. H. Auden, who left Europe in the 1930s to escape the looming war, found his entire outlook shaken as he sat in a Manhattan theater watching newsreels of German atrocities. His belief in the goodness of human beings collided with the evidence of appalling evil flashing before him. He concluded, "If I was to say that was evil, I had to have a standard by which to do so. I didn't have one.... I'd spent all my adult life as an intellectual, destroying the absolutes, and now suddenly I needed one to be able to say that this was wrong."

Auden left the cinema in search of some absolute, one stronger than liberal humanism, that would condemn the Nazis as well as defend their victims. He soon made his way to Christian faith. Only God could ask human beings, as he later said in a poem, to "love your crooked neighbour with your crooked heart."

FOR OUR OWN GOOD

I think back once again to my childhood, legalistic though it was, and the moral environment in which I was reared. Good Christians did not smoke, drink, use drugs, divorce, or fool around sexually. The church granted that money, sex, and power may be God's gifts but emphasized their dangers: like volatile explosives they must be handled with care and discipline. I heard far more negative motivation—*you'll pay for your sins!*—than positive. Into that stale environment, the Sixties revolution swept like a gust of fresh air, promising freedom and liberation, and many of my friends happily threw off the subculture's straitjacket.

As it happened, though, time proved the subculture right on many of those issues. In the wake of the sexual revolution came teen pregnancies, family breakups, and fatherless children. Promiscuity led directly to outbreaks of venereal disease, the plague of AIDS, and numerous other health problems. And now secular activists are the ones who warn of the health dangers associated with smoking, binge-drinking, and drug use.*

Hardly an impediment to the good life, religious faith can positively show the way. A study published in the *American Journal of Psychiatry* reported on Harvard undergraduates who experienced a religious conversion in their student days. The students had a "radical change in lifestyle" shown by a marked decrease in the use of drugs, alcohol, and cigarettes. Not only that, their academic performance improved and they seemed less prone to depression, preoccupation with death, and bouts of "existential despair."

Many nonbelievers have the notion that God is somehow against them and that Christians are determined to keep them from enjoying life. Ironically, I took away from a legalistic church a different version of the same message: *God is trying to keep me from something better and more exciting.* It is a whisper as old as Eden. I have come to believe just the opposite, that God desires the best life for us, "life to the full," in Jesus' words. I doubt any of those Harvard students miss their former days of angst and addiction.

Somehow we need to communicate to the uncommitted that God wants us to thrive, to live with joy and not repression, trust and not fear. It took me years to realize that the way of life set out in the Bible is intended for our own good. Jesus' images of the kingdom show wellbeing gradually spreading through the rest of society. We thrive best, and society works best, when sex goes along with commitment, when we take care of our bodies, when the strong care for the weak.

---

* In his numerous books, Harold Koenig of Duke University cites two thousand studies that show religious people have better health and live longer, mainly due to lifestyle choices on drugs, promiscuity, smoking, alcohol, and diet.

I have seen many examples of ordinary Christians who cheerfully serve the common good, a fact that gets overlooked in the media's focus on Christians and politics. Robert Putnam, author of the groundbreaking book *Bowling Alone*, documents that religious Americans are more likely to give money to a homeless person, return excess change to a shop clerk, donate blood, help a sick neighbor with shopping or housework, spend time with someone who is depressed, offer a seat to a stranger, or help someone find a job. Regular church attenders give almost four times as much money to charity as their secular neighbors and twice as many of them do volunteer work among the poor, the infirm, or the elderly.

The Clinton administration, no great ally of conservative Christians, first began to promote faith-based agencies because it saw the effectiveness of groups such as Prison Fellowship, the Salvation Army, and Teen Challenge in dealing with crime, alcoholism, and drug addiction. Programs that include a spiritual dimension often have a better success rate than their secular counterparts. As Joseph Califano, former secretary of the Department of Health, Education, and Welfare, observed, "Every individual I have met who successfully came off drugs or alcohol has given religion as the key to rehabilitation."

"Religion is a powerful antidote to crime," argues the respected criminologist Byron Johnson in his book *More God, Less Crime: Why Faith Matters and How It Could Matter More*. It helps reduce the rates of prison recidivism, drug use, violence, and gang activity. For this reason Pastor Eugene Rivers of Brooklyn suggests we should be investing in more church programs, not more prisons, if we want to help underprivileged youth: "It's either barbed wire and more black juvenile superpredators, or civil society and stronger black churches. It's that simple."*

---

* The Jewish medical educator David C. Stolinsky says it more colorfully: "The reason we fear to go out after dark is not that we may be set upon by bands of evangelicals and forced to read the New Testament, but that we may be set

Why do faith-based programs work? Those who run them credit the transforming power of conversion and dependence on God. There is one more factor, though. The motivation to change usually comes about because of love: someone sees an offender not for who they have been but for who they could be. John DiIulio, who once directed the White House Office on faith-based programs, describes the process. Social workers begin by assessing a client's deficits, he says.

> You come in fatherless, abused; you're illiterate; and they say, "We're going to help you. You're going to get literacy, and you're going to get counseling, and you're going to talk to your probation officer. Meanwhile, we're not requiring anything of you. You have so many deficits, you have to make so much progress, it will be some time before we ask anything of you.
>
> Put that alongside the spiritual outreach approach. It's like a martial arts approach. It takes all the negative force that you bring and flips it around. How? It says to the kid, "It may be true that you had nobody, but let me tell you something, God loved you, even when you didn't know. When the world hated you, God loved you. And I'm going to tell you something, I love you, and I'm there for you. And I'm going to be there for you. And where am I? Right over there. Right in that basement over there. Right through that door, 24/7/365, that's where you'll find me."

WHAT GOOD IS CHRISTIANITY?

In early 2014 *Christianity Today* published a cover story on a sociologist named Robert Woodberry, who had wondered why

upon by gangs of feral young people who have been taught that nothing is superior to their own needs or feelings."

some countries take to democracy so well while their next-door neighbors wallow in corruption and bad government. Painstaking research led him to conclude that missionaries made the difference. They taught people to read, built hospitals, and gave a biblical foundation for basic human rights. He concluded,

> Areas where Protestant missionaries had a significant presence in the past are on average more economically developed today, with comparatively better health, lower infant mortality, lower corruption, greater literacy, higher educational attainment (especially for women), and more robust membership in nongovernmental associations.

That does not fit the Hollywood stereotype of missionaries ruining cultures, I know, but so far no one has been able to refute Woodberry's findings.

I wish those who ask "What good is Christianity?" could spend time with some of the remarkable people who dedicate their lives to humble service. I have visited schools for the *Dalits* ("untouchables") in India where the first generation from that caste in five thousand years is obtaining a quality education. I have reported on leprosy hospitals in Asia, AIDS clinics and orphanages in Africa, and a renowned hospital for obstetric fistula sufferers in Ethiopia, all products of missionary work.

I think of Bill Leslie, my pastor for ten years in Chicago. Bill took his family to Zaire to visit the village where his grandfather had served as a medical missionary, only to find that a royal welcome awaited them. Bill's grandfather, he discovered, had treated not only the bodies but also the souls of many villagers. "We want you to see the fruit of your grandfather's ministry here," said the hosts. First they asked all the pastors to stand and around forty did so. Then all the doctors stood, then the nurses, then teachers, masons, and construction workers. In the end several hundred people were standing in the bright African sun beside the banquet table, living proof of his grandfather's faithful service.

Philosophers such as Jürgen Habermas and Alain de Botton debate whether it is possible to produce such effects apart from religious faith. Of course there are many examples of secular individuals and organizations who also serve the common good. Another skeptic, though, points to a kind of internal transformation far more rare. Matthew Parris, a journalist and former member of parliament in the U.K., grew up in Africa. In 2008 he returned to his childhood home after forty-five years and wrote an article for *The Times* of London with the subtitle, "Missionaries, Not Aid Money, Are the Solution to Africa's Biggest Problem — The Crushing Passivity of the People's Mindset."

> Now a confirmed atheist, I've become convinced of the enormous contribution that Christian evangelism makes in Africa: sharply distinct from the work of secular NGOs, government projects and international aid efforts. These alone will not do. Education and training alone will not do. In Africa Christianity changes people's hearts. It brings a spiritual transformation. The rebirth is real. The change is good.
>
> I used to avoid this truth by applauding — as you can — the practical work of mission churches in Africa. It's a pity, I would say, that salvation is part of the package, but Christians black and white, working in Africa, do heal the sick, do teach people to read and write; and only the severest kind of secularist could see a mission hospital or school and say the world would be better without it. I would allow that if faith was needed to motivate missionaries to help, then, fine: but what counted was the help, not the faith.
>
> But this doesn't fit the facts. Faith does more than support

the missionary; it is also transferred to his flock. This is the effect that matters so immensely, and which I cannot help observing....

The Christians were always different. Far from having cowed or confined its converts, their faith appeared to have liberated and relaxed them. There was a liveliness, a curiosity, an engagement with the world—a directness in their dealings with others—that seemed to be missing in traditional African life. They stood tall.

At 24, travelling by land across the continent reinforced this impression. From Algiers to Niger, Nigeria, Cameroon and the Central African Republic, then right through the Congo to Rwanda, Tanzania and Kenya, four student friends and I drove our old Land Rover to Nairobi.

We slept under the stars, so it was important as we reached the more populated and lawless parts of the sub-Sahara that every day we find somewhere safe by nightfall. Often near a mission.

Whenever we entered a territory worked by missionaries, we had to acknowledge that something changed in the faces of the people we passed and spoke to: something in their eyes, the way they approached you direct, man-to-man, without looking down or away. They had not become more deferential towards strangers—in some ways less so—but more open....

What they were was, in turn, influenced by a conception of man's place in the Universe that Christianity had taught.

Elsewhere in his article Matthew Parris reports on the failure of massive aid programs that offer handouts without affecting the people's mindset. Rural Africans have a fatalistic view of life, seeing themselves as helpless pawns before the forces of evil spirits, ancestors, nature, and swaggering leaders. Christianity, writes Parris, "with its teaching of a direct, personal, two-way link between the individual and God, unmediated by the collective, and unsubordinate to any other human being, smashes straight through the philosophical/spiritual framework I've just described. It offers something to hold on to for those anxious to cast off a crushing tribal groupthink. That is why and how it liberates."

Parris confesses that such a conclusion did not come easily: "It confounds my ideological beliefs, stubbornly refuses to fit my world view, and has embarrassed my growing belief that there is no God."

SOMETHING NEW IN HISTORY

I can predict how critics of the church would respond to this chapter. They would cite examples of European countries like Denmark where few claim any Christian commitment and yet society seems to work admirably, yielding a high quality of life. Having visited Denmark and its equally secular Scandinavian neighbors, I would have to agree — though, to be fair, let's admit that the region was populated by warring and pillaging Vikings until the Christian gospel came along. The gospel transforms culture by permeating it like yeast, and long after the people abandon belief they tend to live by habits of the soul. Once salted and yeasted, society is difficult to un-salt and un-yeast.

Critics should also visit countries with little or no history with Christianity and compare their care for the oppressed, their range of freedoms, their treatment of women, and their basic morality. I have traveled to places where you have to double-lock your suitcases and count your change after every transaction, where innocent prisoners rot in jails with no legal recourse, where converting to another religion — or any religion — constitutes a serious, even a capital, offense. The gospel's leavening effect is hard to ignore: nine of ten nations that Freedom House labels "free" it identifies as Christian, and the same pattern applies to nations that Transparency International ranks as least corrupt, the World Giving Index rates as generous, and the World Economic Forum cites for best gender equality.

Don't misunderstand me. I have no desire to tally a balance sheet comparing the net benefits of faith versus a secular approach. Christians should strive to serve God, not some abstract ideal of improving society. We act in accord with Jesus' prayer that God's will be done on earth as it is in heaven, for that is the grand goal that God has promised to accomplish. Yet if we do so, in a humble spirit, we will inevitably contribute to the common good, as has undeniably happened over the centuries. Andy Crouch uses the phrase *posterity gospel* to describe the process of goodness and health spreading through the world, stewarded by the church.

At the same time, we should concede our shortcomings. We live in the shadow of past failures, as critics often remind us. I have learned to appreciate the all-important distinction between the gospel's inherent force and the church's erratic record in channeling it. God has entrusted flawed human beings with a message so powerful that it sometimes does its work in spite of us. Like a flowing stream, the gospel steadily erodes evil even if the church takes the wrong side—as it sometimes has—and even after a society abandons faith.

Gil Bailie points to a modern trend that we take for granted but is actually unprecedented in history: empathy for the marginalized. "Today the victim occupies the moral high ground everywhere in the Western world," says Bailie. He builds on the work of French historian René Girard to argue that the crucifixion of Jesus stands as the central event of history. The cross upset the long-standing categories of weak victims and strong heroes, for at that moment the victim emerged as the hero. The gospel put in motion something new in history, which Bailie calls "the most astonishing reversal of values in human history." Wherever Christianity took root, care for the victims spread. To mention just one example, in Europe of the Middle Ages the Benedictine order alone operated thirty-seven thousand monasteries devoted to the sick.

Moreover, those who condemn the church for its blind spots do so by gospel principles, arguing for the very moral values that the gospel originally set loose in the world. Human rights, civil rights, women's rights, minority rights, gay rights, disability rights, animal rights—the success of these modern movements reflects a widespread empathy for the oppressed that has no precedent in the ancient world; classical philosophers considered mercy and pity to be character defects, contrary to justice. Not until Jesus did that attitude change.

When the rest of the world criticizes us for our failings, we should respond with humility and repentance, qualities that lobby groups and activists don't typically display. Christians know that the church in 2100 will look back on the church of 2000 and shake its head in sad incomprehension. How could we have missed what will seem so obvious to them?

Our challenge as Jesus' followers is to align ourselves with the true gospel, and to reclaim the force it has released to a world in desperate need. George Orwell had it partly right when he declared, "The problem of our time is to restore the sense of absolute right and wrong when the faith that it used to rest on ... has been destroyed." He did not mention one other alternative: a robust renewal of that faith.

THREE DEATHS

Three major public figures died within four days of each other in December 2011. Kim Jong-il, the Dear Leader of North Korea, represented the last holdout of a totalitarian Marxist state with its arbitrary morality enforced from the top down. He called his nation "a Paradise for the People," though anyone with Google satellite mapping can see the concentration camps, execution grounds, and ruined farmlands that belie his Potemkin Paradise.

The second notable who died was the atheist Christopher Hitchens, who wrote some of his bitterest commentary against the tyranny of Kim Jong-il. Yet Hitchens' moral code had no transcendent authority either. On what basis would he judge his own morality superior to that of Kim Jong-il? Peter Hitchens, Christopher's younger brother, turned from atheism and became a Christian after seeing the effects of a spiritual vacuum firsthand in such countries as Somalia, the Soviet Union, and North Korea.

The third, Václav Havel, had lived under a milder form of Communist tyranny, and emerged with a strong conviction about the roots of the modern crisis. The crisis he said, is "due to the fact that we have lost the certainty that the Universe, nature, existence and our lives are the work of creation guided by a definite intention, that it has a definite meaning and follows a definite purpose." Using his platform as the first president of a free Czechoslovakia, Havel gave a prophetic warning to "the first atheistic civilization in the history of humankind," the modern West. He lamented the loss of faith: "As soon as man began considering himself the source of the highest meaning in the world and the measure of everything, the world began to lose its human dimension, and man began to lose control of it."

Predictably, Havel's pronouncement provoked a chorus of outcries. How could an intellectual call for a return to religion? Doesn't he know that religion gives rise to violence, racism, censorship, and intolerance?

Havel, however, had lived under an atheistic regime that outdid any misguided religion in those categories. As he told the U.S. Congress, "The salvation of this human world lies nowhere else than in the human heart.... The only backbone to our actions, if they are to be moral, is responsibility. Responsibility to something higher than my family, my firm, my country, my success—responsibility to the order of being where all our actions are indelibly recorded and where, and only where, they will be properly judged."

Does faith matter to an individual or a society? Apparently, yes.

CHAPTER 9

IS THERE ANYONE ELSE? THE GOD QUESTION

In order to be prepared to hope in what does not deceive,
we must first lose hope in everything that deceives.

GEORGES BERNANOS

One weekend this paragraph ranked as the most popular post on Google's social network:

> Philosophy is like being in a dark room and looking for a black cat. Metaphysics is like being in a dark room and looking for a black cat that isn't there. Theology is like being in a dark room and looking for a black cat that isn't there and shouting "I found it!" Science is like being in a dark room and looking for a black cat using a flashlight.

The "Black Cat Analogy" captures a common opinion these days that religion is mostly fantasy. Like a placebo, religious faith may make you feel better, but it has no real substance. For truth about reality, we must look to science.

A gap between science and faith now yawns open. Science

rules, in part because it has solved some of the most bedeviling human problems: we can cure many diseases, mitigate the effects of weather, control pests, communicate across vast distances. Meanwhile, many in the modern world think of believers as "anti-science" — with good reason in view of the battles waged over science-and-faith issues.

To be honest, I find it hard not to be affected by this point of view. After all, we have no certain proof of an invisible God and only a few wispy hints of an afterlife. We know the material world of rocks and trees, sun and moon exists; anything else requires faith.

At certain key moments, however, I realize there are some rooms where science doesn't attempt to shine a flashlight. They lie outside its realm, as even the scientists agree. Among these are the questions of meaning that all of us wonder about at times, questions any serious faith must address.

Earlier I mentioned one of America's top scientists, who headed the Human Genome Project and went on to direct the National Institutes of Health. Reared as an atheist, Dr. Francis Collins was practicing medicine early in his career when an elderly woman suffering from an untreatable illness asked him, "What do you believe about God and life after death?" That conversation became a turning point for Collins because he had no idea how to answer some of life's most important questions. He traces his conversion to that hinge moment with a patient, which prompted a spiritual search.

Although as a scientist he had always insisted on collecting rigorous data, Collins realized that in matters of faith he had never even sought data. After consulting with a minister he read the gospel of John and then the writings of C. S. Lewis, starting with *Mere Christianity*. As Lewis himself once said, an atheist can't be too careful about what he reads; the reluctant young doctor soon fell into the arms of faith.

I had my own encounter with science and questions of meaning at a conference where I found myself assigned to a panel on "Science and Faith." I was feeling secure since a scholar from Harvard Divinity School would help hold up the faith end of things until I read in the program that each of the three representatives from science had won a Nobel Prize in physics. My collar suddenly felt tight and the room grew noticeably warmer.

When my turn came I quoted Sir William Bragg, a pioneer in the field of X-ray crystallography, who was asked whether science and theology are opposed to one another: "They are: in the sense that the thumb and fingers or my hand are opposed to one another. It is an opposition by means of which anything can be grasped." For much of history the great scientists—Copernicus, Kepler, Galileo, Newton, Leibniz—believed their discoveries in "the book of nature" comprised a form of revelation, teaching us clues about a creator God.

I suggested to the panel that although science had contributed much to modern life, there are at least three important questions for which it has no answers since they lie beyond its bounds. (1) Why is there something rather than nothing? (2) Why is that something so beautiful and orderly? (3) How ought we to conduct ourselves in such a world? After some discussion the other panelists agreed that the answers do lie beyond science.

Yet we cannot avoid these basic questions. They help us grasp what it means to be a human being and for what purpose we exist. For centuries the Western world had a rough Christian consensus. Nowadays, with no clear consensus, many answers are being proposed. I sense a need, for myself if no one else, to consider how some of them stack up against a Christian alternative. Unless we can grasp our own beliefs as truly good news, we cannot easily communicate them to a thirsty world.

I will reframe the questions from the panel as follows, devoting a chapter to each.

- Is there anyone else? The God question.
- Why are we here? The human question.
- How should we live? The social question.

SCIENCE ANSWERS

Are we alone in this vast universe of a hundred billion galaxies and countless solar systems, or is there anyone else? For more than fifty years scientists have been trying to determine just that by means of an expensive undertaking called Search for Extraterrestrial Intelligence (SETI). In their heyday the Soviets swept the sky with huge antennas listening for messages. Some scientists estimated the universe would reveal a hundred thousand, perhaps a million advanced civilizations. Enthusiasm cooled as, one by one, the projects failed to turn up any evidence of intelligent life.

The most outspoken scientists pointedly exclude God from consideration. The late Carl Sagan, a strong proponent of SETI, began his television lectures with the presumptuous statement, "The Cosmos is all there is, all there ever was, and all there ever will be." More recently, New Atheists such as Richard Dawkins and Daniel Dennett have insisted that the universe came into being on its own with no outside agent — despite the daunting odds against such an event.

Scientists themselves who calculate the odds of the universe coming into existence by accident suggest such boggling figures as one in 10^{60}. Physicist Paul Davies explains, "To give some meaning to those numbers, suppose you wanted to fire a bullet at a one-inch target on the other side of the observable universe, twenty billion light years away. Your aim would have to be accurate to that same part in 10^{60}." Stephen Hawking admits that if the rate of expansion one second after the big bang had varied by even one part in a hundred thousand million million, the universe would have recollapsed. That's only the beginning: if the nuclear force in certain atoms varied by only a few percentage points then the sun and other stars would not exist. Life on earth depends on similarly delicate fine-tuning; a tiny change in gravity, a slight tilting of earth's axis, or a small thickening in its crust would make conditions for life impossible.

Confronted with the staggering odds against random existence, Richard Dawkins simply shrugs and says, "Well, we're here, aren't we?" He, along with many others, sees no need to assume a Designer behind such apparent evidence of cosmic design (although in a conversation with Francis Collins, Dawkins admitted that the fine-tuning of the universe is the most troubling argument for nonbelievers to counter). Scientists in the U.S. are equally divided, with 51 percent believing in some form of deity.

It occurred to me, as I later reflected on the "Science and Faith" panel I had participated in, that if the odds were reversed we likely would not have had a discussion. If someone calculated the odds of God's existence at one in 10^{60}, I seriously doubt any scientists would waste their time discussing faith issues with people who believed in such an improbable God. Yet they happily accept those odds of a universe randomly coming into existence on its own.

When I talked with the Nobel laureates later, I asked about their own belief or disbelief in God. All three spoke of a strict Jewish upbringing against which they later reacted. Martin Perl, discoverer of the Tau lepton particle, said candidly, "Ten percent of Americans claim to have been abducted by aliens, half are creationists, and half read horoscopes each day. Why should it surprise us if a majority believe in God? I oppose all such superstition, and in my experience religion is mostly harmful. I limit my beliefs to observation, not revelation."

The most renowned scientist of modern times, Albert Einstein, was more receptive to faith: "The scientist must see all the fine and wise connections of the universe and appreciate that they are not of man's invention. He must feel toward that which science has not yet realized like a child trying to understand the works and wisdom of a grown-up. As a consequence, every really deep scientist must necessarily have religious feeling."

Einstein marveled that our minds are able to assemble patterns of meaning. As he told a friend, *"A priori*, one should expect a chaotic world which cannot be grasped by the mind in any way." The fact that this isn't the case, that the cosmos is comprehensible and follows laws gives evidence of a "God who reveals himself in the harmony of all that exists." Yet Einstein could not bring himself to believe in a personal God such as the Bible portrays. He sensed in the universe a unitary spirit, certainly a creative spirit, though anything beyond that—a loving spirit, say—eluded him. For that leap, as Martin Perl says, we need revelation, not just observation.*

CLUES BUT NOT PROOF

Other scientists share Einstein's childlike wonder. Alexander Tsiaras, a professor at the Yale Department of Medicine, entranced a sophisticated crowd at a TED conference with a video of the fetal stages from conception to birth. He had written the software to utilize an MRI technique that had earned its inventor a Nobel Prize. The video compresses nine months of growth and development into a nine-minute film and is available on YouTube.

The human body largely consists of collagen—hair, skin, nails, bones, tendon, gut, cartilage, blood vessels—Tsiaris explains in his introduction. A rope-like protein, collagen changes its structure in only one place, the cornea of the eye, where it spontaneously forms a transparent grid pattern. As the video of speeded-up fetal development plays, this mathematician drops his objectivity, awed by a system "so perfectly organized it's hard not to attribute

---

* The theologian would agree. Louis Berkhof writes, "In the study of all other sciences man places himself *above* the object of his investigation … but in theology he does not stand above but rather *under* the object of his knowledge. In other words, man can know God only in so far as the latter actively makes Himself known."

divinity to it … the magic of the mechanisms inside each genetic structure saying exactly where that nerve cell should go."

All the eggs and sperm that resulted in the total population of this planet could fit in two quart jars, and from those tiny cells seven billion human beings emerged. On the time-lapse video of one fetus, sixty thousand miles of capillaries and blood vessels take shape where needed, following the genetic script built into a single cell. Aware of the intricate coding required to direct such a project, the programmer Tsiaras remarks, "The complexity of the mathematical models of how these things are done is beyond human comprehension. Even though I am a mathematician, I look at this with marvel: How do these instruction sets not make mistakes as they build what is us? It's a mystery, it's magic, it's divinity."

Unlike the scientists, most ordinary people intuit the answer to *Is there anyone else?* just by looking around. We see the fragile beauty of a luna moth, the intricate design of an ordinary wood duck, the marvel of childbirth, and simply assume that Someone must be behind all this. Nadia Bolz-Weber, an edgy Lutheran pastor in Denver, tells of her stint as a hospital chaplain during seminary. She went into the room of an elderly woman recovering from surgery, expecting to be asked to pray or read her Bible. "Oh, that's all nonsense, dear. I'm an atheist," the woman said. Nadia writes, "Before realizing I was saying it, I blurted out admiringly, 'Man, good for you. I wish I could pull that off.'"

Centuries ago the apostle Paul wrote to the Romans, "For since the creation of the world God's invisible qualities — his eternal power and divine nature — have been clearly seen, being understood from what has been made, so that people are without excuse." Even in a secular culture, many would agree.

Nevertheless, the evidence for a Creator is not overpowering, or else everyone would believe in God. Perhaps, as Dorothy Sayers suggests in *The Mind of the Maker*, we err by imagining God as an engineer when instead creation shows more evidence of God as an artist. Shortly after the conference with the scientists I visited a butterfly museum. After watching the exquisite patterns of living art flit around the glass enclosure, I examined under a microscope the bejeweled, golden chrysalises from which they had burst. Their beauty seemed superfluous—a stage that could have been accomplished by a dull cocoon, with better camouflage at that—and each chrysalis was discarded as soon as the adult butterfly emerged. What or Who lavished such gratuitous beauty on our planet?

While hiking in the Rocky Mountains I'll turn a corner and see a lush carpet of wildflowers: columbine, Indian paintbrush, elephant's head, bishop's cap. On our planet beauty abounds, shouting forth wordless praise. Scientists Alexander Tsiaras and Francis Collins see God's hand in the coding of the DNA double helix. And from nature writers such as John Muir, Henri Fabre, Loren Eiseley, and Lewis Thomas I have gained appreciation for a master Artist they might not even believe in; yet their precise and reverent observations help inform my own gratitude and praise.

Nevertheless, science limits itself to what can be empirically verified, and an invisible God lies outside that realm. In an exchange of letters with Robert Seiple, then president of World Vision USA, Carl Sagan clarified that even he remained open to belief in God. He viewed with wonder the beauty and simplicity in the laws governing the cosmos. Summing up, he wrote, "As a scientist, I hold that belief should follow evidence, and to my mind the evidence for the universe being created is far from compelling. I neither believe nor disbelieve. My mind is, I think, open, awaiting better data."

A friend who is a physicist and also a committed Christian wondered whether celebrating creation can be a form of worship, even by those who do not acknowledge the Creator. He told of a conversation with someone who praised one of his books while admitting he could not recall the author's name—totally unaware he was speaking to the author. "The praise was strangely more genuine for its inarticulate anonymity. I suspect, as C. S. Lewis once speculated, that God may have more connection with honest atheists than many think."

Christians can learn much from science while at the same time giving attention to what lies beyond its bounds. As the quantum pioneer Erwin Schrödinger admitted, "The scientific picture of the world around me is very deficient. It gives me a lot of factual information, puts all our experience in a magnificently consistent order, but is ghastly silent about all that is really near to our heart, that really matters to us. It cannot tell a word about the sensation of red and blue, bitter and sweet, feelings of delight and sorrow. It knows nothing of beauty and ugly, good or bad, God and eternity."

Another scientist expressed a similar thought: "Everything that can be counted does not necessarily count; everything that counts cannot necessarily be counted."

NEW AGE ANSWERS

Is there anyone else? Although scientists and laypersons alike may appreciate the wonders of creation, such regard does not necessarily lead to traditional faith. In recent times a floodgate of other beliefs has opened instead. Given the revival of interest in witches, New Age channeling, and angels, the spirit world has made a strong comeback even in the midst of our materialistic age.

In the 1980s Shirley MacLaine introduced millions to the world of psychics, channelers, and spirit guides. "God lies within," she said, "and therefore we are each part of God." She drew the remarkable conclusion, "I created my own reality.... I had created everything I saw, heard, touched, smelled, tasted.... I was my own universe.... Was this what was meant by the statement I AM THAT I AM?" Carlos Castaneda, Oprah Winfrey, Eckhart Tolle, Marianne Williamson, *The Celestine Prophecy*, Druidism, goddess worship, *Conversations with God*, Wicca, Kabbalah, *A Course in Miracles*, the Unity Church—each puts forth a different understanding of reality than that proposed by Christianity or by science.

Robert Bellah interviewed one young woman, a nurse named Sheila, who practiced a faith so personalized that she gave it her own name. "My faith has carried me a long way," she said. "It's Sheilaism. Just my own little voice. . . . It's just try to love yourself and be gentle with yourself. You know, I guess, take care of each other."

Elizabeth Gilbert recounted her own spiritual quest in *Eat, Pray, Love*, which spent almost four years on the *New York Times* bestseller list and was made into a movie starring Julia Roberts. Unlike Sheila, Gilbert made a determined effort to find truth, searching in Italy, India, and Indonesia. She landed, though, in a place not far from Sheila. "You have every right to cherry-pick when it comes to moving your spirit and finding peace in God," she concludes. And her highest spiritual wisdom? "God dwells within you as you yourself, exactly the way you are."

I admit to little interest in New Age religion, which seems to me as slippery as a wet bar of soap. I shudder to imagine a universe run by a God who resembles me, exactly the way I am. Still, I decided I should listen more carefully since so many post-Christians find New Age beliefs appealing. Out of journalistic curiosity I visited a Unity church, and though I enjoyed their upbeat, smiling spirit I could never get a grip on what its adherents believe, or why.

Next I paid forty-eight dollars for a ticket to hear Wayne Dyer, a guru often featured on PBS television and author of books with titles like *How to Get What You Really, Really, Really Want*. I arrived early for Dyer's gathering. As a harp and violin played soothing music Dyer himself circulated through the crowd, nodding to acquaintances and shaking hands. Then a local fan introduced him in fawning terms and Dyer took the microphone.

"The most profound sentence I ever heard," he began, "is 'I am God.'" Dyer proceeded to speak for ninety minutes nonstop. He set out the goal of connecting with the All, for each of us is part of the one universal source. The worst thing is whatever excludes. Religion excludes. Therefore we need to rise, on our own, to a higher level of consciousness.

"I have within me a knowing," Dyer said. "I was born close to heaven, and I simply need to remember that state." Sprinkling his talk with words like *energy*, *vibration*, and *harmonics*, he presented a faith that is positive, self-fulfilling, and crystal clear. He mentioned Jesus with respect, yet I could not help noticing how much his program differed from the sacrificial, narrow path that Jesus described. Dyer took his concept of Jesus not from the four Gospels, which he sees as redacted many years after Jesus' death, but rather from Mary Magdalene's Gospel, which he said refers to Good but never God.

With a personal-testimony style reminiscent of a Southern tent revival, Dyer told of his own ascent from an orphanage ward that he shared with eleven other boys to a position of fame and wealth. "God gave me the gift," he said proudly, and recounted how he had used that gift to achieve success, becoming the first nonmedical person to receive the Einstein award. Along the way he had learned to calibrate God-consciousness. Jesus stands alone at the top, with a score of 900; Mother Teresa ranks at 700; Dyer's own daughter Sky, surprisingly, scores 640 when she sings one particular song.

I confess that as I listened to Wayne Dyer I had to fight a tendency to dismiss him outright. His *Da Vinci Code*–style conspiracy theories of church history were unconvincing. His God seemed far too tame to govern a universe; I could not even tell whether he believed in a God separate from human beings. He certainly had no concept of the Fall, and I wondered how evil fit into his system. Just as I was sliding toward condescension I reminded myself that I had come to listen, not to judge. I looked around the room and saw seven hundred fans beaming, interrupting Dyer with applause, nodding in enthusiastic agreement. All had paid at least forty-eight dollars for a ticket, and the most devoted had contributed an additional fifty dollars for the privilege of joining him for dinner.

The brochure in my lap spelled out the core message: "God is LOVE. Love is LIFE. I am LIFE. I AM." Love, life, meaning, God—in that hotel conference room I was witnessing an expression of deep thirst. To me the fuzzy mysticism, the blatant self-promotion, and even the quality of the music did not measure up to what I normally hear at church. Yet many in the audience had by their own admission tried church and found no remedy for their thirst. It would be easy to blame them for preferring self-fulfillment to radical discipleship, but I had heard far too many stories from people wounded by the church and turned off by Christians who distort the message.

I wondered how these people would have responded to Jesus, who managed to rattle the religious establishment and present uncompromising demands while at the same time offering a Living Water that fully satisfies. I once heard a rabbi address a group of Army chaplains: "Where others see rebellion, we see thirst," he said. "Where others see apathy, we see yearning. Where others see alienation, we see quest." His words, describing the chaplain's role in postmodern society, echo those of another rabbi who lived two thousand years before.

RELIGION ANSWERS

Is there anyone else? Researchers have yet to find a single society on earth, no matter how "primitive," that does not have some system of religious belief. In his account of the voyage of the *Beagle*, Charles Darwin was amazed to find such advanced belief even among tribes at the tip of Argentina, the Tierra del Fuego, which seemed to him the end of the world. Religion is hard-wired into the human psyche, some scientists contend. We cannot help asking ultimate questions about life, death, and meaning—the very questions that lie beyond the bounds of science.

"Sure, those questions are important," an acquaintance said to me. "But every religion has its own answers, and most people simply accept the religion in which they were raised. How can anyone decide what is true?"

When the Willow Creek Community Church did a survey they found that some in their congregation, and especially their post-Christian friends, believed that all world religions are essentially the same. If their doctrines are similar and point in the same direction, why is it important to choose the "right" one? In response to the survey, the church invited a learned representative from each of the major faiths to a service. A Hindu, a Buddhist, a Muslim, a Jew, and a Christian sat together on the platform and answered questions from the moderator Bill Hybels. I will condense some of the main points.

What is your understanding of God?

Hindu: God was All-consciousness, before creation, and out of his playtime he created the universe. So God in one form is the creation, and also to put life into it he entered the creation, countless times. Indeed, anyone can attain Godhood status by following the rules set out.

Buddhist: We focus not on God or gods, but on the teachings of Gautama Buddha who lived in the fifth century BC. We strive, like the Buddha, to become enlightened human beings, who serve out of compassion and try to end suffering in the world.

Muslim: God is a mercy-giver. He is peace. He is the first and last. He is the owner of the Day of Judgment. He is the owner of the universe. He is the guide. He is the light. He is the Mercy.

Jew: I would suspect everyone here would recognize the God of Judaism through Judaism's daughter religions, Christianity and Islam, both of which have patterned their own theology after the mother religion, Judaism.

Christian: God is all-powerful, all-knowing, and everywhere present. God is spirit and exists eternally in three persons, God the Father, God the Son, and God the Holy Spirit. Also, God is personal, which means he invites me to get to know him and to grow in a deep, loving relationship with him.

What do you think of Jesus Christ? According to your tradition, who was Jesus of Nazareth?

Hindu: This world is God's drama. He created so many religions, and he wanted variety for his own pleasure. When Jesus Christ came and Christianity came about, this was God manifesting himself in Jesus Christ. We have tolerance for all the gods, and we tell everyone you go pray to your god, if you have that belief, and continue what you are doing.

Buddhist: Jesus was a human being, a wise and compassionate human being who was concerned for the suffering of humanity. And the Buddhist tradition would also recognize the perspective that Jesus is the son of God, though not the only way to God.

Muslim: We believe in the prophets of God, which include Jesus, peace be upon him. But we do not believe he died on the cross. The Koran says he was not killed or crucified. He has been lifted by God and will be coming back to guide all mankind according to Islam.

Jew: As for the preeminence of Jesus over any other religion's central figure, we leave that up to anybody to decide for themselves. We have our Bible and our prophets, and they have their Bible and their prophets, and we let it go at that.

Christian: Jesus Christ is the one and only Son of God, fully human and fully God, without sin, the only one worthy or qualified to forgive sin. He proved he was God when he was resurrected, and he also proved that he could defeat death and forgive sin.

One final question: What about the life after this life? If you were to die after this service, what would happen?

Hindu: The Hindus believe in reincarnation, a continuation of life. Before my birth, there must have been thousands of births before. Based on my actions and my next birth, I might go into a lower creature, or I might elevate myself, at least until I reach the state of full consciousness.

Buddhist: Afterlife is problematic. If enlightenment has occurred before death then there is complete liberation, or complete nirvana, which cannot be described or explained. It is neither eternal consciousness or annihilation. It is not in our intellectual capacity to comprehend it.

Muslim: Every human being has a reserved seat in heaven and in hell. The angels will ask you what happened in your life, who was your God, who was your prophet, what was your religion, what was your book. So at the moment of death, those who are going to heaven will be shown their reserved place in hell — and what happened by the grace of God that they were saved from going to that hell — then they will be sent to heaven. Otherwise, people will be shown the other way. We all have to be prepared.

Jew: Rabbis have said that the quality of your life after death depends on the character of your life on earth. "The righteous among all the nations of the world have a share in the world to come."

Christian: The soul will live forever in eternity, and the choices that we make here and now will determine our eternal destiny. If we choose to ignore God or reject God, or to ignore the separation [sin] problem, we will spend an eternity separated from God, and that place is called hell. On the other hand, if we choose to solve the separation problem God's way by receiving Jesus Christ into our lives, and allowing him to forgive our sins and bridge the gap, we will spend an eternity with God in heaven.

Clearly, not all religions teach the same answers to ultimate questions. (I should note that, of course, other representatives of the same religions might have expressed their beliefs differently.)

"We live in a very diverse world, and we have to learn to get along with and respect and show deference and kindness to people who represent different religions," Bill Hybels said at the end of the service. "I hope, as we leave, you will leave with the words of Jesus on your mind: the highest kingdom law or value is the law of love. While we may disagree about where we drive our stake of conviction and belief, we are called to be compassionate, understanding, and respectful of those who believe differently."

HOW TO DECIDE?

Each major religion addresses important questions—Who is God? How should I live? What happens after death?—and presents its own answers. As a Christian, my main concern is not to downgrade others' beliefs but to examine my own. We have no Final Proofs to offer, nothing that would convince a scientist who looks only at empirical data. And in a diverse religious environment, arguments from the Bible don't work well because not everyone accepts its authority. Instead, people make choices based on which faith best corresponds with how they perceive reality.

More than a century ago William James remarked that all religions revolve around a common nucleus consisting of "an uneasiness" about life and "its solution." The world contains beauty, but also violence and death. Human beings feel love and joy, and also longing and despair. Which beliefs best reflect that sense of incompleteness and imperfection? Which solution offers hope and quenches thirst? More soberingly, which religion's followers best live out the reality they claim to believe?

In my own search for answers, I start with the big picture, the view of all creation. Though not everyone agrees, to me the universe, earth, life, and human beings simply show too many "coincidences" to be the products of randomness. So, then, how do I choose among the religious options? New Age holds little attraction for me because the universe requires a God very different from me, one who inspires awe and worship. I line up the main alternatives. As C. S. Lewis noted, on the one side stand Judaism, Christianity, and Islam, which share a common heritage. On the other side are Hinduism and its cousin Buddhism. For many reasons that would require another book to explain, Christianity has for me the most convincing appeal.

Obviously, we shouldn't decide on ultimate issues by what makes us feel good. But as I try to look at my own beliefs from the vantage of an outsider, the Christian gospel does seem to correspond with reality, and in a way that stands out as truly good news. It begins with the assurance that the universe came into being not through random, impersonal forces but rather through a loving Creator who designed a splendid home for us human beings. Yet all of creation shows signs of having been spoiled, and God's followers have the mission of bringing *shalom* — a state of justice, peace, and health — to a broken world. We also have the promise of ultimate restoration to the Creator's original design. "I am going there to prepare a place for you," Jesus assured those he left behind.

The essence of Christian faith has come to us in story form, the story of a God who will go to any lengths to get his family back. The Bible tells of flawed people — people just like me — who make shockingly bad choices and yet still find themselves pursued by God. As they receive grace and forgiveness, naturally they want to give it to others, and a thread of hope and transformation weaves its way throughout the Bible's accounts.

A loving God naturally would want to connect with those

who bear God's own image, leading to an unimaginable feat of condescension: the decision to join us on Earth. The good news comes to a focal point in God's Son, who showed us at once what God is like and what we should be like. In Jesus' story we have proof of God's abiding love ("For God so loved the world that he gave his one and only Son ...") and a template of how God can wrest life out of death and good out of evil.

Here is how *The Message* paraphrase expresses Paul's summary in the book of Ephesians:

> Long before he laid down earth's foundations, he had us in mind, had settled on us as the focus of his love, to be made whole and holy by his love. Long, long ago he decided to adopt us into his family through Jesus Christ. (What pleasure he took in planning this!) ...
>
> It's in Christ that we find out who we are and what we are living for. Long before we first heard of Christ and got our hopes up, he had his eye on us, had designs on us for glorious living, part of the overall purpose he is working out in everything and everyone.

As the New Testament itself admits, Jesus is at once the capstone of creation and also the greatest stumbling block for nonbelievers. All those on the Willow Creek panel agreed that Jesus represents a point of common ground: an esteemed rabbi to the Jew, a god to the Hindu, an enlightened one to the Buddhist, a great prophet to the Muslim. Even to the New Age guru, Jesus is the pinnacle of God-consciousness. At the same time, Jesus is the divider. None but Christians see him as a member of the Godhead on an exclusive mission to repair the broken world.

For us his followers the good news centers on Jesus, like sunlight concentrated by a magnifying glass. He forgave sinners, loved enemies, healed the sick, extended grace to the undeserving, and triumphed as a victim. In short, he demonstrated a different way of being human. That model represents startling good news, though no one finds Jesus' way easy to embrace. And none will, unless we Christians live out what we believe.

For the post-Christian, Jesus remains the central figure, the one not easily dismissed, not easily refuted. A few years ago a rap poem by Jeff Bethke, "Why I hate religion but love Jesus," went viral, attracting almost thirty million views on YouTube. A *Newsweek* cover story the week of Easter 2012 put the message simply: "Forget the church, follow Jesus." Such slogans indicate that a church of moralism, judgment, and spiritual ranking has failed to represent Jesus.

In the end, it is up to Jesus' followers to convey the good news. The thirst endures. Do we help slake it? We are the ones who must convincingly answer the question, "Is there anyone else?"

REALITY CHECK

A reality check came for me in 2012 when I was asked to speak in Newtown, Connecticut, shortly after the shootings at Sandy Hook Elementary School that killed twenty first-graders and six teachers and staff. Yes, people were asking, "How could God allow such a tragedy?" More urgently, though, they were asking, "Will I ever see those children again? Did these six- and seven-year-old lives have any lasting meaning?" In other words, is there any good news we can cling to at such a terrible time?

I could stand before the community of sorrow and offer hope. Unable to soften their grief, I could at least affirm it: the outrage they felt against a calculated slaughter was a true and righteous outrage against despicable evil. I could also affirm that God is on the side of the sufferer, for we have Jesus' clear example of demonstrating that in person. Most important, I could hold out the hope that those young lives did not end that awful day, and that parents could one day reunite with children denied all but a few brief years on this planet.

Our faith rests not just on Jesus' example but on his resurrection. As the apostle Paul said, "If there is no resurrection of the dead, then not even Christ has been raised. And if Christ has not been raised, our preaching is useless and so is your faith. More than that, we are then found to be false witnesses about God ... If only for this life we have hope in Christ, we are of all people most to be pitied."

On my website I received this message from a woman who sees Christianity less as an adversary than as a delusion:

I just ate my lunch looking over your book *Disappointment With God*. I cried a little, something I don't often do. I'm a 51-year-old nurse, raised in a Christian home. I cried because I just looked you up on the Internet and it appears that all these years since you've written the book, you haven't been able to come to grips with the truth — that there really isn't a God. I cried because I understand why you haven't been able to face it, I cried because you are still leading people down a dead-end path because you think you're bringing them comfort when in fact you're leading them astray, I cried because you led my parents astray, thus inspiring them to teach me that a personal God exists who cares about me which has totally skewed my world view for years when in fact I could have been happier than I'd ever thought possible with the truth — that we don't really know why we're here, but that it's nature, an enormous cosmos that we're exploring and that if there really was a God who existed and cared about us, he would never ever ever ever not reveal himself to us in a way we could understand because that just does not make sense. I BEG of you to open your mind to the possibility that, through no fault of your own, you have been mistaken. I BEG of you for the sake of our humanity. I BEG of you for yourself and your family to just LOOK at what you're doing and saying. If you care about ANYONE, please explore the possibility that you might actually be causing harm instead of helping. PLEASE.

I stared at that letter for a long time. She was pleading for me to reassess my faith, the most important part of my life. I cannot deny that I have battled doubt, that I have sometimes wondered about the very issues she raised. What struck me was her tone of ultimate concern, a longing for unvarnished reality. I followed her suggestion to read some recommended books by atheists. One of them, Jean Paul Sartre, admitted, "That God does not exist, I cannot deny. That my whole being cries out for God, I cannot forget."

Here is part of my response to the nurse:

I appreciate your compassion, truly I do. And I understand your position perhaps better than you might think. I have read [some of the books she mentioned]. I'm sure you're aware that others have looked at the same evidence as you and reached a different conclusion. Many of us believe that God has indeed revealed himself: through nature, the Bible, and Jesus. Of course we may be mistaken — as indeed you may be.

I think back to the "wager" presented by Blaise Pascal. "The eternal silence of these infinite spaces frightens me," he said. Nonetheless, he could not understand the attitude of glee with which skeptics proclaimed their disbelief in God and immortality. A brief life in a meaningless universe and then annihilation — can anyone truly welcome such a prospect? Is it not, rather, "a thing to say sadly, as the saddest thing in the world?"

You experience disbelief as a kind of liberation. For many of us faith is a consolation. I have been privileged to know (and write about) many wonderful people who are motivated to selfless good — not harmed — by their beliefs. Someday we'll all know for sure; until then we make choices. I respect your choice, and thank you for the work you're doing in a state I once lived in.

Is there anyone else? If not, we who believe are pitifully misguided. If there is, we will know at last the end of all unease, the quenching of all desire.

CHAPTER 10

WHY ARE WE HERE? THE HUMAN QUESTION

You were born without purpose, you live without meaning,
living is its own meaning. When you die, you are extinguished.
From being you will be transformed to non-being.

INGMAR BERGMAN

Each month a quarter of a million Americans query "What is the meaning of life?" on the search engine Google. When I did so, Google reported 640,000,000 results in less than half a second. Scanning the first few pages, I found responses that ranged from the philosophical to the cynical. A quote from Monty Python's film *The Meaning of Life* was typical: "Well, it's nothing very special. Uh, try to be nice to people, avoid eating fat, read a good book every now and then, get some walking in, and try to live together in peace and harmony with people of all creeds and nations."

Various contributors suggested such answers as "To realize my potential," "To seek wisdom," "To do good," "To love God and others," and "To be happy." Someone posted a clip from television's *The Simpsons* in which God promises to enlighten Homer on the meaning of life; only, the credits roll and music cuts in just as God's speech begins.

Answers from the science and faith communities to the question "Why are we here?" could not be further apart. The Baltimore Catechism gives the classic Christian answer: "God made me to know Him, to love Him, and to serve Him in this world, and to be happy with Him forever in heaven." At the other end of the spectrum, Richard Dawkins sees the universe as having "precisely the properties we should expect if there is, at bottom, no design, no purpose, no evil and no good, nothing but blind, pitiless indifference." Science may help answer the "How?" questions, but not "For what purpose?"

IT'S ALL ABOUT ME

As if in response to this identity crisis, the recent field of evolutionary psychology has emerged with a bold new approach. We must look down, not up: to nature, not to a Creator. We best learn about ourselves by studying other species, probing for clues as to why natural selection might prefer certain kinds of behavior. Writers on evolutionary psychology fill their works with vivid descriptions of ants and chimpanzees, proposing theories for the origin of such traits as infidelity, maternal instincts, gossip, and violence. Magazines like *Time* hire these writers to make sense of gang behavior in the inner cities or sexual indiscretions in the capital city. The new behaviorists strive to help us understand ourselves and our role in the cosmos.*

I find the evolutionary psychologists' accounts of animal behavior fascinating. When they apply the same principles to human beings, however, my alarm bells go off. To mention the most important one, displacing God knocks the human species off its pedestal as well. If human beings are not made in the image

---

* Not all evolutionary theorists embrace this school of thought. Notably, Stephen Jay Gould offered a strong critique in successive issues of the *New York Review of Books*, calling the evolutionary psychologists "Darwinian fundamentalists" and "hyper-Darwinian" for their dogged insistence that natural selection alone accounts for all evolutionary development and human behavior.

of God, how can we claim any special rights or privileges? Zoologist Paul Shepard admits, "'Rights' implies some kind of cosmic rule ... something intrinsic or given by God or Nature." Candid atheists agree that any discussion about human or animal rights is pointless—which has a huge impact on how we view ourselves and the world.

"There really is no rational reason for saying a human being has special rights," says Ingrid Newkirk, cofounder of People for the Ethical Treatment of Animals. "A rat is a pig is a dog is a boy."* In 2013 the group Non-human Rights Project (NhRP) filed a series of lawsuits in an attempt to get judges to declare that the great apes are legal persons. Serious ethicists now argue that an animal's rights should sometimes take precedence over a human's. Princeton's Peter Singer suggests that an adult chimpanzee may have more value than a human infant, especially a "defective" child. Infanticide should take place as soon as possible after birth, he says, though it would be acceptable to kill one-year-olds with physical or mental disabilities. This proposal comes from a man *The New Yorker* calls the most influential living philosopher.

Taken to its logical conclusion, the question "Why are we here?" becomes "Should we even be here?" A writer in the journal *Wild Earth* muses about a human-less world: "If you haven't given voluntary human extinction much thought before, the idea of a world with no people may seem strange. But, if you give the idea a chance I think you might agree that the extinction of *Homo sapiens* would mean survival for millions, if not billions, of other Earth-dwelling species.... Phasing out the human race will solve every problem on earth, social and environmental." The movement maintains a website in eleven languages, and under

---

* Theologian Walter Wink comments, "Once we erred by ascribing to animals faculties found only in humans; today behaviorism denies to humans faculties not found in animals. In Arthur Koestler's sardonic phrase, we have substituted for the anthropomorphic view of the rat, a ratomorphic view of humans."

the motto "May we live long and die out," it advocates an end to all new births. The founder envisions a time when "The last humans could enjoy their final sunsets peacefully, knowing they have returned the planet as close as possible to the Garden of Eden."

Fortunately, few are willing to take conclusions about the meaninglessness of human life to that extreme. Evolutionary psychologists have a different approach. Any clue to the meaning of life, they say, must be found in something called the selfish gene, which accounts for all human behavior. We exist for the sole purpose of perpetuating our genes; thus, every decision I make must somehow benefit my gene pool. Some evolutionary theorists herald this notion as the most important single advance in their theory since Darwin. As Richard Dawkins puts it, "We are survival machines—robot vehicles blindly programmed to preserve the selfish molecules known as genes. This is a truth which still fills me with astonishment."

Critics have raised objections to the selfish-gene theory. What about homosexuals or childless couples, who do not perpetuate their genes—how to explain their behavior? How does the voluntary human extinction movement fit into the selfish gene theory? Or consider the case of Robertson McQuilkin, a man I know well. The president of a Christian college, he resigned in his prime in order to care for his Alzheimer's-afflicted wife. How to account for such unselfish behavior? As if explaining algebra to a child, the evolutionary psychologists take up such thorny problems one by one and explain them in terms of the selfish gene.

If Robertson McQuilkin claims, as he does, that he stood by his ailing wife out of his love for her and because of his commitment to biblical standards of fidelity—why, of course he would argue that. He makes a living as a Christian writer and speaker, doesn't he? He is merely propagating the ideas that have served him so well. Challenged to explain Mother Teresa's behavior,

Edward O. Wilson pointed out that she was secure in the service of Christ and in her belief in immortality; in other words, she acted on the "selfish" basis of anticipating a reward.

The same principle applies to me: I am doubtless writing this chapter in response to my own selfish gene in order to spread my Christian beliefs. If you find yourself disagreeing with me, you must be responding to a selfish gene that prompts you to react against Christians. Both of us are following a deterministic script that may not be evident to us or to anyone else—except perhaps the evolutionary psychologists.

DARK NATURE

As I read these modern thinkers I cannot help noticing anomalies. They ask us to protect endangered species and honor animal rights without allowing any basis for those "rights." After describing chilling examples of gang rape, murder, and cannibalism in nature, they urge us to rise above such practices. They call us to "higher" values of nonviolence and mutual respect even though there is no ground for higher and lower and apparently we have no real freedom to act anyway. Most seriously, they have difficulty judging anything as wrong or evil since we are merely acting on our genes.

Robert Wright defends lust as an example of the selfish-gene principle at work. Lust developed as nature's way of "getting us to act as if we wanted lots of offspring and knew how to get them, whether or not we actually do." If a man grows restless after a woman gives him a few children, why shouldn't he spread his genes more widely by taking up with another woman?

Having no category for evil, evolutionary psychologists reach far to explain heinous crimes. Lyall Watson takes up the case of Susan Smith, who rolled a Mazda sedan containing her two infant sons, nicknamed Precious and Sugarfoot, into a lake in order to pursue an affair with a wealthy man. Infanticide, says Watson, is nothing new, being practiced in many animal species. In his book *Dark Nature*, Watson even attempts to fit the atrocities of Rwanda and Auschwitz into a rational framework of genetic behavior. Logically he must, for he assumes that *all* human behavior stems from inbuilt urges chosen through natural selection.

With no outside moral code of right and wrong, many modern scientists teeter on the verge of self-contradiction. Edward O. Wilson's memoir shows a man who possesses the best qualities of a scientist: curiosity, fairness, and commitment to truth. Yet if those qualities came to him genetically, were in fact determined for him, what makes them superior to the qualities of laziness, dishonesty, and superstition against which he so valiantly struggled? Why choose one set of values over another, especially when you do not believe in free choice?

Some evolutionary biologists cheerfully admit the problem. Concludes Robert Wright, "Thus the difficult question of whether the human animal can be a moral animal — the question that modern cynicism tends to greet with despair — may seem increasingly quaint. The question may be whether, after the new Darwinism takes root, the word *moral* can be anything but a joke."

Randolph Nesse, another proponent, feels more unease about grounding all behavior in selfishness:

> When I first grasped it, I slept badly for many nights, trying to find some alternative that did not so roughly challenge my sense of good and evil. Understanding this discovery can undermine commitment to morality — it seems silly to restrain oneself if moral behavior is just another strategy for advancing the interests of one's genes. Some students, I am embarrassed to say, have left my courses with a naïve notion of the selfish-gene theory that seemed to them to justify selfish behavior, despite my best efforts to explain the naturalistic fallacy.

Science increasingly bombards us with a bleak message about what it means to be human. *You result from an accident of natural selection. You have no intrinsic value.* Compared with any other moment in history, human beings have lost a sense of unique destiny, replaced by a cosmic inferiority complex. Scientists, educators, and politicians all strain to come up with any convincing answer to the question "Why are we here?"

THE BROAD WAY

The average person brushes aside philosophical questions and the latest trends in evolutionary science. Most of us drift along in the cultural current, buying the newest electronic gadgets, watching movies and television, paying bills, taking the kids to soccer practice. We live in the "broad way," to borrow Jesus' term, which rarely attends to such grand questions as "Why are we here?" Instead, popular culture provides an endless stream of trivia — news items, games, sports, Hollywood gossip — that have a tranquilizing effect.

I went through adolescence in the 1960s, an era when a youth movement rebelled against the shallowness of popular culture. We openly mocked the dream of a home in the suburbs surrounded by a neatly groomed lawn and housing a family of polite, neatly groomed children. What about the global issues of racism, poverty, and war? What about the meaning of life?

Little did we suspect that the brightest and the best would soon sign on as hedge-fund traders rather than social workers and poets. The big existential questions, people simply stopped worrying about. Kurt Vonnegut's son Mark once asked his father, "What are people for?" He then suggested the only answer modern culture can agree on: "We're here to help each other get through this thing, whatever it is."

Modern society, driven by consumer marketing, excels in offering escapist solutions that keep us from asking the larger

"Why?" questions. Banner ads and pop-ups litter the internet. Eighteen minutes out of every hour television allots to commercials that tempt us to buy the latest products—designer shoes and jeans, exercise machines, video games, smartphones—with such urgency that on special sale days crowds line up all night and trample each other when the doors finally open. A consumer economy fans thirst that only its products can quench.

I feel a wave of culture shock whenever I return from a trip to the developing world to a more "advanced" culture which somehow seems less real. Instead of talking around a village well or sharing a meal with an extended family, I enter a realm of "virtual friends" who communicate in terse text messages and 140-character tweets. And if I look to modern culture for an answer to "Why are we here?" I can only infer that we are here to laugh, make money, become famous, and look as good as possible.

We live in a celebrity culture that glorifies sex, wealth, and success. Pop singers soar to fame as much because of the shape of their bodies as the quality of their voices. We place such a premium on entertainment that a city's favorite athlete can earn more money than several hundred of its schoolteachers. My first instinct is to scorn a culture so shallow that in 2009 *Time* magazine selected a soccer player and Lady Gaga alongside Bill Clinton as its cover subjects for an issue on the "100 most influential people in the world." Once again I fight back the snobbish reflex and force myself to pay attention to the underlying thirst. What does it reveal?

We are all searching for significance. As John Updike said, "No matter in how many ways our lives are demonstrated to be insignificant, we can only live them as if they were not." In a world of seven billion people we want somehow to stand out, to make a mark, to achieve something of worth—and our culture dangles before us the ideals of beauty, wealth, and power. Here's how to succeed, the media proclaim: by having whiter teeth and a swimsuit figure and a diversified portfolio. And if we cannot measure up, at least we can watch our idols on a large HD/3D television screen and find vicarious pleasure by projecting onto them the success we will never achieve.

Some agencies offer a personal paparazzi service that you can hire for a night to follow you with flashing cameras in order to impress the unphotographed crowds around you. For a fee you can pretend that you qualify for a segment on *Entertainment Tonight*, or at least have a role on reality TV. You can get the crowd murmuring, "Who is that?"

"I count," we cry. My life *matters* to the world; it makes a difference. Has any society in history found such effective ways to exploit the human thirst for significance?

ILLUSIONS UNVEILED

Christians often follow the same path, creating our own version of a culture based on celebrity and entertainment. The sociologist Alan Wolfe remarks, "Culture has transformed Christ, as well as all other religions found within these shores. In every aspect of the religious life, American faith has met American culture—and American culture has triumphed." Shouldn't we be presenting an alternative to the prevailing culture rather than simply mimicking it? What would a church look like that created space for quietness, that bucked the celebrity trend and unplugged from noisy media, that actively resisted our consumer culture? What would worship look like if we directed it more toward God than toward our own amusement?

When I signed up with a new television provider I got more than five hundred cable channels on three months' free trial. Over the next ninety days I spent far too much time surfing with the remote control through scenes of sex-obsessed, glamorous, car-chase-filled, lighthearted entertainment. Such a dazzling array easily overpowered Jesus' countercultural message that the poor, not the rich, are truly blessed, as are the meek, the persecuted, and those who mourn. What does it profit a person to gain the whole world? Quite a lot, the television shows insinuated.

I must admit, during those ninety days of free TV I felt the seductive pull of selfish pleasure, the siren call of modern culture. As a Jesus-follower, though, I had recurring doubts about whether a consumer/entertainment culture truly satisfies the deepest thirst. Thomas Aquinas suggests the very opposite, that a person who lacks spiritual joy settles for inferior pleasures. By promising more, does the broad way actually deliver less?

Once my television contract reverted to basic cable, and after a period of withdrawal, I spent some time reflecting on the message I had been absorbing. It seems to me that the broad way fails to satisfy on at least three levels. First, the media culture is built on illusion. Second, its diversions are temporary. Finally, it has little place for losers.

In a strange twist, the very same media that idolize the lucky few then proceed to gossipingly dissect their flawed lives, unveiling the illusion. Fame alone does not satisfy thirst: Hollywood marriages collapse, lottery winners squander their spoils, privileged athletes dabble in drugs and crime. Lindsay Lohan, Barry Bonds, Whitney Houston, Michael Jackson, Amy Winehouse, Lance Armstrong, Paris Hilton, John Edwards, the Kardashians, Tiger Woods, Charlie Sheen — as soon as I write the names they become outdated and a new batch of celebrities rises, only to fall. Still we are not deterred; fame becomes an end in itself, something to pursue for its own sake regardless of the consequences.

We have invented a two-tiered society of watchers and the watched, like the sixty thousand spectators in a football stadium who focus on the tiny figures on the field below. Walker Percy wrote a novel about a small Southern town that suddenly *matters* when a director selects it as the setting for his next movie. Magazine ads trumpet the message "As seen on TV!" as if that fact alone validates the product. "Reality shows" create instant unreality by recording the lives of supermoms and housewives in New Jersey or Orange County or Atlanta—as if anyone could live unaffected by the 24/7 presence of a video crew. We keep falling for the false reality created by media.

Every society has elevated the rich and powerful: Chinese bureaucrats crept on the ground like worms before the emperor, and the serfs of Russia lowered their heads in awe as the carriage of the czar thundered by. What's new is the illusion of intimacy. Justin Bieber or Miley Cyrus tweet and instantly a personal message shows up on thirty million phones. We want to know everything about them, and almost we do. We know their exercise routines, their diets, their taste in clothes, and a little browsing on the internet will expose them in various stages of undress.

Radio personality Garrison Keillor once told a story about Elizabeth June the Human Balloon, a lonely, obese woman "not quite right in the head," often the butt of the locals' jokes. She would go into the woods, spread a picnic blanket, and serve cocktails ("day queeries" she called them, mispronouncing *daiquiris*) to her imaginary friends, whom she had chosen out of a Sears Roebuck catalog. At the end of his monologue Keillor said, with a jolt of honesty rare for an entertainer, "Farewell, my friends in Radioland—and when I say that, remember that you are my friends in the same way Elizabeth June's imaginary friends were to her."

The illusion of intimacy allows me to feel close to my heroes, though actually if I went up to any of them and started a conversation bodyguards would swiftly whisk me away. My only hope is somehow to join that elite group and become one of the watched not the watchers—and the same media feed that illusion with an endless supply of makeover products that will make me more desirable and more successful.

We who follow Jesus know of one other hope: the good news he offered. Most astonishingly, he made possible an intimacy with the God of the universe that can solve the thirst for significance. To a woman shamed by an embarrassing malady, to a social outcast with leprosy, to a thief hanging on a cross hours from death, to a common prostitute—to all these people and many more he held out the bright promise that significance is not something attained but rather bestowed by a gracious God. And thus we who follow Jesus should treat those who rank low on society's scale—"the least of these," in Jesus' phrase—as he did, proclaiming by our deeds what we believe about the image of God in every person.

As a journalist, I have met fulfilled and godly people in the most unlikely places: a leprosarium in Nepal, a prison cell in South Africa, a house church in China, a slum in Chicago, a monastery in Sarajevo. Each of them looks not to the surrounding culture for a sense of worth, but to God. That is good news indeed for one who fails to pass the culture's test of success—and perhaps even one who manages to succeed. The writer John Cheever, whose stories portray the upper crust of society, once commented, "The main emotion of the adult American who has all the advantages of wealth, education, and culture is disappointment."

Here is the honest confession of one witness, the television journalist and author Malcolm Muggeridge, who spent most of his life climbing the social ladder:

> I may, I suppose, regard myself, or pass for being, a relatively successful man. People occasionally stare at me in the streets—that's fame. I can fairly easily earn enough to qualify for admission to the higher slopes of the Internal Revenue—that's success. Furnished with money and a little fame even the elderly, if they care to, may partake of trendy diversions—that's pleasure. It might happen once in a while that something I said or wrote was sufficiently heeded for me to persuade myself that it represented a

serious impact on our time—that's fulfillment. Yet I say to you—and I beg you to believe me—multiply these tiny triumphs by a million, add them all together, and they are nothing—less than nothing, a positive impediment—measured against one draught of that living water Christ offers to the spiritually thirsty, irrespective of who or what they are.

Why are we here? God wants us to flourish, and paradoxically we flourish best by obeying rather than rebelling, by giving more than receiving, by serving rather than being served. Six times in the Gospels Jesus iterated the deeper truth that we succeed not by acquiring more and more but by "losing" life through service to God and others. Centuries later the converted slave trader John Newton wrote in a hymn of the "solid joys and lasting treasure" that far exceed the fading "worldling's pleasure."

Jesus gave a vivid object lesson his last night with the disciples by washing their feet, like a servant. Parents know the self-giving principle by instinct as they pour their energies into their self-absorbed children. Volunteers in soup kitchens and hospices and mission projects learn this lesson by doing.* What seems like sacrifice becomes instead a kind of nourishment because dispensing grace enriches the giver as well as the receiver.

DEATH DEFANGED

Death exposes the second weakness of our culture: all its promises are ephemeral. Jesus said it bluntly: "What good is it for someone

---

* According to *Time* magazine, "A research review published in *BMC Public Health* found that doing volunteer work—in such places as hospitals and soup kitchens that allow direct contact with the people you're helping—may lower mortality rates by as much as 22% compared with those of nonvolunteers. Making such social connections increases life satisfaction and reduces depression and loneliness and in turn lowers the risk of hypertension, stroke, dementia and more."

to gain the whole world, and yet lose or forfeit their very self?"* His disciple James rephrased the thought: "the rich should take pride in their humiliation—since they will pass away like a wild flower."

Accept the twenty, forty, eighty, or however many years of life each of us has on earth as the sum total of all we will ever experience, and a self-obsessed consumer culture makes good sense—even though pampered flesh will decay and luxury goods will get left behind. On the other hand, if we accept that we have no guarantee of one more hour on earth and believe that life extends beyond what we experience here, then everything changes.

A materialist tends to see this life as the goal whereas Jesus held out a different vision, of this life as a preparation for a much longer existence: "Indeed, the water I give will become a spring of water welling up to eternal life." Modern culture diverts attention away from any life beyond this one—until something rudely interrupts it. Two tall towers collapse in a heap on a bright fall morning in 2001, and in the aftermath sporting events, comedy shows, even commercials get canceled. A tsunami wipes out entire villages in Japan, and citizens of a high-tech, secular culture wander around dazed, unable to avoid asking, "Why are we here?" A shooter slaughters twenty children in a school in Connecticut, and at that moment our sex-and-violence entertainment culture seems obscene.

I cannot help noting that at moments of national crisis even secular icons like the *New York Times* open their op-ed pages to priests, rabbis, and pastors. Atheists and evolutionary psychologists maintain a discreet silence, for good reason: What words of comfort and hope might they offer? I have a friend whose agnostic brother tried to comfort their dying mother. "The universe

---

* John Steinbeck updated the question in *Cannery Row*: "What can it profit a man to gain the whole world and to come to his property with a gastric ulcer, a blown prostrate, and bifocals?"

loves you," he said, stroking her arm. As my friend later reflected, "Somehow that didn't do much for her."

The problem of death, no scientist, politician, philosopher, or celebrity has been able to solve. From the day of birth we live under its certain sentence. All animals die, but the outrage against death is uniquely human. I have watched a lion attack a gazelle in Africa: after scattering to a safe distance the other gazelles nonchalantly resume their grazing as the lion devours their relative. Nature has little indignation over death, no scandalous sense that something is wrong—except among us humans.

The apostle Paul staked his faith on the good news that God will one day solve the death problem. In most ways Paul's faith made life harder, not easier, his biography a frightening succession of beatings, riots, stints in prison, and close escapes. Yet his underlying confidence in an eternal destination changed everything. After reviewing those hardships for the Corinthians, he summed up, "Though outwardly we are wasting away, yet inwardly we are being renewed day by day. For our light and momentary troubles are achieving for us an eternal glory that far outweighs them all."

That belief in something beyond this transitory life spread along with the gospel. Churches gradually moved burying places from scary graveyards to church lawns and even into the building itself. "The faithful stood on the bodies of their loved ones as they prayed," remarks a historian of the period, and as a result, " ... a definitive page in the history of death had been turned."

When the missionary Paulinus first presented the gospel to the fierce tribe of Anglo-Saxons in Britain, he explained the Christian view of death and what follows it. According to the historian Paul Johnson,

> There was a moment of silence, and then a wise old earl spoke. Life, he said, was short. It was like a sparrow, in

winter, flying through the king's hall. "It goes from darkness into the light, then into the darkness again—that is life." Human life, he added, "appears for a short space, but of what went before, and what is to follow, we know nothing. If, then, this new teaching gives us certitudes, we should follow it."

The Anglo-Saxons promptly converted. Johnson concludes, "Without God, death is horrific. With God, death is still fearsome, but it can be seen to have a meaning and purpose and a hope. The great strength of Christianity has always been that it brings men and women to terms with death in a way which offers them comfort and an explanation."

Advocates for the disabled sometimes use the term "temporarily abled" to describe unafflicted people, making the point that all of us have health on temporary loan. My friend Tim Hansel lived with relentless and excruciating pain after a rock-climbing accident, though it did not stop him from a productive life as a speaker and author. When he died, his wife Anastasia—her Greek name itself means "resurrection"—asked for his cremated ashes in the least expensive receptacle. The crematorium presented her with a cardboard box labeled in large letters, "Temporary Container." She sent me a whimsical photo of herself holding the box that contained all that remained of her husband's tortured body, a negative image of the newly resurrected body he had long anticipated. Tim saw life as a preparation, not an end, and for him, too, it changed everything.

To a skeptical post-Christian society the promise of resurrection does not have the same novel appeal that it once did. It summons up the old complaint of Christians promising "pie in the sky by and by" at the expense of a fulfilled life on earth. Actually, having the proper destination in mind should transform life here and now. In the words of C. S. Lewis, "If you read history you will find out that the Christians who did most for the present world were precisely those who thought most of the next." He added, "Aim at Heaven and you will get earth 'thrown in.' Aim at earth and you get neither."

A WORLD WITHOUT LOSERS

Finally, modern culture has little place for losers, those who will never measure up to its ideals. I stand at the checkout stand by a magazine rack displaying the beautiful bodies of celebrities and athletes and watch my fellow shoppers. Two-thirds of them are overweight, few seem flush with funds, and none makes a good prospect for *America's Top Model.* By the standards of popular culture they have little to offer.

Canadian novelist Robertson Davies speaks candidly about another kind of loser: "The greatest idiot and yahoo can be saved, the doctrine goes, because Christ loves him as much as he loves Albert Einstein. I don't think that is true. I think that civilization— life—has a different place for the intelligent people who try to pull us a little further out of the primal ooze than it has for the boobs who just trot along behind, dragging on the wheels."

Again, Jesus has a different set of qualifications for his kingdom than does civilization. His stories consistently made the wrong character the hero: the prodigal son not the responsible elder brother, the Good Samaritan not the good rabbi, a scabby beggar not a rich man. Those people most attracted to him included undesirables such as a half-caste woman with a checkered past, a blind beggar, ten exiles with leprosy, a corrupt tax collector, a prostitute, a Roman soldier—all outcasts by the standards of proper Jewish society. Religious professionals, legal scholars, a king, and a governor: these were the ones who arranged Jesus' death.

To the bafflement of the modern elite, the Christian faith continues to grow, and Jesus' somersault values may help explain why. An African American slave named "Old Elizabeth," who narrated her conversion story at the age of ninety-seven, told of getting from Jesus a sense of "somebodiness." In rural India and China and in the sprawling slums of South America and the Philippines, people respond to a gospel that bestows dignity on society's losers. Even in prosperous societies that measure worth by sex appeal, native talent, and celebrity status, the majority realize they will never measure up. Sometimes all of us feel like "the boobs who just trot along behind, dragging on the wheels," and at such a time a thirst for a more lasting satisfaction, for Living Water, wells up.

The good news of the gospel means that every one of us can have a sense of destiny, a part to play in God's great story. We are more than a collection of neurons, more than an organism directed by a script of selfish genes. A receptionist, a truck driver, a kindergarten teacher, a banker, a stay-at-home mom or dad can all realize that destiny: not by adopting cultural standards of wealth and fame but by loving God and neighbor. It's the difference between just living, and living for God's sake.

Why are we here? We, all of us, are here because of the Creator's love, who seeks both our flourishing and our response of love and gratitude. "Find out what pleases the Lord," Paul told the Ephesians. We are here to please God. It brings God pleasure to see us thrive, and we thrive by living as God intended.

The Christian answer to the question "Why are we here?" offers a stark contrast to that given by science and by popular culture. Robertson Davies pointed to one distinction even while disagreeing: Christ loves the greatest idiot and yahoo as much as he loves Albert Einstein. Jesus' early followers understood that every person—slave or free, Jew or Gentile, man or woman—has an absolute value, a radical notion that did not exist before Christianity. Plato valued a person according to behavior. Aristotle saw some men as "slaves by nature." According to the Christians, though, God created all of us as eternal beings, made in God's own image, which holds true for the brilliant or the mentally challenged, for the virtuous citizen or the criminal.

I write these words, and then think of how poorly I live them. Just yesterday I unloaded on a telephone order-taker who kept me waiting half an hour and then accidentally deleted the internet order I had painstakingly typed. Last week in church I heard from a family who had distributed food and blankets to the homeless. The six-year-old son had the most poignant comment. "I think mainly the homeless people want someone to talk to," he said— and I thought of how often I avert my eyes and quicken my pace when I encounter the homeless.

To the degree we live out the message we say we believe, treating everyone with dignity and worth and measuring success by the standards of Jesus and not the broader culture, to that degree only we will succeed in serving up good news to a thirsty world.

CHAPTER 11

HOW SHOULD WE LIVE?
THE SOCIAL QUESTION

On a shattered and deserted stage,
without script, director, prompter, or audience,
the actor is free to improvise his own part.

Jean-Paul Sartre

I got a glimpse of postmoderns and moral issues when my book group tackled the sprawling three-volume *Cairo Trilogy* by Naguib Mahfouz, the Nobel laureate novelist from Egypt. Mahfouz's writings so infuriated Islamic extremists that in 1994 assassins attacked him near his home, stabbing the eighty-two-year-old writer in the neck and leaving him with permanent disabilities (he died in 2006 at ninety-four). Reading the trilogy, I understood why even moderates might wince at his portrayal of their culture.

The novels center on a hypocritical patriarch who spends every evening boozing and womanizing and yet rules as a repressive tyrant at home. He refuses to allow his wife ever to step outside the house, and when at her children's urging she breaks that rule for the one and only time, he tosses her out. Likewise, he controls every aspect of his two daughters' lives, confining them to the house and forbidding them education. He sexually assaults his servants. In short, he embodies the worst kind of male chauvinist oppression, in which men do whatever they want and treat women as property.

I had to force myself to keep reading at times, so great were the injustices that Mahfouz rendered, and so I went to the reading group expecting to hear moral outrage from the women, most of them ardent feminists. Much to my shock, they reacted hardly at all. "It's a different culture," they said. "We can't impose our values on it."

"Wait a minute," I protested. "Locking a woman in her house for thirty years and then ditching her when she goes outside one day is more than a cultural difference. It's wrong! And what about his hypocrisy in ruling his family with an iron fist while he's out partying with prostitutes?" I got the same detached response.

Later we read *The Siege* by an Albanian writer. Set in the fifteenth century, it tells of an armed invasion by Ottoman Turks. In one scene Muslim attackers capture hundreds of Albanian women as prisoners. Unaccustomed to seeing women unveiled, they think the women are laughing when actually they are sobbing. With systematic cruelty the invaders proceed to rape the women repeatedly until some of them die. Surely the book group will condemn this savagery, I thought. Everyone found the scene reprehensible, of course, though they seemed unsurprised by it. As one of the women, a PhD scientist, said with a shrug, "It's genetic, it's spreading the genes — sociobiology. In one word, *men*."

I went away disturbed by that dark view of human nature. It reminded me of a comment I had read in a novel by the feminist Marilyn French: one of her characters proclaimed, "in their relations with women, all men are rapists, and that's all they are." But the men in our reading group had never raped anyone and, as far as I knew, were faithful to their wives. Are we human animals the helpless victims of our scripted genes? Surely we have some capacity to resist our base instincts and make moral decisions.

Members of the book group were trying to avoid Western cultural imperialism. No doubt they were reacting to the days of empire when European nations divided the world among themselves as if playing Monopoly, and perhaps they had seen movie clips of missionaries making the "natives" wear clothes and sing hymns. Fair enough, but can we never pass judgment on cultural practices—including our own? What about bride-burning, slavery, infant sacrifice, cannibalism, bribery, pederasty, wife-beating, sexual trafficking, genocide, toxic pollution, torture, female genital mutilation, child exploitation? I doubt my book group friends would have used such logic with Martin Luther King Jr. in the 1960s: "The South has a different culture and we have no right to impose our values on it."

Today, judgments about right and wrong have a capricious character. Although people continue to use moral terminology—it is *wrong* to own slaves, abuse a child, despoil the environment, prey on the poor, discriminate against women or homosexuals—they may struggle to explain why. A professor at a Texas university told me that his students, when questioned, found it difficult to condemn modern-day slavery in Sudan, or even the Nazi Holocaust, on purely moral grounds. Some of the same students, however, condemned the abuse of children by a prominent football coach and some joined the Occupy Wall Street movement because they thought it wrong for a few to exploit the many.

In his book *Lost in Transition* sociologist Christian Smith documents the difficulty young adults have in making moral judgments. "It's personal," said one respondent. "It's up to the individual. Who am I to say?" Another echoed those sentiments: "I mean, I guess what makes something right is how I feel about it. But different people feel different ways, so I couldn't speak on behalf of anyone else as to what's right and wrong."

NATURAL CONFUSION

How should we live? The moral sense of what's right or wrong traditionally gets passed down through a religion or culture, the collected wisdom of a group rather than an individual. Until recently the West turned to the Bible as a primary source, hence the phrase "Judeo-Christian ethics." Not anymore.

Post-Christians no longer look to religion for guidance. "I don't find the concept of *evil* helpful," said one man, a lawyer, at my book group meeting. "I think in terms of inappropriate behavior, not wrong behavior." Such fundamental questions as the difference between good and evil—or even whether such categories apply—hang in the air, unresolved. Where, then, do secular moderns look for guidance?

The scientist in my book group pointed to sociobiology, the study of animal behavior. Modern science seeks clues in nature because it assumes there is no other source. As one proponent explains:

> But is there any way in which we can decide, with certainty, which actions are right? [Daniel] Dennett's view, which I share, is that there is not, unless you hold that some book, for example the Bible, is the word of God, and that human beings are here to do God's bidding. If a person is simply the product of his or her genetic makeup and environmental history, including all the ideas that he or she has assimilated, there is simply no source whence absolute morality could come.

Charles Darwin was equally forthright: "A man who has no assured and ever-present belief in the existence of a personal God or of a future existence with retribution or reward, can have for his rule of life, as far as I can see, only to follow those impulses and instincts which are the strongest or which seem to him the best ones."

Which of those impulses and instincts do we follow, though? As a moral guide, nature gives decidedly mixed messages. At times animals show admirable behavior: whales and dolphins risking their lives to save injured companions, chimpanzees coming to the aid of the wounded, elephants refusing to abandon slain comrades. Yes, but it all depends on where you point your field binoculars.

Where do you learn about proper behavior between the sexes, for instance? Each fall outside my Colorado home a bull elk bugles together sixty or so cows, bullies them into a herd, and uses his superior rack of antlers to gore all male rivals. Should a human male mimic the elk by forcing himself on a harem of females won through violence? Though elk are conspicuous in their male dominance, in fact nature gives relatively few models of monogamy and even fewer of gender equality. Should our neighborhoods resolve their disputes as do the bonobo chimpanzees, by engaging in a quick orgy in which they all have sex with one another? Should our females, like praying mantises, devour the males who are mating them?

Violence abounds in nature. Zoologists, who once thought murder peculiar to the human species, on closer inspection had to revise their theories. Ground squirrels routinely eat their babies; mallards gang-rape and drown other ducks; the larvae of parasitic wasps consume their paralyzed prey from the inside out; African cichlid fish feed on the eyes of other cichlids. Hyenas get the prize for ruthless cannibalism, for within an hour after birth the stronger of twins will fight its newborn sibling to the death.

Biologist Lyall Watson admits he finds it "disturbing" that hyena cubs seem genetically programmed to attack and kill their siblings on sight. Similarly, researchers who study chimpanzees and gorillas react with dismay when individuals they have grown to love are murdered by others of their species. On what grounds? I wonder. The apes themselves seem undismayed; they are behaving naturally, in response to their genetic script.

Robert Wright draws a parallel between the behavior of urban gangs and that of primates in the wild, who murder and rape their neighbors: "Inner-city violence shouldn't be labeled a 'pathology,'" he writes; "violence is eminently functional — something that people are designed to do." Lyall Watson goes further: though upset by murderous hyenas, he admits that he could not easily condemn human headhunters because their practice keeps certain tribes in ecological balance.

Such notions raise obvious red flags. In response sociobiologists argue, "Don't go from *is* to *ought*." Just because other species are violent, that doesn't mean we ought to do what other species do. How, then, do we decide on the ought? More to the point, where did this whole notion of *ought* come from? When a person does some monstrous deed, we use words like *bestial* and *brutish* to describe it, words that express our innate belief that humans should behave differently.

And often we do behave differently. Spouses resist sexual temptation and stay together. Total strangers will sometimes donate a kidney to save a person's life. We care for patients with terminal illnesses, adopt special-needs children, shelter the homeless, grant benefits to the poor. The Australian philosopher David Strove, an atheist who accepts biological evolution, concedes that its premise of natural selection and survival of the fittest simply doesn't account for all human behavior. By caring for, rather than eliminating, the weak and infirm we forgo a healthier gene pool. "Darwin's dilemma," Strove called the paradox: people supposedly governed by a selfish gene often choose to behave in unselfish ways.

Despite what the evolutionary psychologists may tell us, not everyone acts out of pure selfishness. I mentioned that the philosopher Peter Singer, who wrote the main article on ethics in the *Encyclopædia Britannica*, has suggested that "defective" newborns and some adults no longer qualify as persons and could be euthanized. Yet even he continued to give financial support to his mother after she showed signs of dementia. "I think this has made me see how the issues of someone with these kinds of problems are really very difficult," Singer told one interviewer. "Perhaps it is more difficult than I thought before, because it is different when it's your mother."*

Although polls show that modern Americans continue to behave selflessly, few of them surveyed can articulate a reason why. They act, in Robert Bellah's opinion, from "habits of the heart" rooted primarily in our Christian heritage. Remove those habits of the heart and the true confusion of post-Christian culture comes to light.

PERSONAL CHOICE

We all make moral choices, working out a personal answer to the question "How should we live?" For our main source, Christians accept the moral code revealed in the New Testament, however imperfectly we may understand and follow it. But a postmodern secular culture has no common code, and moral judgments become subjective.

Marilyn vos Savant, listed in *The Guinness Book of World Records* Hall of Fame as having the highest IQ ever measured, answers questions in a weekly "Ask Marilyn" column in *Parade*, a Sunday newspaper insert. Usually she solves mathematical puzzles for readers, but one week a reader asked about a more serious matter: "What do you think is the source of moral authority?" Savant replied, "Most people find the source of moral authority in their religions, but I don't." She looks instead to the lessons of history, which offers an advantage over religion in that it allows us to pick and choose. In essence the source of moral authority for Marilyn

---

* In another interview, though, Singer admitted that his sister — ironically, a lawyer who defends disability rights — shares in the decision to support their mother and that if he were solely responsible, his mother might not be alive today.

vos Savant is herself, and that in a nutshell is the dilemma of post-Christian society.

Nowadays the moral landscape rests on shifting sand. Christina Hoff Sommers tells of a Massachusetts teacher who attempted to teach "values clarification" to her class of sixth-graders. One day her canny students announced that they valued cheating and wanted the freedom to practice it in class. The teacher could only respond that since it was *her* class, she required honesty; they would have to practice their dishonesty in other places. Evidently they do, for surveys show that half of all students cheat. I wonder what restrains the other half.

Feminist thinkers have led the way in challenging sexual norms, with some advocating adultery as a cure for repressed desire. Barbara Ehrenreich suggests, "The only ethic that can work in an overcrowded world is one that insists that ... sex — preferably among affectionate and consenting adults — belongs squarely in the realm of play." But why limit sex to consenting adults? If it's a matter of play, why not sanction pederasty as did the Greeks and Romans? Why choose the age of eighteen as an arbitrary border between child abuse and play? Why the uproar over priests who abuse children? And if sex is mere play, why do we prosecute people for incest?

The author of *Perv: The Sexual Deviant in All of Us*, after examining such practices as rape, pedophilia, and sexual fetishism, concludes with a morally neutral stance: "I see a comfort level growing slowly as the result of rational thought and honest introspection about our hidden tastes. In my opinion, any social change that is the product of careful moral reasoning — grounded in hard-won scientific knowledge and understanding, not 'gut feelings' or religious prescriptions — is moral progress."

James Davison Hunter speculates where a society might be headed once it loses all moral consensus. "Personally I'm into ritual animal sacrifice," says one citizen. "Oh, really," says another. "I happen to be into man-boy relationships." The logical end of such thinking, Hunter suggests, can be found in the Marquis de Sade's novel *Juliette*, which declares, "Nothing is forbidden by nature." In the novel a brute accused of raping, sodomizing, and murdering more than two dozen boys, girls, men, and women, defends himself by saying that all concepts of virtue and vice are arbitrary: "There is no God in this world, neither is there virtue, neither is there justice; there is nothing good, useful, or necessary but our passions."

Lest I sound like a cranky moralist, I should say that to me the real question is not why modern secularists oppose traditional morality; it is on what basis they defend *any* morality. The American legal system vigorously defends a woman's right to choose abortion—but why stop there? Historically, either infanticide or abandonment has been the preferred means of disposing of unwanted children. Romans did it, Greeks did it, and a few centuries ago one-third of babies in Paris were simply abandoned. Yet today if a mother leaves her baby in a Chicago alley, or two teens deposit their newborn in a garbage bin, they face arrest and prosecution.

We feel indignant when we hear news accounts of a middle class couple dumping an Alzheimer's-afflicted parent when they no longer wish to care for him, or when kids push a five-year-old out the window of a high-rise building, or a ten-year-old is raped in a hallway, or a mother drowns her two children because they interfere with her lifestyle. Why? On what grounds, if we truly believe that morality is self-determined? Evidently the people who committed the crimes felt no compunction, just as many of Hitler's SS troops felt no qualms about the extermination ovens.

And if morality is not self-determined, who determines it? As the poet W. H. Auden put it, "If, as I am convinced, the Nazis are wrong and we are right, what is it that validates our values and invalidates theirs?"

A CHRISTIAN RESPONSE

I have painted a bleak, one-sided picture of post-Christian ethics in order to show that the modern West is floundering over a basic sense of right and wrong. As a result we face a continuing moral crisis that spills over into the rule of law. When six renowned moral philosophers argued before the U.S. Supreme Court in favor of assisted suicide, or "the right to die," they contended that people must make their own decisions, "free from the imposition of any religious or philosophical orthodoxy." In deciding issues like marriage, life, and death there is only one acceptable criterion, they said: "Individuals must be allowed to make those decisions for themselves, out of their own faith, conscience, and convictions."

Christian leaders tend to pounce on the new reality. *You see, that's what happens when society loses its Christian roots! We need to return to a time when society looks to us for moral guidance.* They have a point. According to historians Will and Ariel Durant, "There is no significant example in history, before our time, of a society successfully maintaining moral life without the aid of religion." The Durants add a foreboding remark, "The greatest question of our time is ... whether men can live without God."

Amid such confusion, Christians should be positioned to provide the guidance our society needs. With regret I must say frankly that I doubt that will happen. Because of our failure to live out our beliefs, our own lack of moral clarity, and our meddling with partisan politics, Western culture no longer looks to Christianity as its moral source. That reality introduces major problems for lawmakers. And it raises major questions for believers too. How should we relate to, and communicate faith to, those who see the world so differently?

A rearguard attempt to "restore America to its Christian roots" may endanger the very spirit of grace we are called to dispense to a thirsty world. It does little good to shake our heads in dismay and yearn for the Eisenhower days of the 1950s when the U.S. enjoyed more of a Christian consensus (at least on the surface). Rather, we should be asking ourselves, Why do so many people view Christians as bearers of bad news rather than good news that might help the world with these tough issues?

One reason the broader world does not look to Christianity for guidance is that we Christians have not spoken with a credible voice. Churches in my childhood focused on lifestyle issues such as hair- and skirt-lengths, movies, dancing, smoking, and drinking. Meanwhile, conservative churches said little about poverty, racism, war, consumerism, immigration, the treatment of women, and the environment. With some significant exceptions, the church sat on the sidelines of movements that addressed these important causes.

Some further muddle the message of grace by piously casting judgment on society. I heard an all-too-typical example as I was writing this chapter. In the aftermath of historic floods in Colorado that damaged eighteen thousand houses, a Christian radio personality blamed the floods—and also our wildfires the same summer—on legislators who "encourage decadent homosexual activities, vote to kill as many babies as possible, and pass laws approving abominable idolatries such as marijuana." Listening to those words as I watched water creep within inches of flooding my downstairs office, I easily understood how Christians alienate people. I could list scores of such moral pronouncements that foster an "us against the world" mentality rather than "us bringing grace to the world."

Critics of Christianity rightly note that the church has proved an unreliable carrier of moral values. The church has surely made mistakes, as I hope I've made clear. Yet the church also has an inbuilt potential for self-correction because it believes in a higher authority. In recent years Protestant denominations such as the Southern Baptists and South Africa's Dutch Reformed Church repented of their prior support for slavery and apartheid. The Catholic Church admitted the church's errors in opposing science and apologized for wrongs committed against Jews and Muslims. Pope Francis acknowledged that the church's fixation on the social issues of homosexuality, abortion, and contraception has interfered with the main message of God's love for all.

How differently would the world view Christians if we focused on our own failings rather than on society's? As I read the New Testament I am struck by how little attention it gives to the faults of the surrounding culture. Jesus and Paul say nothing about violent gladiator games or infanticide, both common practices among the Romans. In a telling passage, the apostle Paul responds fiercely to a report of incest in the Corinthian church. He urges strong action against those involved but quickly clarifies, "not at all meaning the people of this world. . . . What business is it of mine to judge those outside the church? Are you not to judge those inside? God will judge those outside."

Nowadays, Christians devote enormous energy to judging "those outside the church." To give just one example, many in the millennial generation report that they turned away from the church in part because of its stridency against homosexuals. I heard very little about homosexuality when growing up, though pastors and leaders doubtless knew about it. How did this issue suddenly become the main obsession of prominent Christians?

A friend of mine has documented that the rise in anti-gay rhetoric occurred at precisely the same time that communism fell. Before then, televangelists and Christian lobby groups had raised funds based on fear of the common enemy of godless communism. "Mass movements can rise and spread without belief in a God, but never without belief in a devil," wrote Eric Hoffer in *True Believer*, and my friend theorizes that anti-gay rhetoric surged as a strategy of fundraising, which needed a new enemy. I do not know if that theory is correct, but I do know that singling out one behavior as "sin" and emphasizing it over others provides a convenient way of dodging our own need for grace. High-minded moralism and shrill pronouncements of judgment may help fundraising, but they undermine a gospel of grace.

Opponents sometimes accuse Christians of being "self-righteous." In a discussion on the book of Romans, John Stott reminds us that we are precisely the opposite. The apostle Paul himself confessed, "good itself does not dwell in me ... For I have the desire to do what is good, but I cannot carry it out.... What a wretched man I am!" (He wrote these words after conversion; before then, he took pride in his morality, as "a Pharisee of the Pharisees.") Our only goodness, Stott insists, comes from humble dependence upon God, who alone is righteous. In contrast, non-believers are literally *self*-righteous for they have no moral source to fall back on other than themselves.

In the Sermon on the Mount Jesus raises the ideals so high that none of us can reach them. I have not committed adultery—have I ever lusted? I have not murdered—have I ever hated? Do I love my enemies? Do I give to everyone who asks? What sounds at first like bad news, a moral standard that no one can reach, takes a dramatic shift, for in the same sermon Jesus lowers the safety net of grace. In his ministry Jesus gave vivid proof that no one need fall below the reach of God's grace, not a prostitute, thief, murderer, or traitor. Indeed, Peter the traitor and Paul the human rights abuser, both now forgiven and transformed, proceeded to lead the way in spreading that gospel of grace.

Sadly, Jesus' followers tend to take the reverse approach. Some churches gradually lower the ideals, accommodating moral standards to a changing culture. Others raise the bar of grace so that needy people feel unwelcome: "We don't want that kind of person in our church." Either way we fail to communicate the spectacular good news that everyone fails and yet a gracious God offers forgiveness to all.

LEADING THE WAY

I heard an Australian pastor say that Christians often speak to the broader culture in the same way the prophets addressed Jerusalem, calling it back to a spiritual revival. Actually, he said, we should be thinking of it as more like Athens, a cosmopolitan secular society that views us as a marginal cult. We know how the apostle Paul spoke to Athens in his day, by seeking common ground and awakening a thirst already present in his audience. He used a similar approach with pagan Rome and Corinth, encouraging believers to become a community of contrast that shows the world a better way to live.

I certainly agree that Christians must at times, especially during a period of moral confusion, enter the fray and confront wrong—the subject of the next chapter. Yes, Christians have a role to play in bringing clarity to moral issues, but only if we listen well, live well, and engage well with the rest of society.

I will mention two different models of Christians who engaged well. The first came to the fore more than a century ago. Francis Galton, a cousin of Charles Darwin, sought to apply evolutionary principles to human progress by removing "inferior" or "defective" humans from the gene pool. The resulting eugenics movement got enthusiastic support from scientists, philosophers, and politicians such as Winston Churchill and Theodore Roosevelt.

In the U.S., "Fitter Families" with the desirable traits were exhibited at state fairs next to livestock displays. Southern states passed laws against interracial marriages in an attempt to keep genetic lines "pure," and many states began enforcing the sterilization of criminals, unwed mothers, and the mentally ill. Other countries labeled "degenerate" or "unfit" groups such as the poor, homosexuals, promiscuous women, and those who had hereditary blindness or deafness.

Even the famous Supreme Court justice Oliver Wendell

Holmes Jr. ruled in favor of eugenics. In support of forced sterilization he said, "I see no reason for attributing to man a significance different in kind from that which belongs to a baboon or a grain of sand.... The sacredness of human life is a purely municipal ideal of no validity outside the jurisdiction." Holmes correctly saw the issue as theological at its core. Unless every individual human life—"defective" or not—is sacred, then eugenics represents a positive step in human evolution. Catholic spokesmen, notably the pope and G. K. Chesterton, strongly opposed eugenics, but it flourished into a major industry, supported by academic departments at universities and a series of international conferences.

The eugenics movement fell into disfavor mainly because of Adolf Hitler, who took it to its logical conclusion by systematically exterminating groups he judged undesirable: the Roma (Gypsies), Jews, homosexuals, political opponents, beggars, criminals. Hitler also launched a propaganda campaign to prepare Germans for the medical killing of "unfit children" and the mentally disturbed. At an art theater I watched a Nazi film from the time featuring a politician with budget graphs. It takes a hundred thousand reichsmark to keep one of these defectives alive, he explains; "Fellow Germans, that is your money, too!" Humans should follow the example of nature and allow the weak to die: "The fox catches the weak rabbit, and the hunter shoots the weak deer."

Despite their slick films and propaganda, Nazis failed in their efforts to kill most of the physically and mentally disabled. The turnabout in policy traces back to one brave woman, a Christian nurse who worked at an institution for the mentally ill. When she saw the facility being converted into a gas chamber, she could not keep silent. She carefully documented the facts and reported them to her bishop, who released them to the public. The resulting outcry—from the church—forced the Nazis to back down.

As history has shown, civilized societies are capable of doing all sorts of things out of moral confusion. In a letter to the *New York Times*, novelist Walker Percy wrote that perhaps the most influential book published in German before the start of World War II was *The Justification of the Destruction of Life Devoid of Value*. Percy warned that modern society has some of the same moral blind spots. If right and wrong are determined by opinion polls, he reasoned, "it is not difficult to imagine an electorate or a court ten years, fifty years from now, who would favor getting rid of useless old people, retarded children, antisocial blacks, illegal Hispanics, gypsies, Jews ... Why not?—if that is what is wanted by the majority, the polled opinion, the polity of the time."

We look back with horror on the Nazi campaign to kill the mentally defective. But not long ago a newsletter of Mensa, the organization for people with high IQs, published an article proposing that we eliminate undesirable citizens such as the retarded and the homeless. Modern China mandates abortions for defective fetuses, including those diagnosed with retardation, as well as unauthorized babies beyond the one-child limit. And in some states in the U.S. the incidence of Down syndrome children has dropped by 90 percent; the rest are aborted before birth. My neighbor, who manages group homes for Down syndrome individuals, finds such a policy appalling: "These are wonderful people!" he says. "They live happy, fulfilled lives, and many of them have productive jobs. I can hardly believe a civilized society encourages their elimination."

Americans like to settle moral issues on utilitarian grounds. But Aristotle argued in favor of slavery using such reasoning. In his crusade to abolish slavery William Wilberforce had to oppose utilitarian philosophers like David Hume, who considered blacks inferior, as well as business leaders and politicians who saw slaves as a boon to the economy. Christians allied with Wilberforce made a moral appeal instead, focusing on the slaves' essential worth as human beings created by God.

Christians have an important role to play in contending that no human life is "devoid of value." We can do so through courageous protest, as happened in Germany, as well as in compassionate care for the most vulnerable members of society, as Mother Teresa did. In both approaches theology—what one believes about God and human life—matters. The world desperately needs that good news.

ACCOUNTABILITY AND HOPE

In a very different, more recent example Bishop Desmond Tutu found himself thrust into a moral maelstrom in South Africa. Appointed by Nelson Mandela to lead the Truth and Reconciliation Commission, he daily heard eyewitness testimonies of vicious assaults by both sides in the conflict. As he listened, Tutu realized that his Christian beliefs affected all that he heard and saw.

> Theology reminded me that, however diabolical the act, it did not turn the perpetrator into a demon. We had to distinguish between the deed and the perpetrator, between the sinner and the sin, to hate and condemn the sin while being filled with compassion for the sinner. The point is that, if perpetrators were to be despaired of as monsters and demons, then we were thereby letting accountability go out the window because we were then declaring that they were not moral agents to be held responsible for the deeds they had committed. Much more importantly, it meant that we abandoned all hope of their being able to change for the better. Theology said that they still, despite the awfulness of their deeds, remained children of God with the capacity to repent, to be able to change. Otherwise we should, as a commission, have had to shut up shop ...

What began as a political trial became instead for Tutu an advanced course in theology. The experience convinced him that human beings live in a moral universe and must be held accountable for their acts, "for this universe has been constructed in such a way that unless we live in accordance with its moral laws we will pay the price for it." At the same time, the commission offered a path of hope: those who "repented" by honestly admitting their crimes and apologizing to the victims were set free.

The Truth and Reconciliation Commission affirmed for Tutu that good and evil are real and how we live has lasting consequences. He concluded, "Despite all the evidence that seems to be to the contrary, there is no way that evil and injustice and oppression and lies can have the last word." At the same time, no one is irredeemable: "In this theology, we can never give up on anyone because our God was one who had a particularly soft spot for sinners."

After two years of presiding over the commission, Bishop Tutu came away with his faith strengthened, not shattered. South Africa needed a simultaneous message of accountability and of hope, and his commission provided just that.

Martin Luther King Jr. liked to quote an abolitionist who said that the moral arc of the universe is long, but it bends toward justice. President Barack Obama quoted that same phrase at Nelson Mandela's funeral. Both South Africa and the Southern U.S. have realized the lasting truth of that phrase in my own lifetime.

Individuals and societies are not helpless victims of heredity. We have the power to change — not by looking "down" to nature but "up" to God, who consistently calls us forward to become the people we were designed to be. A confused world urgently needs a model of what that looks like. If Christians fail to provide that model, who will?

PART FOUR

FAITH
AND CULTURE

Standing in the ruins of his native Germany after World War II,
pastor Helmut Thielicke asked, "In the long run can we keep the
Christian West, if we lose this Figure who sustains, animates,
and inspires it? Is it possible to hold on to certain Christian
ideas about humanity, love of one's
neighbor, and faith, if the figure
of Christ himself disappears
and we hold in our hands only
copies of copies instead of the
original?"

CHAPTER 12

UNEASY PARTNERS:
CHRISTIANS AND POLITICS

People say we need religion,
when what they really mean is we need police.

H. L. MENCKEN

In 2012 I toured Croatia and Bosnia-Herzegovina, two of the Balkan countries that split off from the former Yugoslavia in the midst of a brutal war. Religion played a big part in the violence as Catholic, Orthodox, and Muslims squared off against each other. To my surprise, when I arrived my publisher host announced he had arranged a meeting with the president of Croatia, Ivo Josípović.

Bodyguards with shaved heads and walkie-talkie earpieces met us at the gate of the forested grounds and whisked us in black BMWs to the presidential palace. There we waited in an ornate, Versailles-style room overlooking trees resplendent in fall foliage high above the city of Zagreb. A wire-tapping scandal dubbed "Croatian Watergate" was occupying the president that day, and so for an hour we sipped strong coffee and admired the view and artwork on the walls. Finally we were ushered into the president's office, where he greeted us and apologized for the delay.

Before entering politics Josípović had combined a legal career with a serious hobby of composing classical music. During the election campaign he made clear his agnostic religious beliefs, which stirred up opposition from the Catholic hierarchy. Yet during his tenure he had managed to bring together representatives from all the area's religions — Catholic, Protestant, Jewish, Eastern Orthodox, Muslim — to work toward peace. During that process he got a whiff of the antagonism that exists between religion and politics, as well as the potential for cooperation.

My publisher explained the purpose of my visit to Croatia (to release translations of two of my books) and told of our visit to Sarajevo, where Josípović had recently made a plea for peace and unity among religious leaders. As we talked, I mentioned the agnostic German philosopher Jürgen Habermas's remark, "A liberal democracy requires of its citizens qualities that it cannot provide." In a similar vein, Martin Luther King Jr. said that the government can require a white man to serve blacks in his restaurant, and can stop whites from lynching blacks, but no government can force a white person to *love* a black one. That requires a transformation of the heart, the province of religion.

I then mentioned surveys in the U.S. that show a higher rate of volunteerism and charitable giving and a lower rate of crime among those with robust religious commitment. The president smiled and asked mischievously, "Are you saying Christians are better than non-Christians like me?" No, I replied, but they can be some of your best citizens.

A few days later I returned home to the 2012 presidential contest between Barack Obama and Mitt Romney, the most heated campaign in recent history. Republicans were making strong appeals to evangelicals as an essential base (they ultimately got 80 percent of their votes), sometimes by slandering the incumbent president. An evangelical talk show host with a million followers pronounced that Obama "despises the Constitution" and "nurtures a hatred for the white man." His ministry posted a picture of the president's face doctored with a Hitler mustache and superimposed on a background of swastikas.

President Obama kept talking about his Christian faith even as a fifth of the country thought him a Muslim. In a lengthy article the CNN.com religion editor explored how Obama has gradually turned to evangelicals such as Joel Hunter and T. D. Jakes as his spiritual mentors. He begins each morning reading Christian devotionals on his Blackberry and prays with Christian leaders before major events. Yet my inbox contained emails from Christians spelling out Obama's "devout Muslim" faith and secret Marxism: "He is purposely overwhelming the U.S. economy to create systemic failure, economic crisis and social chaos — thereby destroying capitalism and our country from within."

I couldn't help wondering how much of the overwrought opposition from evangelicals had made its way to President Obama's desk.* Is it any wonder that the Democratic Party and mainstream media view Christians with suspicion? Nevertheless, my visit to the Balkans made the fractious disputes in my own

---

* A famous letter sent by James Dobson back in 2008 details events "that are likely or at least very possible" to take place "by 2012" if Barack Obama is elected and far-left Democrats gain control of government, including:

Campus organizations such as Campus Crusade for Christ [now known as Cru], Navigators, and InterVarsity will shrink to skeleton organizations and in many states will cease to exist.

Elementary schools will mandate homosexuality as a choice to children, and the Boy Scouts will no longer exist because of the same issue. Churches that refuse to allow their buildings for same-sex weddings will lose their tax-exempt status.

Christian radio stations will be subject to new regulations on "hate speech" like those in Sweden, and conservative talk radio will be virtually shut down. Evangelical publishers will be banned from Amazon.com and Barnes & Noble.

Because of severe restrictions on home schooling, dedicated parents will emigrate to places like Australia and New Zealand.

Four US cities will have been bombed by terrorists, with Obama doing little in response.

Taking advantage of Obama's weakness, Russia will retake much of Eastern Europe.

Tel Aviv will be destroyed when Iran launches a nuclear attack against Israel.

Due to health care rationing, people older than eighty will have essentially no access to hospitals or surgical procedures. Euthanasia [will become] more and more common.

country seem like a family quarrel. At least we weren't massacring each other!

With thoughts of Croatia and the U.S. election in mind, I turned again to some of the questions about faith and politics that have long interested me. I care about such questions in part because so many nonbelievers judge faith by politics, singling out evangelicals as just another shrill lobbying group. The media often use "right-wing" as an adjective inseparably connected with evangelicals. James Davison Hunter says, "It is possible to argue that at the same time the Christian Right acquired and exercised its greatest power—culminating in the 2004 presidential election—this movement also generated greater hostility toward the Christian faith than ever before in the nation's history." Hunter adds that evangelicals on the left follow a parallel course of political involvement, looking to government to enact the policies they hold dear.

How should Christians engage in a democracy that includes a diversity of beliefs and that grows increasingly post-Christian? And how do we live out convictions in a way that still conveys grace?

CHRIST AND CULTURE

Jesus himself showed little concern for secular politics, calling Herod "that fox," stonewalling Pontius Pilate with his lack of self-defense, and leaving us with the enigmatic rule, "Give back to Caesar what is Caesar's and to God what is God's." The apostle Paul, in contrast, used the full privilege of Roman citizenship. He confronted culture with the new message of Jesus while simultaneously showing respect for political authority. He testified before imperial officials and at times relied on the Roman military to protect him from his religious enemies. When arrested, he appealed his case up the ladder of the Roman justice system, where he got a final hearing with a tragic end.

In short, the New Testament presents government as necessary, even ordained by God, but certainly no sponsor or friend to faith. Jesus, Paul, and most of the twelve disciples died as martyrs, after all, and the early Christians faced periodic waves of persecution from Roman emperors.

Two centuries later Christians viewed with thanksgiving and relief the conversion of the emperor Constantine, who granted Christianity protected status. Soon it became the official state religion. Over the next millennium in Europe, church and state interplayed like dancing partners, sometimes locked in tight embrace and sometimes flinging each other across the ballroom floor. The global spread of Christianity introduced new church/state variations in places like Africa and the Americas.

During the Eisenhower era of the 1950s, about the time "In God We Trust" was added to U.S. coins, theologian H. Richard Niebuhr published a book that became a classic. *Christ and Culture* describes five different approaches to how religion and government, or church and state, might relate to each other.

Niebuhr called one approach "Christ *above* culture," referring to times when the church wielded the real power. Europe's Holy Roman Empire perfected this model: royalty kneeled before the pope, not vice versa. At the other end of the spectrum, Anabaptists and other splinter groups separated themselves from the surrounding culture; "Christ *against* culture," Niebuhr labeled their approach. The dissenters' refusal to take oaths, to doff their caps to authorities, and to serve in the army and on juries infuriated their governments, and as a result European countries cruelly persecuted them. North America served as a haven for many of these groups, including Quakers, Amish, Mennonites, and Hutterites.

John Calvin's model, adopted by Puritans in America, calls for Christ to *transform* culture, bringing society in line with Christian values as far as possible. Around the same time, Lutherans developed a doctrine of Christ *in paradox with* culture. On earth we are subject to two kingdoms, said Martin Luther: the kingdom of God and the kingdom of the world. (Of course, sometimes the government may ask Christians to do what goes against their convictions, bringing the two kingdoms into conflict: in Luther's homeland many of Hitler's soldiers used the excuse, "We were obeying the secular kingdom.")

Finally, a fifth group identifies Christ *with* culture. This approach may take many forms, such as the ethnic groups (like Orthodox Serbs and Catholic Croats) who blend religion and culture. Niebuhr used the Social Gospel movement as an American example: as they work to reform society, these folks tend to absorb the culture around them, and in time the distinctives of their faith may disappear.

Reading Niebuhr's book in my college days left me feeling enlightened but as confused as ever. All five approaches seemed to have something to contribute, and in fact I could point to biblical examples of each one, especially in the Old Testament. Kings such as David and Solomon virtually combined church and state. Prophets often denounced the surrounding culture — yet even as the prophet Elijah was violently opposing Ahab's regime, a "devout believer in the Lord" named Obadiah ran Ahab's palace while sheltering God's true prophets on the side. Amos and Hosea thundered against the state; Isaiah acted as a kind of court prophet. Daniel held high office in two different pagan governments and Nehemiah led a detachment of Persian cavalry.

Theologian John Howard Yoder pointed out that Christians will never wholeheartedly embrace or reject culture, but rather we must discriminate among its various parts. We will categorically reject some elements (pornography, tyranny, human trafficking), accept others within limits (commerce, transportation, taxes), and provide a new motivation to others (family life, education, peacemaking). We will use some aspects of culture (music, art, language), albeit in our own way, and we will heartily promote certain activities (hospices, care for orphans, homeless shelters, soup kitchens).

Is there one best way for Christians to relate to politics and culture, especially in a democracy where we have a rightful voice? Should we withdraw into a counterculture and devote our energies to the kingdom of God, or should we actively work to transform society? And if we choose the second path, can we do so in a way that does not drown out our core message of love and grace? As Lesslie Newbigin posed the question, "Can one who goes the way of the Cross sit in the seat of Pilate when it falls vacant?"

I am writing in the wake of an election year when candidates eagerly courted the evangelical vote. With all the God-talk in politics today, younger voters may be surprised to learn that evangelicals' love affair with politics is a recent phenomenon. During my childhood, conservative churches did little "meddling" in politics, emphasizing instead personal behavior and preparation for the next life. In Niebuhr's term we were mostly Christ-*against*-culture, and only in the 1980s did anyone start talking about a Moral *Majority*.

In the next decades a clear pattern emerged, as many polls attest: the more vocal Christians became in the political arena, the more negatively they were viewed. Not long ago a huge majority of the uncommitted still viewed Christians favorably. Now, as I have mentioned, a diminishing minority of young "outsiders" have a favorable impression of Christianity and only 3 percent have a good impression of evangelicals. Have Christians obscured the good news by their efforts to restore morality to the broader culture?

The state has one overriding concern, that of controlling bad behavior: how to keep citizens from killing each other, breaking into houses, cheating customers at the market, and yielding to a sexual license that would undermine families. The modern world faces a dilemma. On important issues, such as those discussed in the last chapter, society badly needs moral guidance. Religion seems an obvious resource, yet one rejected by much of secular society. Already the media treat opinion polls as the primary arbiter of such matters as sexual behavior, abortion, the death penalty, and assisted suicide.

In nations with a religious consensus, church and state can work hand in hand to encourage moral values they both agree on. For example, in more religious times the British king issued a proclamation for the "Encouragement of Piety and Virtue, and for the Preventing and Punishing of Vice, Profaneness, and Immorality." The world has changed, however. Diverse societies now contain many different religions — Yugoslavia ruptured into seven countries over its inability to deal with this very predicament.

President Obama irked some Christians when, on a visit to Turkey, he said that although the United States has a large Christian population, "we do not consider ourselves a Christian nation or a Jewish nation or a Muslim nation; we consider ourselves a nation of citizens who are bound by ideals and a set of values." Fair enough, but if Christians comprise a majority, as they do in the U.S., shouldn't they have a strong influence in determining those ideals and values?

FIVE SUGGESTIONS

The shift in American society from admiring Christians to fearing and criticizing them provides an opportunity for self-reflection. How *have* we been presenting the message we believe in? Might there be a more grace-filled way?

Some want to focus on personal morality and leave public morality to secular politicians. Others seek ways to guide the broader culture while still communicating grace. Rather than propose a single path, I will instead make a series of observations and suggestions for Christians to consider as we interact with a world that does not always share our views.

1. Clashes between Christ and culture are unavoidable

John Howard Yoder recounted fifty-one separate times in which Jesus himself confronted injustices, and throughout history Jesus' followers have followed suit. Early Christians were instrumental in ending the Roman practices of gladiatorial games and infanticide, and in the years since Christians have led moral campaigns against abuses such as slavery and sexual trafficking. Even separatist groups must engage with culture—the Anabaptists' pacifism, for instance, stands as a powerful moral statement.

Christians must always discern which injustices merit a fight, but complete withdrawal is bad for both church and state. Nazi Germany posed the severest test to Luther's doctrine of two kingdoms, a test the church mostly failed. Practicing a personal faith, with no real tradition of opposing the state, German church leaders waited far too late to protest. Indeed, many Protestant leaders initially welcomed the Nazis as an alternative to communism and some adopted a motto that now seems obscene: "The Swastika on our breasts, the Cross in our hearts."*

Eventually some Christians did wake up to the threat. Martin Niemöller published a series of sermons with the in-your-face title *Christus ist mein Führer* ("Christ [not Hitler] is my Führer"). Niemöller spent seven years in a concentration camp; Dietrich Bonhoeffer was executed in another. In the end, faithful Christians were one of the few groups within Germany to oppose Hitler. Trade unions, parliament, politicians, doctors, scientists, university professors, lawyers—all these capitulated. A small but determined minority of Christians who understood their loyalty to a higher power resisted, and their courageous stand attracted the world's attention: from 1933 to 1937 the *New York Times* ran nearly a thousand news accounts on the German church struggle.

After World War II the eastern part of Germany found itself under a different kind of totalitarian rule, the onset of four decades

---

* Jürgen Moltmann, who served in Hitler's army as a teenager, reflects, "But what we got to hear from the ruling politicians at that time was that a suspension of the Sermon on the Mount was necessary out of political responsibility—an echo of Bismarck's brusque statement that 'no country can be governed with the Sermon on the Mount.' But anyone who excludes the precepts of the Sermon on the Mount from certain parts of his life also loses the assurance of its Beatitudes."

of Soviet domination. A few years ago I interviewed a pastor in Saxony who recalled the difficulties that Christians faced under Communism. In those days his children had limited educational opportunities, and he had to work as a plumber to supplement his meager pastor's salary. When the Berlin Wall came down everything changed. Although less than 20 percent of Saxony's citizens now belong to a church, he estimates that 70 percent of those in parliament are active, practicing Christians. Having lived under Nazism and then Communism, Christians quickly stepped into a cultural vacuum to help the newly free society lay a foundation for morality and law. They knew all too well what can happen when Christians are excluded from the public square.

As the pastor learned, working within a democracy presents a different kind of challenge. It involves tiresome work and tricky compromises. Stephen Monsma, a Christian who served in the Michigan state legislature, has written of the painstaking struggles to get drunk-driving legislation—an issue that invites a clear moral consensus—passed in his state. He likens his original vision of doing good to sitting by a cozy fire in his living room choosing luscious vegetables and beautiful flowers from a seed catalog; the actual work, he said, more resembles the gardener's chores of digging furrows, pulling weeds, and battling insects.

There are a variety of ways to engage with culture. Some Christians express their pro-life beliefs by picketing; others volunteer at hospices and pregnancy counseling centers; still others work with Mothers Against Drunk Driving or campaign against the death penalty. Some debate ethical issues within the academy while others take up the tedious work of writing laws.

Democracy always requires bargaining and compromise. While he was Surgeon General, C. Everett Koop attracted the ire of fellow conservatives who had an all-or-nothing approach to morality and resisted any compromise on abortion. Koop, who shared their iron-clad belief that all abortion is wrong, came to conclude, "One of the problems with the pro-life movement is that they are 100-percenters. Historically it is true that if the pro-life movement had sat down in, say, 1970 or 1972 with the pro-choice people, we might have ended up with an agreement on abortion for the life of the mother, defective child, rape and incest, and nothing more. That would have saved ninety-seven percent of the abortions since then." Only after losing the absolute battle did the pro-life movement change tactics to restrict rather than abolish abortion; since then hundreds of such laws have passed in state legislatures.

Modern democracy, which grew out of Christian soil, compels us to recognize others' rights even when we deeply disagree with their positions. We seek to persuade but not to coerce. More, the gospel commands me to love my enemy as well as my neighbor. Christians may work within institutions, but always wary of their limitations and always conscious of our primary charge to love. Institutions cannot really express love; justice is as close as they come.

2. Christians should choose their battles wisely

The sociologist Peter Berger has written of the "world maintaining" and "world shaking" functions of religion. Founders of the United States recognized that a democracy, with less top-down control and more freedom, needs a religious foundation to guide and motivate its citizens. In John Adams' words, "Our constitution was made only for a moral and religious people. It is wholly inadequate to the government of any other." The nation's leaders counted on the church for this world-maintaining role, to teach and equip citizens to act responsibly.

When the church moves into the world-shaking business, however, it must do so wisely and with care. Alas, Christians involved in politics have tended to go off on tangents. In the 1840s and 1850s the aptly named "Know-Nothing movement" demonized

Catholics and raised hysterical fears about them. Historian Mark Noll has written about a fracas in 1844 that was sparked when a Catholic bishop requested that Catholic schools be allowed to read from their own version of the Bible rather than the King James Version; rioters in Philadelphia burned several Catholic churches and killed more than a dozen people. As late as 1960 the National Association of Evangelicals urged all evangelical clergy to proclaim the dangers of a Catholic president on Reformation Day, just before the election of John F. Kennedy.

The church's landmark moral campaign was Prohibition, which absorbed more sheer energy from Protestant Christians than any other political effort. The leaders understood well how democracy works and how to attain a public consensus. Its advocates persuaded the general public that alcohol had dire costs in terms of health, life expectancy, poverty, family breakdown, inefficient workers, and social decay. Prohibition legislation succeeded because of relentless education and skillful lobbying. Early feminists joined the cause, broadening its base. A Prohibition party actually ran candidates for president, and in two decades the United States went from having five dry states to passing a constitutional amendment for the entire nation; only two states failed to ratify the amendment.

For five years the nation mostly complied. Then drinking began to increase, accompanied by organized crime and corruption. The legislation was too severe, and it alienated other religious groups such as Jews and Catholics who saw no problem with moderate drinking. In the final analysis, judges historian Paul Johnson, "what looked at first like the greatest victory for American evangelicalism turned instead into its greatest defeat." The failure of this moral crusade drove Protestants out of the political arena, and not until the late twentieth century would they return in large numbers.

The more Christians focus on tangential issues, the less we

will be heard on matters of true moral significance. I hear very little from evangelicals about the impact of gun proliferation on violent crime, much less an issue like nuclear disarmament. I hear almost nothing about healthcare for the poor and protecting widows and orphans, all biblical mandates. Only recently have evangelicals taken up the cause of creation care. Evangelicals trumpet family values, but when an administration proposed legislation to allow mothers to take *unpaid* leave after childbirth, conservative religious groups opposed it.

Too often the agenda of religious groups matches line for line that of conservative—or liberal—politics and not the priorities of the Bible.

3. Christians should fight their battles shrewdly

Once again evangelicals do not have the best track record. On one occasion an engineer working for the Christian Broadcasting Network used satellite-transmission equipment to interrupt the Playboy Channel during its broadcast of *American Ecstasy* with this message: "Thus sayeth the Lord thy God. Remember the Sabbath and keep it holy. Repent, the kingdom of God is at hand!" (He was later indicted by a federal grand jury.) His boss, Pat Robertson, has made several outlandish statements over the years, including a famous description of feminism as "the socialist, anti-family political movement that encourages women to leave their husbands, kill their children, practice witchcraft, destroy capitalism and become lesbians."

To gain the hearing of a post-Christian society already skeptical about religion will require careful strategy. We must, in Jesus' words, be wise as serpents and harmless as doves. I fear that our clumsy pronouncements, our name-calling, our stridency—in short, our lack of grace—has proved so damaging that society will no longer look to us for the guidance it needs. Such tactics, let alone comments about hurricanes and terrorism as acts of

God's judgment,* undermine the credibility of Christians engaging culture.

In one commendably shrewd tactic, Protestant Christians have formed alliances with Catholics, Jews, and Muslims on some issues. All these groups share a belief in one God who has revealed moral principles we ought to live by, and in engaging culture each group has something to contribute. The self-described fundamentalist Tim LaHaye agrees that "we have more in common with each other than we ever will with the secularizers of this country." It has become common to see Orthodox rabbis, Catholic priests, and evangelical pastors linking arms in protests outside abortion clinics.

Fifty evangelicals and Roman Catholics met with fifty Jews to identify areas of mutual concern: adoption reform, divorce reform, opposition to gratuitous sex and violence, character education in the schools. And Jewish rabbis have raised some of the loudest alarms about the dangers of a purely secular society. Rabbi Joshua Haberman wrote a much discussed article in *Policy Review* in which he, a survivor of Hitler's Germany, said,

> As a Jew, I differ with a variety of Bible-believing Christians on theology, our nation's social agenda, and matters of public policy. I am, at times, repelled by fits of fanaticism and narrow-minded, rigid dogmatism among fundamentalist extremists. Yet far greater than these differences and objections is the common moral and spiritual frame of reference I share with Christians, including fundamen-

---

* An evangelical Republican Senator, James Inhofe, suggested on the Senate floor that 9/11 was divine punishment for America's inadequate support for Israel; later he described global warming as "the second-largest hoax ever perpetrated on the American people, after the separation of church and state" and the Environmental Protection Agency as a "Gestapo bureaucracy." Other prominent evangelicals linked the 2012 Newtown, Connecticut, school shooting in which twenty children died to the policy of "removing God from the public schools."

talists. The Bible gave our nation its moral vision. And today, America's Bible Belt is our safety belt, the enduring guarantee of our fundamental rights and freedoms.

A friend of mine in England stirred up a hornet's nest among residents when he hired a chaplain for a character-based charter school; Muslims and Hindus rose to his defense, even though the chaplain was a Christian. These religious leaders are willing to set aside their differences in common cause because they sense a desperate need for a shared moral vision.

4. In engaging with culture, Christians should distinguish the *immoral* from the *illegal*

President Bill Clinton tried to make that distinction. As a Christian, he said, he sought guidance on moral issues from the Bible. As president of the United States, though, he could not automatically propose that everything immoral should therefore be made illegal. A well-known national columnist seized on his comment and devoted an entire column to attacking Clinton's "situational ethics and false religiosity."

But President Clinton was surely right. "Thou shalt not covet" is a moral issue that ranks as one of the Ten Commandments. What municipality or national government could enforce a law against coveting? Pride is a sin, even the root of sin, but can we make pride illegal? Jesus summed up the Old Testament law in the command, "Love the LORD your God with all your heart and with all your soul and with all your strength and with all your mind" — what human authority could police such a commandment?

Although Christians have an obligation to obey God's commands, it does not necessarily follow that we should enact those moral commands into law. Not even John Calvin's Geneva would dare turn the Sermon on the Mount into a legal code. The late Kurt Vonnegut, a satirical American author, wrote: "For some reason, the most vocal Christians among us never mention the beatitudes. But—often with tears in their eyes—they demand that the Ten Commandments be posted in public buildings. And of course that's Moses, not Jesus. I haven't heard one of them demand that the Sermon on the Mount, the beatitudes, be posted anywhere."

An Alabama Supreme Court chief justice made headlines in 2001 when he defied authority by installing a 5,280-pound granite monument of the Ten Commandments in his courthouse. The Ten Commandments are a bedrock on which laws should be based, he explained. As a Christian I too accept the Ten Commandments as a God-given rule for life, especially since Jesus reaffirmed them. But as I stared at a news photo of the judge standing beside his monument, it struck me that only two of the ten ("You shall not murder" and "You shall not steal") have been enacted into law. The other eight, regardless how important, no pluralistic society can codify into law.

Christians are currently debating the pros and cons of gay rights—a moral issue, as both sides would agree. A few decades ago the Church of England debated an issue with close parallels: divorce. The Bible has far more to say about the sanctity of marriage and the wrongness of divorce than it says about homosexuality. C. S. Lewis shocked many people in his day when he came out in favor of allowing divorce, on the grounds that we Christians have no right to impose our morality on society at large. Although he continued to oppose divorce on moral grounds, he maintained the distinction between morality and legality.

5. The church must use caution in its dealings with the state

Historian Edward Gibbon said that in ancient Rome all religions were to the people equally true, to the philosophers equally false, and to the government equally useful. Society needs the restraint offered by religion, and the state welcomes it—as long as it can call the shots.

The Christians who supported Hitler were startled to learn one day that the German government would now appoint church officials. Soon all pastors were required to take a loyalty oath to Hitler and his government. In Russia, Stalin compelled the church to grant the Party full control over religious instruction, seminary education, and the appointment of bishops. In China today the Communist government pays the salaries of official Three-Self pastors, a way of keeping them under its thumb, and appoints "illicit" Catholic bishops who do not have Vatican approval.

The church works best as a separate force, a conscience to society that keeps itself at arm's length from the state. The closer it gets, the less effectively it can challenge the surrounding culture and the more perilously it risks losing its central message. Jesus left his followers the command to make disciples from all nations. We have no charge to "Christianize" the United States or any other country—an impossible goal in any case.

When the church accepts as its main goal the reform of the broader culture, we risk obscuring the gospel of grace and becoming one more power broker. That is how many in the secular world view us now, as a right-wing conspiracy intent on passing laws against them. In the process, they miss the good news of the gospel, that Christ died to save *sinners*, to free us from guilt and shame so that we can thrive in the way God intended.

The state will often try to use religion for its own purposes, but when it does so, the gospel itself changes. Civil religion invites us to share in a nation's military glory; the gospel calls us to take up a cross. Civil religion offers prestige and influence; the gospel calls us to serve. Civil religion rewards success; the gospel redefines success and forgives failure. Civil religion values reputation; the gospel calls us to be "fools for Christ."

During the Brezhnev era at the height of the Cold War, Billy

Graham visited Russia and met with government and church leaders. Conservatives in the West harshly criticized him for treating the Russians with such courtesy and respect. He should have taken on a more prophetic role, they said, by speaking out against the abuses of human rights and religious liberty. One of his critics said, "Dr. Graham, you have set the church back fifty years!" Graham lowered his head and replied, "I am deeply ashamed. I have been trying very hard to set the church back 2000 years."

CHAPTER 13

HOLY SUBVERSION

Every self-respecting writer of any significance
is a saboteur and as he surveys the horizon wondering
what to write about, more often than not he
will choose some forbidden topic.

ANDREI SINYAVSKY (RUSSIAN DISSIDENT)

Shortly before his death novelist Graham Greene grew disillusioned to the point of despair. He had lived a long, dissolute life, all the while conducting a love-hate affair with the Catholic Church. God-haunted, he contemplated a modern world in danger of losing its soul, a prospect that seemed to him bleakest of all. In that somber mood he wrote one of his final short stories, "The Last Word," set in the future when a world government has exterminated all Christians except one, Pope John XXIX.

The pope, a pathetic old pensioner, has few reminders of his former life apart from a wooden crucifix with a broken arm, which he has somehow kept hidden from authorities. One day he receives a summons to report to the general who rules over the United World. A uniformed officer helps him dress in a white papal surplice, a historical relic borrowed from the World Museum of Myths. Thus costumed, he is ushered into the presence of the general.

"The last Christian. This is a moment of history," says the general, placing a gun on the table between them.

"Do you intend to kill me?" asks the pope.

"Yes."

It was relief the old man felt, not fear. He said, "You will be sending me where I've often wanted to go during the last twenty years."

"Into darkness?"

"Oh, the darkness I have known was not death. Just an absence of light. You are sending me into the light. I am grateful to you."

... The General poured out two glasses. His hand shook a little as he drained his glass. The old man raised his as though in salute. He said in a low voice some words which the General could not properly catch, in a language which he did not understand. "Corpus domini nostri ..." As his last Christian enemy drank, he fired.

The story ends with this sentence: "Between the pressure on the trigger and the bullet exploding a strange and frightening doubt crossed his mind: is it possible that what this man believed may be true?"

MUTUAL FEAR

I return to where I began, the great divide between Christians and a society that seems increasingly post-Christian. Fear abounds on both sides. The secular world sees Christians as a threat, a breed of morals police intent on reforming society by their own rules and punishing those who object. On the other side, Christians see themselves as a harassed minority holding out against forces hostile to religion—the nightmare vision of Graham Greene's short story.

The distinguished philosopher Alasdair MacIntyre weighs the

conflicts in recent times and doubts whether we will ever achieve consensus on key moral questions. Our differences on issues such as euthanasia, abortion, war, and social justice have a kind of "interminable character," writes MacIntyre in *After Virtue*. In the current climate "modern politics is civil war carried out by other means." His book ends on an ominous note:

> What matters at this stage is the construction of local forms of community within which civility and the intellectual and moral life can be sustained through the new dark ages which are already upon us.... This time however the barbarians are not waiting beyond the frontiers; they have already been governing us for some time.

His image calls to mind much of church history: early Christians huddling together as barbarians batter the gates of Rome, Benedictine monks burying parchment manuscripts while darkness descends around them, Russian and Chinese believers worshiping in secret as the Red Army or Red Guards prowl outside. Rightly or wrongly, some Christians feel a similar sense of siege in modern times.

The anxieties of both sides, secular and Christian, have some basis, though I do not share the extreme pessimism of Alasdair MacIntyre. I am concerned, however, about how we respond to others in an adversarial environment. I care about vanishing grace, the erosion of a gospel that, for many, sounds less and less like good news.

From my reading of the New Testament, two responses strike me as out of bounds. First, we dare not withdraw and hunker down in a defensive posture, raising a drawbridge against "the barbarians." According to Jesus, a hostile reception by the world should neither surprise nor deter us. "Go! I am sending you out like lambs among wolves," he warned one group of followers—

sending you out, not *hiding you away in the safety of the barn.* To complicate matters, he commanded us to love our enemies, the wolves themselves. As the Book of Acts makes clear, the first Christians did not shrink in the face of violent opposition but boldly proclaimed the good news that the world needs to hear.

Second, we dare not fulfill the fears of the secular world by resorting to power. When Christians use such phrases as "getting our country back," "restoring morality," and "making America Christian again," it brings up stereotypes of the Inquisition and the Crusades—or perhaps the sort of religious theocracy being pursued by Islamic extremists today.

Several years ago a Muslim man said to me, "I have read the entire Koran and can find in it no guidance on how Muslims should live as a minority in a society. I have read the entire New Testament and can find in it no guidance on how Christians should live as a majority." He pointed out that Islam seeks to unify religion and law, culture and politics. The courts enforce religious (sharia) law, and in a nation like Iran the mullahs, not the politicians, hold the real power.

The United States and its allies fought a long and costly war in Afghanistan in part to free Afghans from the tyranny of Taliban fanatics, who forbade the education of girls, banned all music, and held weekly public exhibitions in a soccer stadium in which they chopped off the hands of thieves and stoned adulterers. In some Islamic countries the morals police publicly beat women who drive a car or who dare to ride in a taxi unaccompanied by their husbands. Such examples make secularists wary of any religion gaining power.

In contrast, as the Muslim man reminded me, Christians best thrive as a minority, a counterculture. Historically, when they reach a majority they too have yielded to the temptations of power in ways that are clearly anti-gospel. Charlemagne ordered a death penalty for all Saxons who would not convert, and in 1492 Spain decreed that all Jews convert to Christianity or be expelled. British Protestants in Ireland once imposed a stiff fine on anyone who did not attend church and deputies forcibly dragged Catholics into Protestant churches. Priests in the American West sometimes chained Indians to church pews to enforce church attendance.

After many such episodes in Christendom it became clear that religion allied too closely to the state leads to the abuse of power. Much of the current hostility against Christians evokes the memory of such examples. The blending of church and state may work for a time but it inevitably provokes a backlash, such as that seen in secular Europe today.

Over time Christians learned that the faith grows best from the bottom up rather than being imposed from the top down. Viewing the United States from the perspective of Europe and its long history of church-state blending, the British historian Paul Johnson identifies this as one of our finest contributions: "The assumption of the voluntary principle, the central tenet of American Christianity, was that the personal religious convictions of individuals, freely gathered in churches and acting in voluntary associations, would gradually and necessarily permeate society by persuasion and example."

Today, Christians and Muslims face opposite challenges. We in the West have something to learn from cultures that do not push faith to the margins. Meanwhile, Islamic nations have something to learn from the Christian West, which has settled on liberal democracy as the best way to protect minorities' rights in a multicultural world. Not to learn those lessons leads to disaster, as is playing out in the "clash of civilizations" right now.

The very things we disapprove of in Islam, some Christians still find tempting; they too seek political power and a legal code that reflects revealed morality. Will Christians in the U.S. and elsewhere turn once again toward a coercive style that forces its will on the rest of society? Doing so would betray our founder, who resisted a temptation to authority over "all the kingdoms of the world," and who died a martyr at the hands of a powerful state. In the words of Miroslav Volf, "Imposition stands starkly at odds with the basic character of the Christian faith, which is at its heart about self-giving—God's self-giving and human self-giving—and not about self-imposing."

Self-giving always involves risk. Yet that is a risk God took in granting humans freedom in the first place. A respect for freedom has led to the very term *post-Christian* as people in some places choose to opt out of the faith. (Notably, there are no "post-Muslim" societies except in regions where Islam was evicted by force.) Whoever desires to remain faithful to Jesus must communicate faith as he did, not by compelling assent but by presenting it as a true answer to basic thirst.

Rather than looking back nostalgically on a time when Christians wielded more power, I suggest another approach: that we regard ourselves as subversives operating within the broader culture. At times Jesus acted in overtly subversive ways: against a corrupt religious establishment by forcibly cleansing the temple, and against an oppressive government by breaking out of a guarded tomb.

I will revisit how this might work for us today within the three categories already suggested: pilgrim, activist, and artist.

PILGRIM

Graham Greene later commented on his short story that in the split second of hesitation before the firing of the gun lies hope for the world. In a real-life event with haunting parallels to "The Last Word," one of the Columbine High School killers pointed a gun at his terrified victim and asked, "Do you believe in God?" She said yes.* That instant of courage inspired millions of teenagers

---

* Originally attributed to Cassie Bernall, the subject of the bestselling book *She Said Yes*, it later came out that the exchange may have taken place between the shooter Dylan Klebold and Valerie Schnurr, who had already been hit with thirty-four shotgun pellets.

and captured the attention of a society dazed by such deeds of evil. Perhaps her brave answer even caused a split second of hesitation in the gunman. It was a dangerous act of subversion that made a sharp contrast to the calculated nihilism of the killers.

As the year 2013 came to a close, Malcolm Gladwell, a staff writer for the *New Yorker* and author of such bestsellers as *Blink*, *The Tipping Point*, and *Outliers*, spoke out publicly about his own rediscovery of faith. He credits a visit with a Mennonite couple in Winnipeg, Canada, who lost their daughter to a sexual predator. After the largest manhunt in the city's history, police officers found the teenager's body in a shed, frozen, her hands and feet bound. At a news conference just after her funeral the father said, "We would like to know who the person or persons are so we could share, hopefully, a love that seems to be missing in these people's lives." The mother added, "I can't say at this point I forgive this person," stressing the phrase *at this point*. "We have all done something dreadful in our lives, or have felt the urge to."

The response of this couple, so different from a normal response of rage and revenge, pulled Gladwell back toward his own Mennonite roots. As he says, "Something happened to me when I sat in Wilma Derksen's garden. It is one thing to read in a history book about people empowered by their faith. But it is quite another to meet an otherwise very ordinary person, in the backyard of a very ordinary house, who has managed to do something utterly extraordinary. Their daughter was murdered. And the first thing the Derksens did was to stand up at the press conference and talk about the path to forgiveness." He adds, "Maybe we have difficulty seeing the weapons of the spirit because we don't know where to look, or because we are distracted by the louder claims of material advantage. But I've seen them now, and I will never be the same."

Our confused society badly needs a community of contrast, a

counterculture of ordinary pilgrims who insist on living a different way. We can make the world stop and think before pulling a trigger or exacting revenge or neglecting the vulnerable or euthanizing those it deems "devoid of value." Unlike popular culture, we will lavish attention on the least "deserving," in direct opposition to our celebrity culture's emphasis on success, wealth, and beauty. "The world looks with some awe upon a person who appears unconcernedly indifferent to home, money, comfort, rank, or even power and fame," said Winston Churchill. "The world feels not without a certain apprehension, that here is someone outside its jurisdiction; someone before whom its allurements may be spread in vain ..." Here is a true subversive.

By acting against society's norms, Christians will sometimes seem like troublemakers. We are "foreigners and exiles" in the world, according to 1 Peter, called to subvert whatever dishonors God or God's image bearers. Though we will not sweep all evil from the world, we can at least present a shining alternative.

I keep turning back to Karl Barth's summary of the church's mission: "To set up in the world a new sign which is radically dissimilar to [the world's] own manner and which contradicts it in a way which is full of promise." No idealist (he saw firsthand the German church's tepid response to Hitler), Barth added a qualifier to his description of the church: "That fellowship that goes through history in obedience and in disobedience, in understanding and in misunderstanding of the lofty good God has given us." We must always remember that we bear the news of that lofty good as humble pilgrims, not as haughty power brokers.

Somehow Christians have gotten the reputation as being morally superior when in fact we turn to God only when we have recognized our moral *inferiority*. As the recovery movement teaches, naked honesty and helplessness are what drive us to God. The truth, about ourselves and about our need for outside help, sets us free. We don't need to pretend that things are fine or that goodness comes easily. We admit we are needy and look to God for both vision and strength to subvert the world.

In his introduction to the book of James, Eugene Peterson explains this unsettling truth:

> When Christian believers gather in churches, everything that can go wrong sooner or later does. Outsiders, on observing this, conclude that there is nothing to the religion business except, perhaps, business—and dishonest business at that. Insiders see it differently. Just as a hospital collects the sick under one roof and labels them as such, the church collects sinners. Many of the people outside the hospital are every bit as sick as the ones inside, but their illnesses are either undiagnosed or disguised. It's similar with sinners outside the church.
>
> So Christian churches are not, as a rule, model communities of good behavior. They are, rather, places where human misbehavior is brought out in the open, faced and dealt with.

Herein is grace: "While we were still sinners, Christ died for us." Christians are simply pilgrims who acknowledge their lostness and their desire for help in finding the way. Or, in Peterson's analogy, we are sick patients who have found a remedy and want to introduce it to others.

ACTIVIST

A few years ago on a trip to London I visited the newly opened George Friedrich Handel Museum, situated in the composer's three-hundred-year-old home—which incongruously also houses a museum dedicated to Jimi Hendrix. I knew of Handel's charitable bent, for his *Messiah* debuted in Ireland as a fundraiser for hospitals and prison work. The museum told about the immigrant musician's support of another charity, London's Foundling Hospital.

In the eighteenth century, parents of unwanted children simply abandoned them, and so each morning horse carts would collect the bodies of street children who had frozen or died of disease or malnutrition. Touched by their plight, a sea captain gave the seed money for a combination orphanage/school/hospital, and when Handel learned of this facility in his neighborhood he offered to organize a benefit concert. It proved so successful that he staged a performance of *Messiah* annually until his death, providing a vital source of income for the charity. In addition, Handel donated a pipe organ, composed the Foundling Hospital Anthem, "Blessed Are They that Considereth the Poor," and joined the board of governors. At his death he willed the orphanage an original copy of the *Messiah* score and other valuable papers.

A pastor in modern-day South Korea runs his own small-scale version of a foundling hospital. Lee John-rak cares for a son born with crippling cerebral palsy, and it disturbed him greatly to learn that hundreds of babies born with disabilities — deafness, blindness, cerebral palsy, Down syndrome — are abandoned on the streets of Seoul every year. He constructed an ingenious "drop box" in the wall of his home. From the outside it resembles an after-hours deposit box at a bank. A parent who wishes to remain anonymous can open the baby box and deposit the unwanted infant in a warm, blanketed compartment fitted with a motion sensor and an alarm. Thus alerted, Pastor Lee or a volunteer comes to collect the baby and bring it into their bustling orphanage. As many as eighteen babies a month have been left in the baby box.

Every Christian can be an activist, whether full- or part-time. Subversively, we act out our beliefs as they go against the grain of surrounding culture. When parents discard unwanted children, Christians make a home for them. When scientists seek ways

to purify the gene pool, Christians look for special-needs babies
to adopt. When politicians cut funding for the poor, Christians
open shelters and feeding stations. When law enforcement con-
fines criminals behind barbed wire, Christians run programs for
them.

Out of the media spotlight, Christian activists have found creative ways to fight moral battles. Prison Fellowship International
has shown such expertise in caring for prisoners that several governments have asked them to take over the management of entire
prisons. A sister organization, International Justice Mission, tackles sexual trafficking overseas by working with local authorities.
An IJM representative learns about a corrupt mayor and visits his
office. "We know you are getting kickbacks from a prostitution
ring. And we both know that your own laws forbid that. We want
to stop the exploitation of these women, and can handle it one of
two ways. We can bring in cameras and expose you to the world
press. Or we can make you a hero, letting you partner with us in
a public campaign to break up this ring. Your choice."

When I write about such organizations I often feel a pang
of regret that my own work is so vicarious. While I may visit
prisons and IJM sites and then report on their activities, I write
about them from the security of my home. I am not venturing
on the frontlines, as do these activists. I take some small comfort
in the fact that my financial gifts contribute to their work. And
both of these organizations rely on the prayers of their supporters.
Through volunteer work, prayer, and financial contributions, all
of us can have a share in activism.

Some, however, sense a special calling for more extreme action.
I think of the Old Testament prophets, activists for justice. Sometimes they engaged in civil disobedience and sometimes they acted
bizarrely in order to grab the attention of a numb society. ("...
to the hard of hearing you shout, and for the almost-blind you
draw large and startling figures," said the Catholic novelist Flan-

nery O'Connor.) The erudite Isaiah went naked and barefoot for three years. Jeremiah staggered around under an ox yoke and once invited teetotalers in for a wine party. Hosea married a prostitute. Extreme situations call for extreme actions, especially when dealing with institutions.

The prophets were singlehandedly confronting the corrupt institutions of temple and kingdom. In a more modern context, Reinhold Niebuhr drew a contrast between the individual and the institution (banks, churches, the military, governments, corporations). We think of evil as an individual trait, he said, but actually the institution may represent the greater evil, more resistant to change and more likely to abuse power. How can a Christian confront institutions in a way that does not undercut our message of grace for the people who run those institutions?

In the 1960s Martin Luther King Jr. struggled with this very issue. "Prior to reading Gandhi," he said, "I had about concluded that the ethics of Jesus were only effective in individual relationships." He found a solution by combining the power of love as described in the Sermon on the Mount with Mahatma Gandhi's method of nonviolent resistance. King saw that activism could indeed be expressed in a loving way. "I came to feel that this was the only morally and practically sound method open to oppressed people in their struggle for freedom." That creative strategy has since been adapted to many causes in many countries.

Institutions do not respond well to subversives, as the life of King makes clear. Yet his nonviolent campaign has a continuing effect on an entire society long after his adversaries have faded from memory. Church history has seen many activists who take on causes such as slavery, racism, war, poverty, and women's rights. Gradually, like the melting of a glacier, change takes place and what first seemed subversive becomes an accepted feature of the landscape.

ARTIST

The Catholic novelist Walker Percy describes his approach: "[In art] you are telling the reader or the listener or the viewer something he already knows but which he doesn't quite know that he knows, so that in the action of communication he experiences a recognition, a feeling that he has been there before, a shock of recognition."

Art may be the most effective subversion tactic. It certainly was for me. In different ways books like *To Kill a Mockingbird*, *The Lord of the Rings*, and *The Brothers Karamazov* slid around my defenses and cut right to the heart. My early reading subverted the fragile world of fundamentalism I grew up in; later, great art beckoned me back to faith with a sudden shock of recognition.

Tony Rossi, a blogger on the Patheos website, was surprised to get favorable comments from self-professed atheists in response to his review of the movie version of *Les Misérables*. "This is the only Christian story I have ever connected with and I love it," wrote one. He admitted to having a chip on his shoulder about Christianity, but he loved the musical because Jean Valjean manifested all the Christian virtues without being obnoxious or condescending. Another commented wistfully, "While I find that faith, once lost, is nearly impossible to find again, I found this a very touching story and had more Christians acted like Jean Valjean and the bishop and less like Javert, I might never have lost my faith to begin with."

When Victor Hugo first wrote the novel, some of his French compatriots objected that it treated the church too kindly. Hugo's son wanted him to substitute a lawyer or doctor for the merciful bishop who forgave Jean Valjean. The novelist, however, decided to portray a good priest who actually lives out the Christian message of grace and redemption. A century-and-a-half later, audiences are still responding to the story, which began as a novel and found new life as one of the most popular musicals of all time.

Art involves an exchange between two parties: the creator and the receiver. C. S. Lewis explains the act of reading as "less concerned with altering our own opinions—though this of course is sometimes their effect—than with entering fully into the opinions, and therefore also the attitudes, feelings and total experience" of the author. While reading a good book I temporarily suspend my own life and enter an imaginative world created for me. Prior to that, the author has done almost the reverse: entering into the attitudes, feelings and total experience of the reader. And here, I believe, is where Christians sometimes err in attempts to communicate faith: we fail to take into account the point of view of the other party.

Alexander Solzhenitsyn learned an important lesson after his release from the Gulag, when his writing first began to appear in Soviet literary journals. In his memoir he recalls, "Later, when I popped up from the underground and began lightening my works for the outside world, lightening them of all that my fellow countrymen could hardly be expected to accept at once, I discovered to my surprise that a piece only gained, that its effect was heightened, as the harsher tones were softened."

Reading religious books sometimes reminds me of traveling through a mile-long mountain tunnel. Inside the tunnel, headlights provide crucial illumination, without which I might drift dangerously toward the tunnel walls. But when I emerge from the tunnel I need a "Check Headlights" sign to remind me that I still have them switched on. Christian books are usually written from a perspective outside the tunnel, in blinding daylight. From that vantage, the writer easily forgets the blank darkness inside the tunnel where many readers live.

As one of the atheists commented on the blog about *Les Misérables*, "Modern Christian storytelling seems to steer away from the fear and despair because expressing that might show a lack of faith. Instead, avoiding those feelings just whitewashes the religion and makes it seem weak." One of John Updike's characters in *The Witches of Eastwick* made a similar point less delicately: "I want art to show me something, to tell me where I'm at, even if it's hell." Doubt must sound like true doubt, not a caricature; otherwise, Christian literature will be read only by those predisposed to belief.

Whenever I need a good model, I pick up the Bible. God must love art because most of the Bible is expressed in the form of story or poetry. And no one could accuse the authors of Samuel, Kings, and Chronicles of whitewashing history, or the book of Job of sentimentalizing suffering. What protagonists in literature demonstrate a more subtle mixture of good and evil than David or Jacob? From the despair of Ecclesiastes to the conversion stories of Acts, the Bible renders the full spectrum of doubt and faith, struggle and resolution, sin and redemption. In a book of sacred scripture that message itself is subversive.

A master artist, Jesus gave his most enduring truths in the form of parables, homespun stories shaped out of his listener's daily lives. "Tell all the truth but tell it slant," wrote Emily Dickinson; "The truth must dazzle gradually / Or every man be blind—." Eugene Peterson, who borrowed her phrase for the title of his book *Tell It Slant*, notes that as Jesus approaches the end of his life, his language becomes even more oblique. "Instead of high decibel rhetoric, calling for decisions before it is too late, he hardly, if at all, even mentions the name of God, choosing instead to speak of neighbors and friends, losing a lamb, and the courtesies of hospitality."

Peterson draws a contrast to Christian communicators of the current day. "Because it is so much more clear and focused we use the language learned from sermons and teachings to tell others what is eternally important. But the very intensity of the language can very well reduce our attentiveness to the people to whom we are speaking—he or she is no longer a person but a cause."

A MODERN PARABLE

Pilgrim, activist, artist — whatever our calling, we join together to proclaim the good news that God has commissioned us to announce to the world. As Karl Barth points out, the church has done so erratically, "in obedience and in disobedience, in understanding and in misunderstanding of the lofty good God has given us." A post-Christian society is quick to remind us of our faults, which we should humbly acknowledge. Yet wherever the gospel has taken root, it has borne fruit. Much that we value in the modern world — freedom, democracy, education, healthcare, human rights, social justice — traces back to a Christian origin. The smallest seed in the garden has become a great tree in which the birds of the air come to nest.

Christ-followers need not live in fear, even when it seems that society may be turning against us. We rest in full confidence that God, in control of human history, will have the final word: "The kingdom of the world has become the kingdom of our Lord and of his Messiah, and he will reign for ever and ever." We each of us do our part, loving others as God loves us, tending the world as stewards of a gracious landlord. The yeast spreads, the salt preserves, the tree survives, even in dark and foreboding times.

This chapter begins with an excerpt from "The Last Word" by Graham Greene, which he wrote in 1988. Despairing of what lay ahead, Greene painted an exaggerated picture of a United World intent on destroying the last remaining alternative to its authority. In truth, however, Greene's story now seems quaintly naive, for his best model for the United World — communist regimes that systematically tried to eliminate religious faith — collapsed in a heap in 1989, the year after he wrote the story. *

---

* The full history has yet to be written, but no one doubts that subversive artists played a major role, both in exposing the lies of the regime and in upholding values that its materialistic philosophy excluded. To mention only a few: Alexander Solzhenitsyn, Joseph Brodsky, Mstislav Rostropovich, Galina Vishnevs-

A neighbor of mine visited Russia both before and after the fall of communism there. During his visit in 1983 some exuberant young tourists were arrested for unfolding a banner in Red Square on which was printed in large letters the traditional Easter Sunday greeting, "Christ is Risen!" Soldiers surrounded the hymn-singing subversives, tore up their banner, and hustled them off to jail. In 1993, exactly one decade after that act of civil disobedience, again my neighbor visited Red Square on Easter Sunday. This time all across the plaza Russians were openly greeting each other: "Christ is risen!" ... "He is risen indeed!"

That same year the Bolshoi Theater sponsored a performance of Handel's *Messiah*, broadcast on state television. At the close of the performance the conductor lifted up a huge Orthodox cross and the lead soprano testified to a national audience that her Redeemer really did live. "What is that beautiful music?" my neighbor's Russian hosts asked during the concert. They had never before heard Handel's *Messiah*, banned in Russia for seven decades. (History repeats itself: in 2008 the Communist government in China banned public performances of *Messiah* and other Western religious music.)

Faith survived in Russia not because of a power struggle between church and state but because poets in the Gulag, faithful babushkas, persecuted priests, and ordinary pilgrims kept the flame alive throughout the grimmest days. As the apostle Paul wrote, "Brothers and sisters, think of what you were when you were called. Not many of you were wise by human standards; not many were influential; not many were of noble birth. But God chose the foolish things of the world to shame the wise; God chose the weak things of the world to shame the strong. God chose the lowly things of this world and the despised things—and the

kaya, Aleksandr Galich, Václav Havel, Irina Ratushinskaya, Anna Akhmatova, Boris Pasternak, Czesław Miłosz.

things that are not—to nullify the things that are, so that no one may boast before him."

I have interviewed some of the faithful in places like Russia, China, Kazakhstan, Ukraine, Albania, and Romania. "Why did you take such a risk?" I ask. "Why did you choose to follow Jesus when your government, your teachers, and perhaps even your family insisted it was all a lie?" Again and again I have heard a two-pronged answer. They speak of their spiritual thirst, an inner longing that no amount of noisy propaganda could silence. And then they tell me of a humble Christian who loved them, who held out the possibility of a power that could help in their battle against alcoholism or drugs or meaninglessness or whatever demon happened to be tormenting them.

One of the faithful, the Soviet Union's most renowned sculptor, who had designed Nikita Khrushchev's tombstone, eventually went into forced exile in Switzerland. "If I had not come out," Ernst Neizvestny declared, "the artist in me would have died." Knowing the sculptor's talent, the authorities tried at first to hold on to him. "We need Neizvestny," said one official, "but we cannot use him. We must create a Communist Neizvestny."

His final rupture with the regime took place over a commission he did for a Communist Party building. Neizvestny constructed a huge sculpture, some fifty feet high and fifty feet wide, that covered the entire facade. He submitted the design in sections, each of which was approved by Party officials. Only at the unveiling did they see it as a whole—and gasped in horror. A huge cross covered the front of the Communist headquarters.

"A cross?" said Neizvestny. "Can't you see it's a face?" But, knowing his Christian beliefs, authorities took it for a cross and expelled him from the country.

The cross stayed in place. The state that opposed it did not.

SOURCES

Epigraph

9: *"See to it that no one ..."*: Hebrews 12:15 NIV 1984.

Part One: A World Athirst

13: *"I cannot be sure they don't have ..."*: Walker Percy, *The Second Coming* (New York: Washington Square Press, 1980), 218–19.

Chapter 1: A Great Divide

15: *"In general the churches ..."*: John Updike, *A Month of Sundays* (New York: Ballantine, 1985), 30.

15: *a few telling statistics ...*: cited in David Kinnaman and Gabe Lyons, *UnChristian: What a New Generation Really Thinks about Christianity ... and Why It Matters* (Grand Rapids, Mich.: Baker, 2007), 24–25.

17: *"Evangelicals were called illiterate ..."*: Cited in "Define 'Evangelical' — Again," *Terry Mattingly On Religion*, September 10, 2008, http://www.patheos.com/blogs /tmatt/2008/09/define-evangelical-again.

17: *"the aroma of Christ"*: 2 Corinthians 2:15–16 NIV 1984.

17: *"There's no easy way ..."*: Marc Yoder, "10 Surprising Reasons Our Kids LEAVE Church," *Church Leaders*, February 2013, http://www.churchleaders.com/children /childrens-ministry-articles/169292–10-surprising-reasons-our-kids-leave-church.html.

18: *(footnote) According to Barna ..."*: "Most Twentysomethings Put Christianity on the Shelf Following Spiritually Active Teen Years," *Barna Group*, September 11, 2006, www.barna.org/barna-update/article/16-teensnext-gen/147-most-twentysomethings -put-christianity-on-the-shelf-following-spiritually-active-teen-years#.Uv0WX_ldU9I.

18: *"When Christians talk to you ..."*: Daniel Hill, "Reaching the Post-Christian," *Leadership Journal*, Fall 2004, 71–74.

18: *C. S. Lewis's analogy ...*: C. S. Lewis, *God in the Dock: Essays on Theology and Ethics* (Grand Rapids, Mich.: Eerdmans, 1970), 172.

21: *"An enemy is one ..."*: Gene Knudsen Hoffman, *The Compassionate Listening Project*, http://www.compassionatelistening.org.

21: *"All religions are the same ..."*: Cathy Ladman, quoted in "Religion Quotes," *Tentmaker*, http://www.tentmaker.org/Quotes/religionquotes.htm.

22: *I turned on CNN ...*: "Pastor's Anti-Gay, Anti-Obama Sermon," in "Belief Blog," *CNN,* http://religion.blogs.cnn.com/2012/05/22/video-of-north-carolina -pastors-plan-to-get-rid-of-gays-goes-viral.

22: *"Ain't no homos ..."*: "Toddler Sings in Church," *TMZ,* http://www.tmz .com/2012/05/30/indiana-toddler-church-song-no-homos-heaven.

22: *The 2004 movie ...*: *Saved!* Directed by Brian Dannelly. British Columbia, Canada: United Artists, 2004.

23: *"Most people I meet ..."*: quoted in David Kinnaman and Gabe Lyons, *UnChristian: What a New Generation Really Thinks about Christianity ... and Why It Matters"* (Grand Rapids, Mich.: Baker, 2007), 26.

23: *"Is religion a force ..."*: "Is Religion a Force for Good in the World?" *Ipsos Global,* http://www.ipsos-na.com/news-polls/pressrelease.aspx?id=5058.

25: *an article Tim Stafford wrote ...*: Tim Stafford, "This Samaritan Life," *Christianity Today,* February 2008, 47–49.

25: *"Jews do not associate ..."*: John 4:9.

25: *"a Samaritan and demon-possessed"*: John 8:48.

26: *"I've decided I'm against abortion ..."*: Andy Rooney, "Coming Out Against Abortion," *Chicago Tribune News,* February 10, 1985.

27: *"great joy"*: Acts 8: 8–17.

27: *"I don't like these atheists ..."*: Heinrich Böll, quoted in Jürgen Moltmann, *A Broad Place: An Autobiography* (Minneapolis: Fortress, 2009), 64.

27: *Jesus "came from the father ..."*: John 1:14.

28: *"incomparable riches"*: Ephesians 2:7.

28: *John records one close-up encounter ...*: John 4: 1–42.

28: *"I'm a priest ..."*: Henri Nouwen, conversation with author, cited in Philip Yancey, *Soul Survivor: How My Faith Survived the Church* (New York: Doubleday, 2001), 293 ff.

29: *"Deo Gratias, Deo Gratias!"*: Graham Greene, *A Burnt-Out Case* (New York: Bantam Books, 1960), 50.

Chapter 2: Grace Endangered

31: *"But you take pleasure in the faces ..."*: Rilke: Rainer Maria Rilke, *Rilke's Book of Hours: Love Poems to God,* trans. Anita Barrows and Joanna Macy (New York: Berkley Publishing Group, 1996), 61.

31: *"It is not as easy as one might suppose ..."*: Theodore Dalrymple, "What the New Atheists Don't See," *City Journal,* Autumn 2007, city-journal.org/html/17_4_oh_to_be .html.

32: *One therapist lists the complaints ...*: Thomas Moore, *Care of the Soul: A Guide for Cultivating Depth and Sacredness in Everyday Life* (New York: HarperCollins, 1992), xvi.

32: *"whole life was a search for God ..."*: Quoted in Anthony Flew, *There Is A God: How the World's Most Notorious Atheist Changed His Mind* (New York: HarperCollins, 2007), xx–xxi.

SOURCES

32: *"There is darkness without..."*: Bertrand Russell, *Mysticism and Logic*, quoted in James Le Fanu, *Why Us? How Science Rediscovered the Mystery of Ourselves* (New York: Vintage, 2009), 234.

33: *"You never really understand a person..."*: Harper Lee, *To Kill a Mockingbird* (New York: Popular Library, 1962), 34.

34: *"Love your neighbor..."*: Matthew 22:39.

34: *"You don't listen to me..."*: T. Suzanne Eller, "Seekers Speak Out," *Today's Christian Woman*, November/December 2004, 78.

35: *"As I have loved you..."*: John 13:34–35.

35: *"No one has ever seen God..."*: 1 John 4:12.

36: *"Don't think in terms of what..."*: quoted in "Tim Keller: The Reason for God," *Servant Magazine* 88 (2011): 10.

37: *"The Hebrew Bible [Old Testament]..."*: Jonathan Sacks, *The Dignity of Difference* (New York: Continuum, 2002), 58–60.

37: *"I quit being a Christian..."*: Anne Rice, quoted in "Gleanings," *Christianity Today*, August 2, 2010, http://www.christianitytoday.com/gleanings/2010/august/anne-rice-today-i-quit-being-christian.html.

37: *"Imagine, suing them!"*: Will Campbell, from a personal conversation with author. See also: Will D. Campbell, *Soul Among Lions: Musings of a Bootleg Preacher* (Louisville: Westminster John Knox, 1999), 43.

37: *Norma Leah McCorvey*: Norma Leah McCorvey, in " 'Roe' and 'Doe' Tell Their Stories," *Christianity Today*, June 17, 1996, http://www.christianitytoday.com/ct/1996/june17/6t762b.html. See also Norma McCorvey and Gary Thomas, *Won by Love* (Nashville: Nelson, 1998).

38: *"Love your enemies..."*: Matthew 5:44.

38: *an Army reserve chaplain...*: Thomas Bruce, *Adopt a Terrorist for Prayer* website, https://atfp.org.

39: *"that you may be children..."*: Matthew 5:45.

39: *"You will be children..."*: Luke 6:35.

39: *"To our most bitter opponents..."*: Martin Luther King Jr., *Strength to Love*, first edition (Minneapolis: Fortress Press, 1981), 56.

40: *"Lord, do not hold this sin..."*: Acts 7:60.

40: *"a virus of the mind"*: Richard Dawkins, *A Devil's Chaplain: Reflections on Hope, Lies, Science, and Love* (New York: First Mariner, 2003), 128ff.

40: *"I have had a most shameful..."*: Virginia Woolf, quoted in Peter Hitchens, *The Rage Against God* (Grand Rapids, Mich.: Zondervan, 2010), 24.

41: *"the quiet service of love..."*: Dietrich Bonhoeffer, *Spiritual Care* (Philadelphia: Fortress Press, 1988), 50.

41: *A gentle answer turns away wrath...*: Proverbs 15:1.

41: *"I don't want American Science..."*: Peter J. Boyer, "The Covenant," *The New Yorker*, September 6, 2001, http://www.newyorker.com/reporting/2010/09/06/100906fa_fact_boyer?currentPage=all.

41: *"He's not a bright guy"*: "Is God-Fearing, Gene-Hunter Francis Collins Fit to Run NIH?" *Examiner*, July 8, 2009, http://www.examiner.com/article/is-god-fearing -gene-hunter-francis-collins-fit-to-run-nih.

41: *"As NIH director I approve ..."*: Dr. Francis Collins, from a personal conversation with the author, November 9, 2010.

42: *"he got cancer in the one part ..."*: Christopher Hitchens, "Unanswerable Prayers," *Vanity Fair*, October 2010, 158–63.

42: *"See to it that no one misses ..."*: Hebrews 12:15 NIV 1984.

42–43: *advice "to myself and anyone else ..."*: Martin Marty, "Atheism Redux," *Christian Century*, July 24, 2007, www.christiancentury.org/article/2007–07/atheism-redux.

44: *"Humanity is the real Christian virtue ..."*: Henri Nouwen, *Gracias! A Latin American Journal* (Maryknoll, N.Y.: Orbis, 1993), 162.

45: *"Jesus said to feed the poor ..."*: Donald Miller, *Blue Like Jazz: Nonreligious Thoughts on Christian Spirituality* (Nashville: Nelson, 2003), 117–25.

46: *"I'm ready for that fight"*: Craig Detweiler, *A Purple State of Mind* (Eugene, Ore.: Harvest House, 2008), 133–34.

Chapter 3: Soul Thirst

49: *"The soul knows for certain ..."*: Simone Weil, quoted in Robert Coles, *Simone Weil: A Modern Pilgrimage* (Reading, Mass.: Addison-Wesley, 1987), 29.

50: *"In fact, spiritual dryness ..."*: Thomas Merton, *Run to the Mountain: The Story of a Vocation (The Journals of Thomas Merton, Volume 1 1939–1941)* (New York: Harper SanFrancisco, 1996), 452.

51: *"In my life, I have lost ..."*: Barbara Brown Taylor, *An Altar in the World: A Geography of Faith* (New York: HarperOne, 2009), 72–3.

52: *"This brother of yours was dead ..."*: Luke 15:32.

53: *"The church is where Christ is"*: Jürgen Moltmann, *A Broad Place: An Autobiography* (Minneapolis: Fortress, 2009), 203.

53: *(footnote) "Christianity has been denounced ..."*: H. G. Wells, *The Outline of History: Being a Plain History of Life and Mankind* (Garden City, New York: Doubleday, 1971), 418.

53: *"When I assented to the faith ..."*: Christian Wiman, *My Bright Abyss: Meditation of a Modern Believer* (New York: Farrar, Straus & Giroux, 2013), 12.

54: *devotion to an "unknown God"*: Acts 17:23.

54: *"would seek him and perhaps reach out ..."*: Acts 17:27.

54: *"I went looking for spirit ..."*: Bono, quoted in Steve Stockman, *Walk On: The Spiritual Journey of U2* (Winter Park, Fla.: Relevant, 2001), 138.

55: *Bono answers his questions*: Michka Assayas, *Bono: In Conversation with Michka Assayas* (New York: Riverhead, 2005).

55: *"He sat at meat with publicans ..."*: Dag Hammarskjöld, *Markings*, trans. Leif Sjöberg and W. H. Auden (New York: Random House, 1993), 157.

55: *"Like a whispering in dark streets ..."*: Rainer Maria Rilke, *Rilke's Book of Hours: Love Poems to God*, trans. Anita Barrows and Joanna Macy (New York: Berkley Publishing Group, 1996), 67.

56: *"Why I—and incidentally my six ..."*: Sigmund Freud, quoted in Dr. Armand M. Nicholi Jr., *The Question of God: C.S. Lewis and Sigmund Freud Debate God, Love, Sex, and the Meaning of Life* (New York: The Free Press, 2002), 75.

57: *"Do you love me?"*: Albert Camus, *The Stranger* (New York: Vintage, 1954), 52–53.

57: *"There is but one truly serious ..."*: Albert Camus, *The Myth of Sisyphus and Other Essays* (New York: Vintage, 1991), 3.

57: *"Either life is holy with meaning ..."*: Frederick Buechner, *Secrets in the Dark: A Life in Sermons* (New York: HarperOne, 2006), 137.

58: *"their politics of hatred ..."*: Rosaria Champagne Butterfield, "My Train Wreck Conversion," *Christianity Today*, January/February 2013, http://www.ctlibrary.com/ct/2013/january-february/my-train-wreck-conversion.html?utm_source=ctlibrary-html&utm_medium=Newsletter&utm_term=2016670&utm_content=153855392&utm_campaign=2013.

59: *"Jesus looked at him ..."*: Mark 10:21.

59: *"Everyone who drinks this water ..."*: John 4:13.

60: *"If there is no God ..."*: Ivan, in the movie *Sunshine*. Directed by István Szabó. Berlin: Alliance Atlantis Communications, 1999.

60: *Affliction and beauty pierce ...*: Simone Weil, quoted in Brent Curtis and John Eldridge, *The Sacred Romance: Drawing Closer to the Heart of God* (Nashville: Nelson, 1997), 185.

61: *"One of my greatest difficulties ..."*: George MacDonald, quoted in William Raeper, *George MacDonald: The Major Biography of George MacDonald, Novelist and Victorian Visionary* (Batavia, Ill.: Lion, 1987), 62.

62: *"Definite beliefs enable us ..."*: Christian Wiman, *My Bright Abyss: Meditation of a Modern Believer* (New York: Farrar, Straus & Giroux, 2013), 123.

62: *"neither joy, nor love, nor light ..."*: Matthew Arnold, "Dover Beach," *Poetical Works of Matthew Arnold* (New York: Macmillan, 1905), 227.

62: *"Dear God, yes, I do believe ..."*: Kelly James Clark, ed., *Philosophers Who Believe: The Spiritual Journeys of 11 Leading Thinkers* (Downers Grove, Ill.: InterVarsity, 1993), 216.

63: *"When we have overcome absence ..."*: Nicholas Wolterstorff, *Lament for a Son* (Grand Rapids, Mich.: Eerdmans, 1987), 72–73.

63: *"A buddy and I were assigned ..."*: See Philip Yancey, *I Was Just Wondering* (Grand Rapids, Mich.: Eerdmans, 1989), 76–78.

66: *"the God of all comfort"*: 2 Corinthians 1:3.

66: *"We love because he first loved us ..."*: 1 John 4:19.

Chapter 4: Reclaiming the Good News

69: *"Between the time a gift comes ..."*: Lewis Hyde, *The Gift: Creativity and the Artist in the Modern World* (New York: Vintage, 2007), 60.

70: *"I look at him and I force myself ..."*: Alicia Nash, in *A Beautiful Mind*. Directed by Ron Howard. New Jersey: Universal Pictures, 2001.

70: *"So from now on we regard ..."*: 2 Corinthians 5:16.

70: *"Turn around and believe ..."*: Frederick Buechner, *Secrets in the Dark: A Life in Sermons* (New York: HarperOne, 2006), 161.

71: *"leads us by example ..."*: Reynolds Price, *Clear Pictures: First Loves First Guides* (New York: Scribner Classics, 1998) 74.

71: *"For God so loved the world ..."*: John 3:16.

71: *Mark Rutland whimsically recalls ...*: Mark Rutland, *Streams of Mercy: Receiving and Reflecting God's Grace* (Ann Arbor, Mich.: Vine, 1999), 39.

72: *"I like my way of doing it ..."*: D. L. Moody, quoted in James S. Hewett, *Illustrations Unlimited* (Wheaton: Tyndale House, 1988), 178.

73: *"God didn't go to all the trouble ..."*: John 3:16; Eugene H. Peterson, *The Message: The Bible in Contemporary Language* (Colorado Springs: NavPress, 2005), 1664.

73: *"They marry, like everyone else ..."*: "Letter to Diognetus," Chapter 5, *Christian History for Everyman*, http://www.christian-history.org/letter-to-diognetus.html.

74: *"in the world ..."*: John 17:11, 14.

74: *Gabe Lyons recommends inviting ...*: Roxanne Stone, "Gabe Lyons: The Culture and the Church," *Outreach Magazine*, January/February 2014, 95.

74: *"Salvation took such hold in her ..."*: Kathleen Norris, *Amazing Grace: A Vocabulary of Faith* (New York: Riverhead, 1998), 297.

76: *"Married, divorced or single here ..."*: bulletin, Highlands Church, Denver, Colorado, http://highlandschurchdenver.org/about/our-beliefs.

78: *"sharing God's wisdom"*: Miroslav Volf, *Public Faith: How Followers of Christ Should Serve the Common Good* (Grand Rapids, Mich.: Brazos, 2011) 99–117.

78: *"Do you want to get well?"*: John 5:6.

79: *Ignatius of Loyola defined sin ...*: David G. Benner, *Sacred Companions: The Gift of Spiritual Friendship and Direction* (Downers Grove, Ill.: InterVarsity, 2002), 39.

79: *"Instead of telling them they are sinning ..."*: Tim Keller, "The Gospel in All Its Forms," *Leadership Journal*, Spring 2008, 15.

80: *"the root meaning in Hebrew ..."*: Eugene Peterson, *Reversed Thunder: The Revelation of John and the Praying Imagination* (New York: HarperSanFrancisco, 1991), 153.

80: *"I run in the path of your commands ..."*: Psalm 119:32 NIV 1984.

80: *"participate in the divine nature ..."*: 2 Peter 1:4.

81: *"I have come to think that the challenge ..."*: Stanley Hauerwas, *Hannah's Child: A Theologian's Memoir* (Grand Rapids, Mich.: Eerdmans, 2010), 159.

81: *"When asked to identify their activities ..."*: (Barna Group study) David Kinnaman and Gabe Lyons, *unChristian: What a New Generation Really Thinks about Christianity ... and Why It Matters* (Grand Rapids, Mich.: Baker, 2007), 47–48.

82: *"The astonishing quality of the early believers' lives ... "*: Ronald J. Sider , "Revisiting Mt. Carmel through Charitable Choice," *Christianity Today*, June 11, 2001, 84–90.

83: *"I am convinced that if we lose kids ..."*: Shane Claiborne, *Irresistible Revolution: Living as an Ordinary Radical* (Grand Rapids, Mich.: Zondervan, 2006), 225–26.

83: *Dorothy Day used to say ...*: Quoted in Jonathan Wilson-Hartgrove, *The Awakening of Hope: Why We Practice a Common Faith* (Grand Rapids, Mich.: Zondervan, 2012), 27.

84: *"Live such good lives among the pagans ..."*: 1 Peter 2:12, 3:15–16.

84: *"For who is greater ..."*: Luke. 22:27.

84: *"What you do in the present ..."*: N.T. Wright, *Surprised by Hope: Rethinking Heaven, the Resurrection, and the Mission of the Church* (New York: HarperOne, 2008),193.

85: *"I have found that the longer ..."*: Michael Cheshire, *How to Knock Over a 7-Eleven and Other Ministry Training* (n.p.: Cheshire, 2012), 31–32.

86: *a community called Miracle Village*: Linda Pressly, "The Village Where Half the Population Are Sex Offenders," *BBC News Magazine*, July 30, 2013, http://www.bbc.co.uk/news/magazine–23063492.

86: *(footnote)*: Amy Sherman, *Kingdom Calling* (Downers Grove, Ill.: InterVarsity, 2011) and Timothy J. Keller, *Ministries of Mercy: The Call of the Jericho Road* (Phillipsburg, N.J.: P & R, 1997).

Part Two: Grace-Dispensers

89: *"There are three kinds of Christians ..."*: Thanks to Kathryn Helmers for this insight.

Chapter 5: Pilgrims

91: *"Jesus came announcing the Kingdom ..."*: quoted in Richard John Neuhaus, *The Naked Public Square: Religion and Democracy in America* (Grand Rapids, Mich.: Eerdmans, 1986), 168.

91: *"I considered him a homophobe ..."*: Gina Welch, *In the Land of Believers: An Outsider's Extraordinary Journey into the Heart of the Evangelical Church* (New York: Metropolitan, 2012), 2.

95: *John Bunyan wrote* The Pilgrim's Progress ...: John Bunyan, *The Pilgrim's Progress* (London: Penguin, 1988).

96: *"we minister above all with our weakness"*: Henri Nouwen, *Gracias! A Latin American Journal* (Maryknoll, N.Y.: Orbis, 1993), 19.

97: *"Why is Brennan Manning lovable ..."*: Brennan Manning, "Healing Our Image of God and Ourselves," a speech given at the Omni Hotel, Atlanta, July 8, 2007.

98: *"If Jesus came back and saw ..."* Hannah and Her Sisters. Directed by Woody Allen. New York: Orion Pictures, 1986.

98: *"some doubted"*: Matthew 28:17.

99: *"the ends of the earth"*: Acts 1:8.

99: *"Why do you stand here looking..."*: Acts 1:11.

100: *"Anyone who has seen me..."*: John 14:9.

100: *"It is for your good..."*: John 16:7.

100: *"When the Advocate comes..."*: John 15:26–27.

101: *"Lord, are you at this time going..."*: Acts 1:6.

101: *"Whoever believes in me..."*: John 14:12.

101: *"The Holy Spirit is just what Christ..."*: Henry Drummond, *The Greatest Thing in the World and 21 Other Addresses* (London: Collins, 1966), 151.

102: *"Again and again I tell God..."*: Anne Lamott, *Traveling Mercies: Some Thoughts on Faith* (New York: Pantheon, 1999), 120.

102: *"Go out into the world uncorrupted..."*: Philippians 2:15; Eugene H. Peterson, *The Message: The Bible in Contemporary Language* (Colorado Springs: NavPress, 2005), 1847.

104: *"I thirst"*: John 19:28 KJV.

104: *"We carry in our body and soul..."*: Mother Teresa, quoted in "A Thirsty God," *Theology and Monkey Business, Dr. Louie's Teaching Blog*, June 24, 2011, http://theologyand monkeybusiness.blogspot.com/2011/06/thirsty-god-mother-teresa.html.

104: *"please God in every way..."*: Colossians 1:10, paraphrase. NIV says, "please him in every way."

105: *"a nice, pleasant, bland person ..."*: Steve Brown, "Only Sinners Welcome," *Crosswalk*, http://www.crosswalk.com/print/510220/.

106: *"the only cooperative society ..."*: Archbishop William Temple, in John Stott, *The Living Church: Convictions of a Lifelong Pastor* (Downers Grove, Ill.: InterVarsity, 2007), 51.

106: *"serve others faithfully administering ..."*: 1 Peter 4:10, NIV 1984; emphasis added.

106: *"One thing that had always troubled me ..."*: Barbara Brown Taylor, *Leaving Church* (New York: HarperCollins, 2007), 147–48.

107: *"There is neither ..."*: Galatians 3:28.

107: *"That they may be one"*: John 17:11.

107: *sermons on the phrase "one another"*: Wayne Hoag, *The One Another Project* (Maitland, Fla.: Xulon Press, 2012), 172–73.

108: *"For the joy set before him ..."*: Hebrews 12:2.

109: *"One sees the pleasure ..."*: John Hick, quoted in John Polkinghorne, *The God of Hope and the End of the World* (New Haven, Conn.: Yale University Press, 2002), 145–46.

Chapter 6: Activists

111: *"We lead our lives well ..."*: Miroslav Volf, *A Public Faith: How Followers of Christ Should Serve the Common Good* (Grand Rapids, Mich.: Brazos, 2011), 72.

111: *"God, don't you care ..."*: Bono, from a personal conversation with the author.

112: *"The Spirit of the Lord is on me ..."*: Luke 4:18.

112: *"Why do you stand here looking ..."*: Acts 1:11.

113: *"in the world ..."*: John 17:13, 16.

113: *"a minority of the minorities"*: Miroslav Volf, *Allah: A Christian Response* (New York: HarperCollins, 2011), 214.

113: *"As you sent ..."*: John 17:18.

114: *"When the missionaries came to Africa ..."*: Bishop Desmond Tutu, quoted in Steven Gish, *Desmond Tutu: A Biography* (Westport, Conn.: Greenwood, 2004), 101.

114: *(footnote) Albanian evangelicals ...*: Deborah Meroff, *Europe: Restoring Hope* (Linz, Austria: OM Books, 2011), 79.

115: *"No other religion has ever ..."*: Soho Machida, "Jesus, Man of Sin: Toward a New Christology in the Global Era," *Buddhist-Christian Studies* 19 (1990): 81–91.

117: *"My social circle at Brown ..."*: Kevin Roose, *The Unlikely Disciple: A Sinner's Semester at America's Holiest University* (New York: Grand Central, 2009), 9, 38.

119: *"Evangelicals in the Middle East ..."*: Leonard Rodgers (Director of Evangelicals for Middle East Understanding), in personal correspondence with the author.

120: *"How can I worship a homeless person ..."*: Shane Claiborne, *Irresistible Revolution: Living as an Ordinary Radical* (Grand Rapids, Mich.: Zondervan, 2006), 56. Claiborne is quoting a banner he saw displayed in a church.

121: *Studies in Latin America document ...*: See W. E. Hewitt, *Base Christian Communities and Social Change in Brazil* (Lincoln, Neb.: University of Nebraska Press, 1991); Richard Shaull and Waldo A. Cesar, *Pentecostalism and the Future of the Christian Churches: Promises, Limitations, Challenges* (Grand Rapids, Mich.: Eerdmans, 2000); Anthony Gill, *Rendering unto Caesar: The Catholic Church and the State in Latin America* (Chicago: University of Chicago Press, 2008); and Manuel A. Vasquez, *The Brazilian Popular Church and the Crisis of Modernity* (Cambridge, UK: Cambridge University Press, 1998).

121: *"as it is in heaven"*: Matthew 6:10.

121: *(footnote)*: See Tom Krattenmaker, *Evangelicals You Don't Know: Introducing the Next Generation of Christians* (Lanham, Md.: Rowman & Littlefield, 2013); and Amy L. Sherman, *Kingdom Calling* (Downers Grove, Ill.: InterVarsity, 2011).

124: *James Davison Hunter published a book ...*: James Davison Hunter, *To Change the World: The Irony, Tragedy, and Possibility of Christianity in the Late Modern World* (New York: Oxford University Press, 2010), 5.

125: *"I'm looking for a second reformation ..."*: Rick Warren, quoted in Hunter, Ibid., 221.

126: *"caring for those who believe ..."*: Gabe Lyons, quoted in Andy Crouch, "What's So Great about the 'Common Good'?" *Christianity Today*, November 2012, 40.

126: *"foreigners and strangers on earth"*: Hebrews 11:13.

126: *"Each one should use whatever gift ..."*: 1 Peter 4:10 NIV 1984.

127: *"We had whites, blacks, Hispanics ... "*: John Marks: *Reasons to Believe: One Man's Journey among the Evangelicals and the Faith He Left Behind* (New York: HarperCollins, 2009), 167–68.

128: *"Let your light shine ... "*: Matthew 5:16.

128: *"Funny how you don't see secular humanists ... "*: Joe Klein, "Can Service Save Us?" *Time*, July 1, 2013, 27–34.

128: *"nearly all of us in the news business ... "*: Nicholas D. Kristof, "Evangelicals without Blowhards," *New York Times*, July 30, 2011, http://www.nytimes.com/2011/07/31 /opinion/sunday/kristof-evangelicals-without-blowhards.html?_r=0.

129: *"on earth as it is in heaven ... "*: Matthew 6:10.

130: *One Harlem preacher likens us ...*: Rev. Jeff White of Harlem New Song Church, in Amy Sherman, *Kingdom Calling: Vocational Stewardship for the Common Good* (Downers Grove, Ill.: InterVarsity, 2011), 23.

Chapter 7: Artists

131: *"The Lord who created ... "*: T. S. Eliot, "Choruses from 'The Rock,' " *The Complete Poems and Plays: 1909–1950* (New York: Harcourt, Brace, 1952), 111.

131: *"They also serve who only sit ... "*: See chapter with that title in Philip Yancey, *Finding God in Unexpected Places* (Colorado Springs: WaterBrook, 2005), 41–44.

133: *Peter Hitchens, brother of atheist ...*: Peter Hitchens, *The Rage Against God* (Grand Rapids, Mich.: Zondervan, 2010), 102.

133: *"are highways into the center ... "*: N. T. Wright, *Simply Christian: Why Christianity Makes Sense* (New York: HarperOne, 2006), 235.

134: *"The only really effective apologia ... "*: Joseph Cardinal Ratzinger with Vittorio Messori, *The Ratzinger Report* (San Francisco: Ignatius, 1985), 129.

134: *"He pondered and searched out ... "* Ecclesiastes: 12:9–11.

134: *"Be warned, my son ... "*: Ecclesiastes 12:12.

134: *"Did you do that?"*: Russell Martin, *Picasso's War: The Destruction of* Guernica *and the Masterpiece That Changed the World* (New York: Plume, 2002), 166.

135: *"So you are the little woman ... "*: Harriet Beecher Stowe Center website, *Impact of* Uncle Tom's Cabin, *Slavery, and the Civil War*, http://www.harrietbeecherstowe center.org/utc/impact.shtml.

136: *"the permanent things"*: T. S. Eliot, "Four Quartets," *The Complete Poems and Plays: 1909–1950* (New York: Harcourt, Brace, 1952), 133.

137: *"In a universe whose size ... "*: Loren Eiseley, *The Immense Journey* (New York: Vintage, 1959), 161–62.

137: *Remnick cites a story ...*: David Remnick, "Letter From Moscow: Exit the Saints," *The New Yorker*, July 18, 1994.

138: *The novelist Reynolds Price says ...*: Reynolds Price, in Alfred Corn, ed., *Incarnation: Contemporary Writers on the New Testament* (New York: Viking Penguin, 1990), 72.

138: *"The Catholic writer..."*: Flannery O'Connor, *Mystery and Manners: Occasional Prose* (New York: Farrar, Straus & Cudahy, 1986), 146.

138: *"The refracted light through whom..."*: J. R. R. Tolkien, "Mythopoeia," posted by Chester County Interlink, http://home.ccil.org/~cowan/mythopoeia.html.

138: *"As we were saying yesterday..."*: "Luis de León,"*Wikipedia*, http://en.wikipedia.org/wiki/Luis_de_León.

140: *"Whence do we come?"*: Gustav Mahler, quoted in Bruno Walter and Ernst Krenek, *Gustav Mahler* (New York: Dover, 2013), 129.

140: *"Now I have to work very hard..."*: Anton Bruckner, quoted in Harold C. Schoenberg, *The Lives of the Great Composers* (New York: Norton, 1970), 427.

141: *"The performance is divine..."*: Heuwell Tircuit, liner notes of the recording *Brahms: Ein Deutsches Requiem*, performed by the Chicago Symphony Orchestra, James Levine, conductor, recorded 1993, RCA 82876 60861 2, compact disc.

141: *(footnote) "When Yo-Yo Ma visited..."*: Walter Isaacson, *Steve Jobs* (New York: Simon & Schuster, 2011), 425.

142: By way of contrast, James Davison Hunter...: James Davison Hunter, *To Change the World: The Irony, Tragedy, and Possibility of Christianity in the Late Modern World* (New York: Oxford University Press, 2010).

143: *"pessimism, denigration, surreptitious sniping..."*: Aleksandr I. Solzhenitsyn, *The Oak and the Calf: Sketches of Literary Life in the Soviet Union*, trans. Harry Willetts (New York: Harper & Row, 1980), 95.

143: *(footnote) "thrilling, attractive and good news..."*: Jan Morris, in Diarmaid MacCulloch, *Christianity: The First Three Thousand Years* (New York: Viking Penguin, 2010), 78.

144: *"will illuminate the road..."*: Alan Paton, in Robert McAfee Brown, *Persuade Us to Rejoice* (Louisville: Westminster/John Knox, 1992), 103.

144: *"A lot of Christians are afraid..."*: Thanks to Kathryn Helmers for these insights.

146: *"There is only one real deprivation..."*: May Sarton, quoted in Lewis Hyde, *The Gift: Creativity and the Artist in the Modern World* (New York: Vintage, 2007), 189.

146: *"Of making many books..."*: Ecclesiastes 12:12.

147: *"The drawing of those characters..."*: Seamus Heaney, *The Government of the Tongue: Selected Prose, 1978–1987* (New York: Farrar, Straus & Giroux, 1989), 108.

147: *"You yourselves are our letter..."*: 2 Corinthians 3:2–3.

148: *"Such work blesses him..."*: Walt Whitman, in Walter Lowenfels, *Walt Whitman's Civil War* (New York: Da Capo Press, 1960), 193.

148: *"Political social history..."*: W. H. Auden, quoted in Leonard Feinberg, *Hypocrisy: Don't Leave Home Without It* (Boulder, Colo.: Pilgrim's Process, 2002), 66.

149: *"The movie was so filled with images..."*: Henri Nouwen, *Gracias!: A Latin American Journal* (Maryknoll, N.Y.: Orbis, 1993), 57.

149: *"So now, from this mad passion..."*: Quoted in "Moments of Suspension," *Encounter With God*, January 12, 2013, http://sammanjac.wordpress.com/tag/michelangelo.

Part Three: Is It Really Good News?

151: *Simone Weil drew an analogy* ...: Richard Rees, *Simone Weil: A Sketch for a Portrait* (Carbondale, Ill.: Southern Illinois University Press, 1966), 161.

Chapter 8: Does Faith Matter?

153: *"I want my attorney* ...": Voltaire, quoted in David G. Myers, "Wanting More in an Age of Plenty," *Christianity Today*, April 24, 2000, 97.

153: *"We have taller buildings* ...": Dr. Bob Moorehead, "The Paradox of Our Time," *Snopes.com,* http://www.snopes.com/politics/soapbox/paradox.asp; originally from Bob Moorehead, *Words Aptly Spoken* (Redmond, Wash.: Overlake Christian Bookstore, 1995).

154: *"The accumulation of material goods* ...": Al Gore, quoted in David G. Myers, "Wanting More in an Age of Plenty," *Christianity Today*, April 24, 2000, 95.

154: *According to a Gallup poll* ...: J. John, *Just 10: God's Timeless Values for Life Today* (Rickmansworth, UK: Philo Trust, 2013) , 14.

155: *"There's a lot more I could be doing* ...": Bill Gates, quoted in Walter Isaacson, "In Search of the Real Bill Gates," *Time*, January 13, 1997.

155: *Two books by sociologist Rodney Stark* ...: Rodney Stark, *The Rise of Christianity: How the Obscure, Marginal Jesus Movement Became the Dominant Religious Force in the Western World in Just a Few Centuries* (New York: HarperOne, 1996) and *The Triumph of Christianity: How the Jesus Movement Became the World's Largest Religion* (New York: HarperOne, 2011).

156: *Julian the Apostate complained bitterly* ...: quoted in James Davison Hunter, *To Change the World: The Irony, Tragedy, and Possibility of Christianity in the Late Modern World* (Oxford, New York: Oxford University Press, 2010), 55–56. The story is also told in Charles Schmidt, *The Social Results of Early Christianity*, 2 ed. (London: Wm. Isbister, 1889), 328.

158: *"the faith has to all appearance* ...": G. K. Chesterton, *The Everlasting Man* (New York: Image, 1955), 260–61, 255.

159: *"Also, seek the peace and prosperity of the city* ...": Jeremiah 29:7.

159: *"Democracy requires its citizens* ...": Jürgen Habermas, *The Habermas Forum*, May 3, 2009, http://www.habermasforum.dk/index.php?type=news&text_id=451.

160: *Another philosopher, Alain de Botton* ...: Alain de Botton, *Religion for Atheists: A Non-believer's Guide to the Uses of Religion* (New York: Pantheon, 2012).

160: *"Oh, exactly. Very much so"*: Margaret Thatcher, quoted in Gertrude Himmelfarb, *The De-Moralization of Society: From Victorian Virtues to Modern Values* (New York: Vintage, 1996), 3.

161: *"Everyone has different moral standards* ...": surgeon general, quoted in Himmelfarb, Ibid., 241.

161: *"We are now confronting the consequences* ...": Ibid., 242.

161: *"For two hundred years we had sawed* ...": George Orwell, "Notes on the Way," in *George Orwell: My Country Right or Left, 1940–1943* (New York: Harcourt, Brace & World, 1968), 15–16.

162: *"If I was to say that was evil ..."*: W. H. Auden, quoted in Dallas Willard, ed., *A Place for Truth: Leading Thinkers Explore Life's Hardest Questions* (Downers Grove, Ill.: InterVarsity, 2010), 51.

162: *"love your crooked neighbour ..."*: W. H. Auden, *The Collected Poetry of W. H. Auden* (New York: Random House, 1945), 198.

163: *Harvard undergraduates who experienced ...*: Dr. Armand M. Nicholi Jr., "A New Dimension of the Youth Culture," *American Journal of Psychiatry* 131, no. 4 (April 1974): 396–401.

163: *"life to the full"*: John 10:10.

164: *Robert Putnam, author of the groundbreaking book ...*: See Robert D. Putnam, *American Grace: How Religion Divides and Unites Us* (New York: Simon & Schuster, 2010). Also, Arthur C. Brooks of Syracuse University gives much statistical data supporting similar conclusions in *Who Really Cares: The Surprising Truth About Compassionate Conservatism* (New York: Basic Books, 2006).

164: *"Every individual I have met ..."*: Joseph Califano, in Charles Colson and Nancy Pearcey, *How Now Shall We Live?* (Wheaton, Ill.: Tyndale House, 1999), 311.

164: *"Religion is a powerful antidote ..."*: Byron Johnson, *More God, Less Crime: Why Faith Matters and How It Could Matter More* (West Conshohocken, Penn.: Templeton, 2011), xiv.

164: *"It's either barbed wire ..."*: Eugene Rivers, quoted in John DiIulio "The Truth About Crime and Welfare," *First Things*, August/September 1965, 31–35.

164: *(footnote) "The reason we fear to go out ..."*: David C. Stolinsky, quoted in Thomas Reeves "Not So Christian America," *First Things*, October 1996, 17.

165: *"You come in fatherless, abused ..."*: John DiIulio, quoted in Tim Stafford, "The Criminologist Who Discovered Churches," *Christianity Today*, June 14, 1999, 38.

165: *In early 2014* Christianity Today: *Christianity Today*, January/February 2014, 39.

166: *"We want you to see the fruit ..."*: in private conversation with the author.

167: *"Now a confirmed atheist ..."*: Matthew Parris, "As an Atheist, I Truly Believe Africa Needs God," *The Times of London*, December 26, 2008, http://www.thetimes.co.uk/tto/opinion/columnists/matthewparris/article2044345.ece. Used by permission.

170: *Andy Crouch uses the phrase* prosperity gospel ...: Andy Crouch, *Playing God: Redeeming the Gift of Power* (Downers Grove, Ill.: InterVarsity, 2013), 188.

170: *"Today the victim occupies ..."*: Gil Baillie, *Violence Unveiled: Humanity at the Crossroads* (New York: Crossroad, 1997), 29.

171: *"The problem of our time is to restore ..."*: George Orwell, "Notes on the Way," in *George Orwell: My Country Right or Left, 1940–1943* (New York: Harcourt, Brace & World, 1968), 15–16.

172: *"due to the fact that we have lost ..."*: See "Vaclav Havel — A Reflection," *The Sceptical Market Observer*, December 24, 2011, http://scepticalmarketobserver.blogspot.com/2011/12/vaclav-havel-reflection.html. Also see "Vaclav Havel's address to the US

Congress," *Everything*, February 21, 1990, http://everything2.com/title/Vaclav+Havel %2527s+address+to+the+US+Congress%252C+21+February+1990.

Chapter 9: Is There Anyone Else? The God Question

175: *"In order to be prepared to hope ..."*: Georges Bernanos, in Jacques Ellul, *Reason for Being: A Meditation on Ecclesiastes*, trans. Joyce M. Hanks (Grand Rapids, Mich.: Eerdmans, 1990), 47.

175: *"Philosophy is like being in a dark room ..."*: Google's social network, "The Black Cat Analogy," *Google Plus*, https://plus.google.com/115858612877723984178/posts/bD3fQybctbF.

176: *"What do you believe about God ..."*: Francis S. Collins, *Language of God: A Scientist Presents Evidence for Belief* (New York: Free Press, 2006), 20ff.

176: *As Lewis himself once said ...*: C. S. Lewis, *Surprised by Joy: The Shape of My Early Life* (Orlando: Harcourt, 1955), 191: "A young man who wishes to remain a sound atheist cannot be too careful of his reading."

177: *"Yes, but in the sense that any thumb ..."*: Sir William Henry Bragg, "The World of Sound: Six Lectures Delivered Before a Juvenile Auditory at the Royal Institution, Christmas, 1919," *Cornell University Library*, Internet Archive, G. Bell and Sons Ltd., London. Retrieved from Internet Archive, https://archive.org/details/cu31924031233038.

178: *"The Cosmos is all that is ..."*: Carl Sagan, quoted in Dinesh D'Souza *What's So Great About Christianity* (Washington, D.C.: Regnery, 2007), 34.

178: *"To give some meaning to those numbers ..."* Paul Davies, *God and the New Physics* (New York: Touchstone, 1983), 179.

178: *Stephen Hawking admits ...*: Stephen Hawking, *A Brief History of Time* (New York: Bantam, 1996), 156.

179: *"Well, we're here, aren't we?"*: Richard Dawkins, "Viruses of the Mind" (1991), http://www.cscs.umich.edu/~crshalizi/Dawkins/viruses-of-the-mind.html.

179: *Dawkins admitted that the fine tuning ...*: Richard Dawkins in conversation with Francis Collins.

179: *"The scientist must see all the fine ..."*: Albert Einstein, in Walter Isaacson, *Einstein: His Life and Universe* (New York: Simon & Schuster, 2007), 462, 551.

180: *"A priori, one should expect a chaotic world ..."*: Albert Einstein, *Letters to Solovine: 1906–1955* (New York: Open Road, 1987), 117. Also quoted in "Atheism," *Einstein: Science and Religion*, http://www.einsteinandreligion.com/atheism.html.

180: *(footnote) "In the study of all other sciences ..."*: Louis Berkhof, *Systematic Theology* (Grand Rapids, Mich.: Eerdmans, 1941), 34.

180: *"so perfectly organized ..."*: Alexander Tsiaras, "Conception to Birth—Visualized," *TED.com*, http://www.ted.com/talks/alexander_tsiaras_conception_to_birth_visualized.html.

181: *"Oh, that's all nonsense, dear ..."*: Nadia Bolz-Weber, *Pastrix: The Cranky, Beautiful Faith of a Sinner and Saint* (New York: Jericho, 2013), 79.

181: *"For since the creation of the world ..."*: Romans 1:20.

181: *as Dorothy Sayers suggests ...*: Dorothy Sayers, *The Mind of the Maker* (New York: HarperSanFrancisco, 1987), 38.

182: *"As a scientist, I hold that belief ..."*: Robert Seiple, "Commentary: Learning about Faith from Carl Sagan," *Religion News Service*, August 1, 1997.

183: *"The praise was strangely more genuine ..."*: Karl Giberson, "God's Other Good Book," *Christianity Today*, December 12, 2008, 62.

183: *"The scientific picture of the world ..."*: Erwin Schrödinger, quoted in Antony Flew, *There Is a God* (New York: HarperOne, 2007), 104.

183: *"Everything that can be counted ..."*: "Not Everything That Counts Can Be Counted" *Quote Investigator*, May 26, 2010, http://quoteinvestigator.com/2010/05/26 /everything-counts-einstein/.

183: *"God lies within ..."*: Shirley MacLaine: *Going Within* (New York: Bantam, 1989), 100.

183: *"I created my own reality ..."*: Shirley MacLaine, *It's All in the Playing* (New York: Bantam, 1987), 192.

184: *"My faith has carried me ..."*: Robert Bellah, *Habits of the Heart: Individualism and Commitment in American Life* (New York: Harper & Row, 1985), 221.

184: *"You have every right to cherry-pick ..."*: Elizabeth Gilbert, *Eat, Pray, Love* (New York: Penguin, 2006), 208.

184: *"God dwells within you ..."*: Ibid., 208, 192.

190: *"We live in a very diverse world ...*: Bill Hybels, "I Have a Friend Who Thinks All Religions Are the Same," *Willow Creek Association*, Week 11, 2001. Message recording and transcript available: http://www.willowcreek.com/ProdInfo.asp?invtid=PR14924.

190: *William James remarked that all religions ...*: William James, *The Varieties of Religious Experience* (New York: Modern Library, 1936), 498.

191: *"I am going there to prepare a place for you ..."*: John 14:2.

192: *"For God so loved the world ..."*: John 3:16.

192: *"Long before he laid down earth's foundations ..."*: Ephesians 1:4–5, 11–12, Eugene H. Peterson, *The Message: The Bible in Contemporary Language* (Colorado Springs: NavPress, 2005), 1836.

193: *"Why I hate religion ..."* Jefferson Bethke, "Why I Hate Religion But Love Jesus: Spoken Word by Jefferson Bethke," *You Tube*, http://www.youtube.com/ watch?v=QrYUVtAAsDM.

193: *"Forget the church, follow Jesus"*: Andrew Sullivan, "Christianity in Crisis," *Newsweek*, April 2, 2012, http://www.newsweek.com/andrew-sullivan-christianity -crisis–64025.

194: *"If there is no resurrection ..."*: 1 Corinthians 15:13–15, 19.

194: *"I just ate my lunch ..."*: reader comment on "Movin' Down the Road," at *PhilipYancey.com*, http://www.philipyancey.com/archives/2951.

195: *"That God does not exist ... "*: Jean Paul Sartre, "That God Does Not Exist ...", *Think/Exist*, http://thinkexist.com/quotation/that_god_does_not_exist-i_cannot_deny -that_my/189882.html.

Chapter 10: Why Are We Here? The Human Question

197: *"You were born without purpose ... "*: Ingmar Bergman, *The Magic Lantern: An Autobiography* (New York: Viking Penguin, 1988), 204.

198: *"God made me to know Him ...*: *Baltimore Catechism*: "The Catholic Primer," *Preserving Christian Publications*, Lesson First, page 8, www.pcpbooks.net/docs/baltimore _catechism.pdf.

198: *"precisely the properties we should expect ... "*: Richard Dawkins, *River Out of Eden: A Darwinian View of Life* (New York: Basic Books, 1996), 155.

198: *(footnote) Stephen Jay Gould offered ...*: Stephen Jay Gould, "Darwinian Fundamentalists," *New York Review of Books*, June 12, 1997, http://www.nybooks.com /articles/archives/1997/jun/12/darwinian-fundamentalism/.

199: *"'Rights' implies some kind of cosmic rule...."*: Paul Shepard, *The Others* (Washington, D.C.: Island Press, 1996), 308.

199: *"There really is no rational reason ... "* Ingrid Newkirk, quoted in Wesley J. Smith, *Culture of Death* (Jackson, Tenn.: Encounter, 2002), 195.

199: *(footnote) "Once we erred by ascribing ... "*: Walter Wink, *Unmasking the Powers: The Invisible Forces that Determine Human Existence* (Philadelphia: Fortress, 1986), 142.

199: *Peter Singer suggests ...*: Michael Specter, "The Dangerous Philosopher," *The New Yorker*, September 6, 1999, http://www.michaelspecter.com/1999/09/ the-dangerous-philosopher/.

199: *"If you haven't given voluntary ... "*: Les U. Knight, "Voluntary Human Extinction," *Wild Earth* 1, no. 2 (Summer 1991): 72.

200: *"We are survival machines ... "*: See Richard Dawkins, Preface to 1976 edition of *The Selfish Gene* (New York: Oxford University Press, 2006), xxi.

201: *Edward O. Wilson pointed out ...*: Edward O. Wilson, *On Human Nature* (Cambridge, Mass.: Harvard University Press, 2004), 165.

201: *"getting us to act as if we wanted ... "*: Robert Wright, *The Moral Animal: Why We Are the Way We Are: The Science of Evolutionary Psychology* (New York: Pantheon, 1994), 44.

202: *In his book* Dark Nature ...: Lyall Watson, *Dark Nature: A Natural History of Evil* (New York: HarperCollins, 1995), 193.

202: *Edward O. Wilson's memoir ...*: see Edward O. Wilson, *The Naturalist* (Washington D.C.: Shearwater, 1994).

202: *"Thus the difficult question ... "*: Robert Wright, *The Moral Animal: Why We Are the Way We Are: The Science of Evolutionary Psychology* (New York: Pantheon, 1994), 326.

202: *"When I first grasped it ... "*: Randolph Nesse, quoted in Matt Ridley, *Origins of Virtue: Human Instincts and the Evolution of Cooperation* (New York: Viking, 1996), 126.

203: *"What are people for?"*: Kurt Vonnegut, *Conversations with Kurt Vonnegut* (University, Miss.: University Press of Mississippi, 1988), 263.

204: *Time magazine selected...*: Brian Raftery, "The 2009 *Time* 100 Finalists," *Time*, 2009, http://content.time.com/time/specials/packages/0,28757,1883644,00.html.

204: *"No matter in how many ways..."*: John Updike, *A Month of Sundays* (New York: Fawcett Crest, 1975), 212–13.

205: *"Culture has transformed Christ..."*: Alan Wolfe: *The Transformation of American Religion: How We Actually Live Our Faith* (Chicago: University of Chicago Press, 2003), 2–3.

206: *Thomas Aquinas suggests the very opposite...*: Thomas Aquinas, quoted in Peter Kreeft, *Knowing the Truth of God's Love: The One Thing We Can't Live Without* (Ann Arbor, Mich.: Servant, 1988), 171.

206: *Walker Percy wrote a novel...*: Walker Percy, *Moviegoer* (New York: Avon Books, 1980), 55.

207: *"Farewell, my friends in Radioland..."*: Garrison Keillor, "Fall (Hog Slaughter)," *News from Lake Wobegon* (monologue), published by HighBridge Co., April 9, 1990, compact disc.

208: *"the least of these"*: Matthew 25:40.

208: *"The main emotion of the adult American..."*: John Cheever, in David Robert Anderson, *Losing Your Faith, Finding Your Soul: A Guide to Rebirth When Old Beliefs Die* (Colorado Springs: Convergent, 2013). 147.

208: *"I may, I suppose, regard myself..."*: Malcolm Muggeridge, *Jesus Rediscovered* (Wheaton, Ill.: Tyndale House, 1972), 59–60.

209: *"solid joys and lasting treasure"*: John Newton, "'Glorious Things of You Are Spoken': John Newton," *Christian Biography Resources*, http://www.lutheran-hymnal.com/lyrics/lw294.htm.

209: *(footnote) "A research review published..."*: Jeffrey Kluger, "The Art of Living," *Time*, September 23, 2013, http://content.time.com/time/magazine/article/0,9171,2151786,00.html.

209: *"What good is it..."*: Luke 9:25.

210: *(footnote) "What can it profit a man..."*: John Steinbeck, *Cannery Row* (New York: Penguin, 1992), 15.

210: *"the rich should take pride..."*: James 1:10.

210: *"Indeed, the water I give..."*: John 4:14 NIV 1984.

211: *"Though outwardly we are wasting away..."*: 2 Corinthians 4:16–17.

211: *"The faithful stood on the bodies..."*: Paul Veyne, ed., *A History of Private Life: From Pagan Rome to Byzantium* (Cambridge, Mass.: Harvard University Press, 1987), 512.

211: *"There was a moment of silence..."*: Paul Johnson, *The Quest for God: A Personal Pilgrimage* (New York: Harper Perennial, 1997), 32.

212: *"If you read history..."*: C. S. Lewis, *Mere Christianity* (New York: Macmillan, 1960), 118.

213: *"The greatest idiot and yahoo ..."*: Robertson Davies, "Robertson Davies, The Art of Fiction No. 107," interviewed by Elisabeth Sifton, *The Paris Review*, Spring 1989, http://www.theparisreview.org/interviews/2441/the-art-of-fiction-no–107-robertson -davies.

214: *slave named "Old Elizabeth" ...*: Delores S. Williams, "A Womanist Perspective on Sin," in Emelie M. Townes, ed., *A Troubling in My Soul* (Maryknoll, N.Y.: Orbis, 1993), 140–42.

214: *"Find out what pleases ..."*: Ephesians 5:10.

Chapter 11: How Should We Live? The Social Question

217: *"On a shattered and deserted stage ..."*: Jean-Paul Sartre, quoted in Maurice Nathanson, "Jean-Paul Sartre's Philosophy of Freedom," *Social Research* 19, no. 3 (Fall 1952): 378.

218: *"in their relations with women ..."*: Marilyn French, *The Women's Room* (Toronto: Random House of Canada, 1988), 462.

219: *"It's personal"*: Christian Smith, *Lost in Transition: The Dark Side of Emerging Adulthood* (New York: Oxford University Press, 2011), 22.

220: *"But is there any way in which ..."*: John Maynard Smith, "Genes, Memes, and Minds," *New York Review of Books*, November 30, 1995, http://www.nybooks.com/ articles/archives/1995/nov/30/genes-memes-minds/?pagination=false.

220: *"A man who has no assured "*: Charles Darwin, *Autobiographies* (New York: Penguin, 1974), 54.

221: *Biologist Lyall Watson admits ...*: Lyall Watson, *Dark Nature: A Natural History of Evil* (New York: Harper Collins Publishers, 1995), 141–48.

222: *"inner-city violence shouldn't be labeled ..."*: Robert Wright, "The Biology of Violence," *The New Yorker*, March 13, 1995, 68–77.

222: *"Darwin's dilemma"*: David Stove, *Darwinian Fairytales* (New York: Encounter, 1995), 5.

223: *"I think this has made me see ..."*: Steven Drake, "Peter Singer — A Slippery Mind," in *Not Dead Yet*, March 20, 2008, http://www.notdeadyet.org/2008/03/peter-singer -slippery-mind.html.

223: *(footnote)*: Steven Drake, in "Peter Singer — A Slippery Mind," in *Not Dead Yet*, March 20, 2008, http://www.notdeadyet.org/2008/03/peter-singer-slippery-mind. html.

223: *"habits of the heart"*: See Robert Bellah, *Habits of the Heart: Individualism and Commitment in American Life* (New York: Harper & Row, 1985).

223: *"Most people find the source ..."*: Marilyn Vos Savant, "Ask Marilyn," *Parade Magazine*, March 10, 1996, 8.

224: *"values clarification"*: Christina Hoff Sommers, "Teaching the Virtues," *Chicago Tribune*, September 12, 1993, http://articles.chicagotribune.com/1993–09–12/features /9309120147_1_moral-life-ethics-private-morality.

224: *"The only ethic that can work ..."*: Barbara Ehrenreich, "The Bright Side of Overpopulation," *Time*, September 26, 1994, http://content.time.com/time/subscriber /article/0,33009,981506,00.html.

224: *"I see a comfort level growing ..."*: Jesse Bering, in "Not Too Taboo? PW Talks with Jesse Bering," *Publishers Weekly*, August 9, 2013, http://www.publishersweekly .com/pw/by-topic/authors/interviews/article/58651-not-too-taboo-pw-talks-with-jesse-bering.html?utm_source=Publishers+Weekly&utm_campaign=fdc28dfc36 -UA – 15906914 – 1&utm_medium=email&utm_term=0_0bb2959cbb-fdc28dfc36 – 304660917.

224: *"Personally I'm into ritual animal sacrifice ..."*: James Davison Hunter, *Culture Wars: The Struggle to Define America* (New York, Basic Books, 1991), 311 – 13.

225: *"If, as I am convinced, ..."*: W. H. Auden and Edward Mendelson, *Prose, Volume III, 1949 – 1955* (Princeton, N.J.: Princeton University Press, 2008), 578.

226: *"free from the imposition of any ..."*: Ronald Dworkin, Thomas Nagel, Robert Nozick, John Rawls, Judith Jarvis Thompson, et al., "Assisted Suicide: The Philosophers' Brief," *New York Review of Books*, March 27, 1997, http://www.nybooks.com/articles/ archives/1997/mar/27/assisted-suicide-the-philosophers-brief/?pagination=false.

226: *"There is no significant example ..."*: Will and Ariel Durant, *The Lessons of History* (New York: Simon & Schuster, 1968), 50.

228: *"not at all meaning ..."*: 1 Corinthians 5:10, 12 – 13.

228: *"Mass movements can rise and spread ..."*: Eric Hoffer, *True Believer: Thoughts on the Nature of Mass Movements* (New York: HarperCollins, 2010), 86.

229: *"good itself does not dwell in me ..."*: Romans 7:18, 24.

229: *Our only goodness, Stott insists ...*: John R. W. Stott, *The Message of Romans: God's Good News for the World* (Downers Grove, Ill.: InterVarsity, 2001), 206.

231: *"I see no reason for attributing ..."*: Oliver Wendell Holmes Jr., quoted in Mary Ann Glendon, "The Bearable Lightness of Dignity," *First Things*, May 2011, 42.

231: *"Fellow Germans, ..."*: "Selling Murder: The Killing Films of the Third Reich," documentary produced by *The Discovery Channel*, 1993.

232: *"it is not difficult to imagine ..."*: Walker Percy, letter to the *New York Times*, 1988, cited in James Davison Hunter, *Before the Shooting Begins: Searching for Democracy in America's Culture War* (New York: Free Press, 1994), 6.

232: *incidence of Down syndrome children ...*: Gabe Lyons, *The Next Christians: The Good News about the End of Christian America* (New York: Doubleday, 2010), 106.

233: *"Theology reminded me, ..."*: Desmond Tutu, *No Future Without Forgiveness* (New York: Random House, 2000), 83 – 84, 86.

234: *"moral arc"*: Theodore Parker, cited by *Quote Investigator*, http://quoteinvesti gator.com/2012/11/15/arc-of-universe/.

Part Four: Faith and Culture

235: *"In the long run can we keep ..."*: Helmut Thielicke, *Christ and the Meaning of Life: A Book of Sermons and Meditations* (Grand Rapids, Mich.: Baker, 1975), 183 – 84.

Chapter 12: Uneasy Partners: Christians and Politics

237: *"People say we need religion ..."*: H. L. Mencken, quoted in David Robert Anderson, *Losing Your Faith, Finding Your Soul: The Passage to New Life When Old Beliefs Die* (Colorado Springs: Convergent, 2013), 70.

238: *"A liberal democracy requires ..."*: Jürgen Habermas, Rabbi Joshua Haberman, "The Bible Belt Is Our Safety Belt," *Policy Review*, Fall 1987, 40.

238: *An evangelical talk show host...*: Jane Mayer, "Bully Pulpit," *The New Yorker*, June 18, 2012, http://www.newyorker.com/reporting/2012/06/18/120618fa_fact_mayer.

239: *the CNN.com religion editor ...*: Dan Gilgoff, "In Obama's First Term, an Evolving Christian Faith and a More Evangelical Style," *CNN Religion Blogs*, http://religion.blogs.cnn.com/2012/10/27/in-obamas-first-term-an-evolving-christian-faith-and-a-more-evangelical-style/.

239: *(footnote) a letter sent by James Dobson*: Focus on the Family, "Letter from 2012 in Obama's America," *WND*, www.wnd.com/files/Focusletter.pdf.

240: *"It is possible to argue ..."*: James Davison Hunter, *To Change the World: The Irony, Tragedy, and Possibility of Christianity in the Late Modern World* (New York: Oxford University Press, 2010), 128.

240: *"that fox"*: Luke 13:32.

240: *"Give back to Caesar ..."*: Luke 20:25.

241: *"Christ above culture"*: H. Richard Niebuhr, *Christ and Culture* (New York: Harper & Bros., 1951), 40–43.

241: *On earth we are subject to two kingdoms, said Martin Luther ...*: See Paul Althaus, "The Ethics of Martin Luther," www.lutheransonline.com/lo/424/FSLO-1330611424-111424.pdf.

242: *"devout believer in the Lord"*: 1 Kings 18:3.

242: *Theologian John Howard Yoder pointed out ...*: Glen Stassen, D. M. Yeager, and John Howard Yoder, *Authentic Transformation: A New Vision of Christ and Culture* (Nashville: Abingdon, 1996), chapter 1.

243: *"Can one who goes the way ..."*: Lesslie Newbigin, *Foolishness to the Greeks: The Gospel and Western Culture* (Grand Rapids, Mich.: Eerdmans, 1986), 125.

244: *"Encouragement of Piety and Virtue ..."*: King George III of England, "Royal Proclamation For the Encouragement of Piety and Virtue, and for the Preventing and Punishing of Vice, Profaneness and Immorality," issued June 1, 1787.

244: *"we do not consider ourselves..."*: President Barack Hussein Obama, "Joint Press Availability with President Obama and President Gul of Turkey," White House, Office of the Press Secretary, *Whitehouse.gov*, April 6, 2009, http://www.whitehouse.gov/the_press_office/joint-press-availability-with-president-obama-and-president-gul-of-turkey/.

244: *John Howard Yoder recounted*: Glen Stassen, D. M. Yeager, and John Howard Yoder, *Authentic Transformation: A New Vision of Christ and Culture* (Nashville: Abingdon, 1996), chapter 1.

245: *Swastika*: "Nazis and the Church," *Slideshare*, #2, http://www.slideshare.net/garveym593/nazis-and-the-church.

245: *(footnote) "But what we got to hear ..."*: See Jürgen Moltmann, *A Broad Place: An Autobiography* (Minneapolis: Fortress Press, 2009), 256.

245: *"Christ [not Hitler] is my Führer"*: Martin Niemöller, quoted in Robert McAfee Brown, *Unexpected News: Reading the Bible with Third World Eyes* (Philadelphia: Westminster, 1984), 59.

246: *Stephen Monsma, a Christian who served ...*: Stephen V. Monsma, *Pursuing Justice in a Sinful World* (Grand Rapids, Mich.: Eerdmans, 1984).

247: *"One of the problems with the pro-life movement ..."*: C. Everett Koop, from a personal interview with the author.

247: *"world maintaining"*: Peter Berger, *A Sacred Canopy: Elements of a Sociological Theory of Religion* (New York: Anchor, 1990), 100.

247: *"Our constitution was made ..."*: John Adams, "Message from John Adams to the Officers of the First Brigade of the Third Division of the Militia of Massachusetts," *Beliefnet*, http://www.beliefnet.com/resourcelib/docs/115/Message_from_John_Adams_to_the_Officers_of_the_First_Brigade_1.html.

248: *Historian Mark Noll has written ...*: Mark Noll, "A World Without the KJV," *Christianity Today*, May 6, 2011, 35.

248: *"what looked at first like the greatest victory ..."*: Paul Johnson, "God and the Americans," http://adasboro.tripod.com/johnson.htm.

249: *"Thus sayeth the Lord thy God ..."*: Anne W. Branscomb, *Who Owns Information?: From Privacy to Public Access* (New York: Basic Books, 1994), 112.

249: *"the socialist, antifamily political movement ..."*: Pat Robertson, *Wikiquote*, http://en.wikiquote.org/wiki/Pat_Robertson, or "Equal Rights Initiative in Iowa Attacked," *Washington Post*, August 23, 1992.

250: *(footnote) "the second-largest hoax ..."*: Senator James Inhofe, *Congressional Record*, July 28, 2003, http://www.gpo.gov/fdsys/pkg/CREC-2003-07-28/pdf/CREC-2003-07-28-pt1-PgS10012.pdf#page=1.

250: *"we have more in common with each other ..."*: Tim LaHaye, quoted in James Davison Hunter, *Culture Wars: The Struggle to Define America* (New York: Basic Books, 1991), 103.

250: *"As a Jew, I differ ..."*: Rabbi Joshua Haberman, "The Bible Belt Is Our Safety Belt," *Policy Review*, Fall 1987, 40.

251: *"Thou shalt not covet"*: Exodus 20:17 KJV.

251: *"Love the Lord your God with all your heart ..."*: Luke 10:27.

251: *"For some reason, the most vocal Christians ..."*: Kurt Vonnegut, *The Man Without a Country* (New York: Random House, 2007), 98.

252: *C. S. Lewis shocked many people ...*: C. S. Lewis, *Mere Christianity* (New York: HarperSanFrancisco, 2001 [1952]), 112.

252: *Historian Edward Gibbon said ...*: Edward Gibbon, *History of the Decline and Fall of the Roman Empire, Volume 1* (London: Penguin, 1994), 26.

252: *"You shall not murder ... steal"*: Exodus 20:13, 15.

253: *"fools for Christ"*: 1 Corinthians 4:10.

254: *"Dr. Graham, you have set the church ..."*: Rev. Billy Graham, quoted by Senator Sam Nunn in a speech at the National Prayer Breakfast, February. 1, 1996.

Chapter 13: Holy Subversion

255: *"Every self-respecting writer ..."*: Abram Tertz (Andrei Sinyavsky), "The Literary Process in Russia," *Kontinent* I (1976): 84.

256: *"Do you intend to kill me?"*: Graham Greene, *The Last Word and Other Stories* (New York: Penguin, 1990), 17–18.

257: *"modern politics is civil war ..."*: Alasdair MacIntyre, *After Virtue: A Study In Moral Theory* (South Bend, Ind.: University of Notre Dame Press, 1984), 253, 263.

257: *"Go! I am sending you out ..."*: Luke 10:3.

259: *"The assumption of the voluntary principle ..."*: Paul Johnson, *A History of Christianity* (New York: Atheneum, 1976), 429.

260: *"all the kingdoms"*: Luke 4:5.

260: *"Imposition stands starkly at odds ..."*: Miroslav Volf, *A Public Faith: How Followers of Christ Should Serve the Common Good* (Grand Rapids, Mich.: Brazos, 2011), 106.

260: *(footnote) Originally attributed ...*: See accounts of Cassie Bernall's story in Dave Cullen, "Who Said 'Yes'?" *Salon*, September 30, 1999, http://www.salon.com/1999/09/30/bernall/; and in Dave Luzadder and Kevin Vaughan, "Biggest Question of All: Inside the Columbine Investigation; Part Three," *Rocky Mountain News*, http://denver.rockymountainnews.com/shooting/1214col1.shtml.

261: *"We would like to know who ..."*: Malcolm Gladwell, "How I Rediscovered Faith," *Relevant Magazine* 67 (January/February 2014): http://www.relevantmagazine.com/culture/books/how-i-rediscovered-faith.

262: *"The world looks with some awe ..."*: Winston Churchill, *Never Give In!: The Best of Winston Churchill's Speeches* (New York: Hyperion, 2003), 139–40.

262: *"foreigners and exiles"*: 1 Peter 2:11.

262: *"To set up in the world a new sign ..."*: Karl Barth and Thomas Forsyth Torrance, *Church Dogmatics: The Doctrine of Reconciliation, Volume 4, Part 3.2: Jesus Christ, the True Witness* (New York: T&T Clark International, 2004), 779.

263: *"When Christian believers gather in churches ..."*: Eugene H. Peterson, *The Message: The Bible in Contemporary Language* (Colorado Springs: NavPress, 2005), 1901.

263: *"While we were still sinners ..."*: Romans 5:8.

265: *"to the hard of hearing you shout ..."*: Flannery O'Connor, *Mystery and Manners: Occasional Prose* (New York: Farrar, Straus & Cudahy, 1986), 34.

266: *Reinhold Niebuhr drew a contrast ...*: Reinhold Niebuhr, *Moral Man and Immoral Society: A Study of Ethics and Politics* (New York: Scribner's, 1932), *passim*.

266: *"Prior to reading Gandhi"*: Martin Luther King Jr., *Stride Toward Freedom: The Montgomery Story* (Boston: Beacon, 2010), 84.

267: *"[In art] you are telling the reader ..."*: Walker Percy, in Peggy Whitman Prenshaw, ed., *Conversations with Walker Percy* (Jackson, Miss.: University Press of Mississippi, 1985), 24.

267: *"This is the only Christian story ..."*: Tony Rossi, "Why 'Les Misérables' Is Reaching Atheists Too," *Patheos*, http://www.patheos.com/blogs/christophers/2013/01/why-les-miserables-is-reaching-atheists-too/.

267: *Hugo*: Victor Hugo, cited in Doris Donnelly, "The Cleric Behind 'Les Mis'," *The Wall Street Journal*, http://online.wsj.com/article/SB10001424127887324669104 578204281398771420.html.

268: *"less concerned with altering ..."*: C. S. Lewis, *An Experiment in Criticism* (Cambridge, England: Cambridge University Press, 1988), 85.

268: *"Later, when I popped up from the underground ..."*: Aleksandr I. Solzhenitsyn, *The Oak and the Calf: Sketches of Literary Life in the Soviet Union*, trans. Harry Willetts (New York: Harper & Row, 1980), 11.

268: *"Modern Christian storytelling seems to steer ..."*: cited in comments to Tony Rossi, "Why 'Les Misérables' Is Reaching Atheists Too," *Patheos*, http://www.patheos.com/blogs/christophers/2013/01/why-les-miserables-is-reaching-atheists-too/.

269: *"I want art to tell me where I'm at ..."*: John Updike, *The Witches of Eastwick: A Novel* (New York: Random House, 2012), 89.

269: *"Tell the Truth but tell it slant ..."*: Emily Dickinson, *The Laurel Poetry Series: Emily Dickinson*, Poem 103, ed. Richard Wilbur (New York: Dell, 1960), 107.

269: *"Instead of high decibel rhetoric ..."*: Eugene H. Peterson, *Tell it Slant: A Conversation on the Language of Jesus in His Stories and Prayers* (Grand Rapids, Mich.: Eerdmans, 2008), 21.

270: *"in obedience and in disobedience ..."*: Karl Barth, *Dogmatics in Outline* (New York: Harper and Row, 1959), 10–11.

270: *"The kingdom of the world has become ..."*: Revelation 11:15.

271: *"Brothers and sisters ..."*: 1 Corinthians 1:26.

272: *"If I had not come out ..."*: Ernst Neizvestny, cited in Victor Sparre, *The Flame in the Darkness: Russian Human Rights Struggle as I Have Seen It*, trans. A. McKay and D. McKay (London: Grosvenor, 1979), 95ff.

ACKNOWLEDGMENTS

S ome books take shape more easily than others. Writing this one, I felt I was trying to corral and tame a herd of small wild animals, each of which was scratching and clawing against my best efforts. I was motivated by my concern about Christians' stance and reputation in the modern world, but how could I express that in a way that didn't sound like scolding? To complicate matters, I felt a need to take a close look at my own beliefs and to examine how they measure up in a culture that often scorns them. I needed help, and I got it from trusted friends who weren't afraid to tell me to start all over again with a new approach.

My computer hard disk holds many megabytes of early drafts of the book, and now that the process is over I look back with nothing but gratitude for those skilled and honest enough to offer the feedback I needed. Joannie Barth, Laura Canby, Dr. David Graham, and Brenda Quinn all chipped in with enough encouragement to keep me going and enough correctives to keep me reworking. John Sloan, Kathy Helmers, Tim Stafford, and Dr. Kirk Quackenbush suggested major changes that pointed me in new directions. Bob Hudson, Joannie Barth, and Melissa Nicholson shepherded some of the most thankless tasks, such as copy editing and tracking down other sources I quote here and there.

Meanwhile, my wife Janet embodied the grace I commend in these pages while sharing the life of a distracted, obsessed, and sometimes confused writer. As it happens, I am writing this on Valentine's Day, full of appreciation for her sustaining love.

Some of this material has appeared in a different form in *Christianity Today, Books & Culture, First Things, The Beliefnet Guide to Evangelical Christianity,* and the ebook *Christians and Politics,* as well as in a few stray blogs on my website. Truly this has been a work "in process," and I'm enormously grateful for all who helped along the way.

What's So Amazing About Grace?

Philip Yancey, Author of
The Jesus I Never Knew

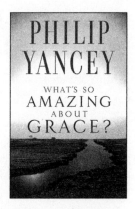

In *What's So Amazing About Grace?* award-winning author Philip Yancey explores grace at street level. If grace is God's love for the undeserving, he asks, then what does it look like in action? And if Christians are its sole dispensers, then how are we doing at lavishing grace on a world that knows far more of cruelty and unforgiveness than it does of mercy?

In his most personal and provocative book ever, Yancey offers compelling, true portraits of grace's life-changing power. He searches for its presence in his own life and in the church. And he challenges us to become living answers to a world that desperately wants to know, *What's So Amazing About Grace?*

Where Is God When It Hurts?

Philip Yancey

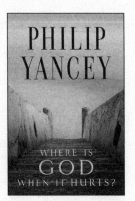

If there is a loving God, then why is it that ...?

You've heard that question, perhaps asked it yourself. No matter how you complete it, at its root lies the issue of pain.

Does God order our suffering? Does he decree an abusive childhood, orchestrate a jet crash, steer a tornado through a community? Or did he simply wind up the world's mainspring and now is watching from a distance?

In this Gold Medallion Award–winning book, Philip Yancey reveals a God who is neither capricious nor unconcerned. Using examples from the Bible and from his own experiences, Yancey looks at pain — physical, emotional, and spiritual — and helps us understand why we suffer. *Where Is God When It Hurts?* will speak to those for whom life sometimes just doesn't make sense. And it will help equip anyone who wants to reach out to someone in pain but just doesn't know what to say.

The Jesus I Never Knew

Philip Yancey, Author of
What's So Amazing About Grace?

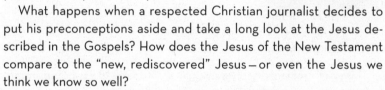

"There is no writer in the evangelical world that I admire and appreciate more."

— Billy Graham

Philip Yancey helps reveal what two thousand years of history covered up.

What happens when a respected Christian journalist decides to put his preconceptions aside and take a long look at the Jesus described in the Gospels? How does the Jesus of the New Testament compare to the "new, rediscovered" Jesus — or even the Jesus we think we know so well?

Philip Yancey offers a new and different perspective on the life of Christ and his work — his teachings, his miracles, his death and resurrection — and ultimately, who he was and why he came. From the manger in Bethlehem to the cross in Jerusalem, Yancey presents a complex character who generates questions as well as answers; a disturbing and exhilarating Jesus who wants to radically transform your life and stretch your faith.

The Jesus I Never Knew uncovers a Jesus who is brilliant, creative, challenging, fearless, compassionate, unpredictable, and ultimately satisfying. "No one who meets Jesus ever stays the same," says Yancey. "Jesus has rocked my own preconceptions and has made me ask hard questions about why those of us who bear his name don't do a better job of following him."

Available in stores and online!

Disappointment with God

Three Questions
No One Asks Aloud

Philip Yancey

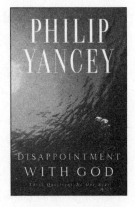

Philip Yancey has a gift for articulating the knotty issues of faith. In *Disappointment with God*, he poses three questions that Christians wonder but seldom ask aloud:

- Is God unfair?
- Is he silent?
- Is he hidden?

This insightful and deeply personal book points to the odd disparity between our concept of God and the realities of life. Why, if God is so hungry for relationship with us, does he seem so distant? Why, if he cares for us, do bad things happen? What can we expect from him after all? Yancey answers these questions with clarity, richness, and biblical assurance. He takes us beyond the things that make for disillusionment to a deeper faith, a certitude of God's love, and a thirst to reach not just for what God gives, but for who he is.

Available in stores and online!

Fearfully and Wonderfully Made

Philip Yancey, Dr. Paul Brand

Mysterious, intricate, pulsing with energy … the human body is an endlessly fascinating repository of secrets. The miracle of the skin, the strength and structure of the bones, the dynamic balance of the muscles … your physical being is knit according to a pattern of incredible purpose. In *Fearfully and Wonderfully Made*, renowned surgeon Dr. Paul Brand and bestselling writer Philip Yancey explore the human body. Join them in a remarkable journey through inner space — a spellbinding world of cells, systems, and chemistry that bears the impress of a still deeper, unseen reality. This Gold Medallion Award-winning book uncovers eternal statements that God has made in the very structure of our bodies, presenting captivating insights into the Body of Christ.

Prayer

Does It Make Any Difference?

Philip Yancey, Author of
What's So Amazing About Grace?

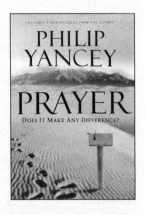

In his most powerful book since *What's So Amazing About Grace?* and *The Jesus I Never Knew*, Philip Yancey explores the intimate place where God and humans meet in Prayer.

Polls reveal that 90 percent of people pray. Yet prayer, which should be the most nourishing and uplifting time of the believer's day, can also be frustrating, confusing, and fraught with mystery.

Writing as a fellow pilgrim, Yancey probes such questions as:

- Is God listening?
- Why should God care about me?
- If God knows everything, what's the point of prayer?
- Why do answers to prayer seem so inconsistent?
- Why does God sometimes seem close and sometimes seem far away?
- How can I make prayer more satisfying?

Yancey tackles the tough questions and in the process comes up with a fresh new approach to this timeless topic.